1 BOOK +
1 MAP

Greater Brussels

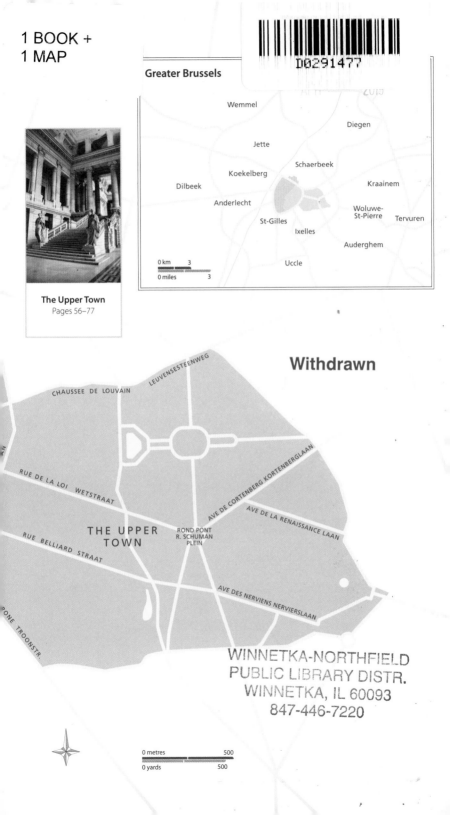

Wemmel

Diegen

Jette

Schaerbeek

Koekelberg

Dilbeek

Kraainem

Anderlecht

Woluwe-
St-Pierre   Tervuren

St-Gilles

Ixelles

Auderghem

0 km   3

0 miles   3

Uccle

The Upper Town
Pages 56–77

Withdrawn

CHAUSSEE DE LOUVAIN

LEUVENSESTEENWEG

RUE DE LA LOI   WETSTRAAT

AVE DE CORTENBERG KORTENBERGLAAN

THE UPPER
TOWN

ROND PONT
R. SCHUMAN
PLEIN

AVE DE LA RENAISSANCE LAAN

RUE BELLIARD STRAAT

AVE DES NERVIENS NERVIERSLAAN

PONE TROONSTR.

0 metres   500

0 yards   500

BRUSSELS
BRUGES, GHENT & ANTWERP

EYEWITNESS TRAVEL

BRUSSELS
BRUGES, GHENT & ANTWERP

LONDON, NEW YORK,
MELBOURNE, MUNICH AND DELHI
www.dk.com

Produced by Duncan Baird Publishers
London, England
Managing Editor Rebecca Miles
Managing Art Editor Vanessa Marsh
Editors Georgina Harris, Michelle De Larrabeiti
Designers Dawn Davies-Cook, Ian Midson
Design Assistants Rosie Laing, Kelvin Mullins
Visualizer Gary Cross
Picture Research Victoria Peel, Ellen Root
Dtp Designer Sarah Williams
Project Editor Paul Hines
Art Editor Jane Ewart
Map Co-Ordinator David Pugh

Contributors
Zoë Hewetson, Philip Lee, Zoë Ross,
Sarah Wolff, Timothy Wright, Julia Zyrianova

Photographers
Demetrio Carrasco, Paul Kenward
Illustrators
Gary Cross, Richard Draper, Eugene Fleury,
Paul Guest, Claire Littlejohn, Robbie Polley,
Kevin Robinson, John Woodcock

Printed and bound by South China Printing Co. Ltd., China

First American Edition, 2000
14 15 16 17 10 9 8 7 6 5 4 3 2 1

Published in the United States by DK Publishing,
345 Hudson Street, New York, New York, 10014

Reprinted with revisions 2003, 2005, 2007, 2009, 2011, 2013, 2015

Copyright 2000, 2015 © Dorling Kindersley Limited, London
A Penguin Random House Company

Published in Great Britain by Dorling Kindersley Limited.

A cataloging in publication record is available from the Library of Congress.

ISSN 1542-1554

ISBN 978-1-46542-565-2

Floors are referred to throughout in accordance with European
usage; ie the "first floor" is the floor above ground level

MIX
Paper from
responsible sources
FSC
www.fsc.org   FSC™ C018179

Front cover main image: Brightly lit façade of the Maison du Roi, Grand Place

◀ Flower carpet in Brussels

Contents

Introducing Brussels

Belgian heroes Tintin, Professor Calculus and Captain Haddock

Le Pigeon, Brussels, home of exiled French novelist Victor Hugo

View of the Rozenhoedkaai, Bruges

Brussels Area by Area

The Lower Town **42**

The Upper Town **56**

Two Guided Walks **78**

Greater Brussels **82**

Lace maker at work in Brussels

Beyond Brussels

Beyond Brussels **90**

Exploring Beyond Brussels **94**

Antwerp Walk **106**

Bruges Walk **130**

Neo-classical façade of the Museum voor Schone Kunsten

Travellers' Needs

Where to Stay **134**

Where to Eat and Drink **142**

Bruges' Bottle Shop has a range of beers

Survival Guide

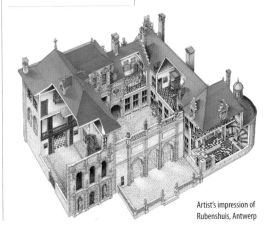
Artist's impression of Rubenshuis, Antwerp

INTRODUCING
BRUSSELS

GREAT DAYS IN BRUSSELS, BRUGES, GHENT & ANTWERP

The charms of Brussels, Antwerp, Ghent and Bruges are always agreeably understated. The pleasures lie in wandering, happening upon hospitable places to eat and drink, and visiting some of their rich and diverse collections of museums, galleries and churches. The following itineraries are aimed at helping you make the most of your time here. They are listed first by theme and then by duration of stay. Be warned that almost all Belgian museums are closed on Monday. Prices shown include admission, but not travel or food.

Brussels in a Nutshell

Two adults allow at least €80

- **The Grand Place, the city's magnificent centrepiece**
- **The Manneken Pis in all his glory**
- **Belgian art: wonderful and weird**
- **The historic sound of music**

Morning
The **Grand Place** (see pp44–5) is one of Europe's finest historic squares, and is a must-see sight. You could spend an hour just looking at the guildhouses, or longer by settling into one of the bar-cafés on the square. Then walk along the Rue de l'Étuve to see that famous icon of Brussels, the **Manneken Pis** (see pp46–7).
  Return to the Grand Place and the Musée de la Ville de Bruxelles to see its surreal collection of costumes and interesting exhibits on the history of the city. There are many places to find lunch

in and around the Grand Place but choose carefully, especially around **Rue des Bouchers** (see p50).

Afternoon
The afternoon can be spent in Brussels' best museums, which are in the Upper Town. It is not far to walk, but you could take a bus to the **Place Royale** (see p61). This is the location of Belgium's great national art collection, the **Musées Royaux des Beaux-Art de Belgique** and the **Musée Magritte** (see pp64–9), which includes unmissable work by Rubens, plus the wonderful alternative art of the Belgian Symbolists. Also nearby is the excellent **Musée des Instruments de Musique** (see p62), which has fine views over Brussels from its top-floor Café Du Mim. Alternatively, continue by tram or bus to the **Musée Horta** (see p84), a shrine dedicated to Art Nouveau, stopping perhaps on the way back for some shopping in the upmarket boutiques of Avenue Louise and Avenue de la Toison d'Or (see pp160–63).

Het Modepaleis, the principal boutique of Dries van Noten in Antwerp

Antwerp: Fashion, New and Old

Two adults allow at least €80

- **Rubens' home, the 17th-century seat of fashion**
- **High art from the age of Rubens**
- **A dynamic museum of modern fashion**
- **High-class boutiques**

Morning
Start the morning with a glimpse of Antwerp's 17th-century golden age at the **Rubenshuis** (see pp104–105). Next, take a short walk, or hop on a tram, to see Antwerp's fine-art collection, currently at the **Museum Aan De Stroom** (see p97). Followers of fashion will want to see Ann Demeulemeester's store, which shares Leopold de Waelplaats with the museum. From here, it is just a short walk along the river to the **Koninklijk Museum voor Schone Kunsten** (see pp102–103), and the excellent **FotoMuseum** (see p101).

Gabled buildings of the Grand Place, Brussels

◀ The Archduchess Isabella Shooting Down a Bird at the Grand Serment, Sablon 1615 (studio of Antoon Sallaert)

Afternoon

After lunch in one of the pleasant cafés located in Grote Markt *(see pp156–7)* or the nearby streets, visit Antwerp's museum of fashion, the **ModeMuseum** or **MoMu** *(see p100)*. Nearby is Het Modepaleis, the main outlet of designer Dries van Noten (on Nationalestraat 16), and there are other good fashion-hunting grounds in the area. To seek refuge from all this high-octane fashion, head for the more stately charms of Antwerp's great cathedral, the **Onze Lieve Vrouwe Kathedraal** *(see p97)* and back to the old city square, the Grote Markt *(see p96)*.

Korenlei on the bank of the River Leie in Ghent

Ghent: Sacred and Profane

Two adults allow at least €80

- Jan van Eyck's outstanding masterpiece
- One of Europe's best design museums
- Cutting-edge modern art

Morning

First, make a pilgrimage to Jan and Hubert van Eyck's exquisite panel painting, *The Adoration of the Mystic Lamb* in St Baafskathedraal *(see p116)*. Then walk to the **Graslei** and **Korenlei** *(see p117)*, stopping to admire the views from the St Michielsbrug bridge over the canal. Continue to **Design Museum Ghent** *(see p117)*, a superb museum tracing the history of interiors, furniture and furnishings. You could also take a 40-minute canal trip from the Korenlei, which gives an insight into the importance of the waterways in the city's medieval life. For lunch, there is a good choice of restaurants in the area *(see pp159)*.

Afternoon

Take a tram from the Korenmarkt to Charles de

Detail from *The Adoration of the Mystic Lamb, Ghent*

Kerchovelaan and walk across the Citadelpark to the **Stedelijk Museum voor Actuele Kunst**, or **SMAK** *(see p119)*. This great collection of contemporary art is bound to leave an impression. Returning to the historic centre of the town, try an aperitif of jenever gin in one of the bars by the canal or in the Vrijdagmarkt.

Bruges: Medieval Glory

Two adults allow at least €100

- A view of medieval Bruges
- Supreme art from its Golden Age
- A relaxing canal trip
- Beer "academies"

Morning

Start the day with an energetic climb up the 366 steps of the **Belfort** *(see p123)*, the city's bell tower, for some exhilarating views across Bruges. Afterwards, walk the short distance to the **Burg** *(see p122)*, a delightful square lined with historic buildings, including the **Stadhuis** *(see p122)*, and the double church of the **Heilig Bloed Basiliek** *(see p122)*. It is a short and pretty walk from here, along the canals, to the **Groeninge Museum**

(see pp126–7), celebrated for its small but fabulous collection of late medieval paintings. There are plenty of places to eat nearby, especially around the Vismarkt back near the Burg, or head further west at Gruuthusestraat, Mariastraat and Walplein.

Afternoon

Begin with a restful canal trip; tours last about 30 minutes and most start from landing stages near the Burg. Next, walk back along the Dijver canal to **Onze Lieve Vrouwekerk** *(see p123)*, one of Bruges' most attractive churches. On the other side of Mariastraat is the **Memling in Sint-Jan Hospitaalmuseum** *(see p125)*, a medieval hospital that is now a museum with an array of late medieval paintings by Hans Memling. From here, take a short walk to the **Gruuthuse Museum** *(see pp124–5)* for a taste of medieval life.

View of Bruges from the top of the Belfort

2 days in Brussels

Two adults allow at least €90

- Take a deep look into the heart of Brussels

- Browse the boutiques of Europe's most historic shopping arcade

- See how royalty lived in the Quartier Royal

Day 1
Morning Any exploration of Brussels should start at the **Grand Place** *(see pp44–5)*. Every building on the square is a gem, especially the **Hôtel de Ville** *(see pp46–7)*, the city's finest building. It is worth taking the guided tour to fully appreciate its ornate interiors. Often overlooked, Palais de la Bourse just behind the Grand Place is no less spectacular: **La Bourse** *(see p49)* itself boasts sculptures by Rodin on its façade. From here, make the short walk across to Rues de l'Etuve and du Chêne to gaze at the **Manneken Pis** *(see pp46–7)*, still by far the most famous sight in Brussels.

Afternoon After lunch in the Grand Place, head for the **Galeries St-Hubert** *(see p49)*, Europe's oldest and the most elegant shopping arcade. Next, take the short walk north to the **Centre Belge de la Bande Dessinnée** *(see pp52–3)*, a unique museum dedicated to the comic strip, which has become one of the city's must-sees. If you have the energy and the time, top off your day with a stroll around the glorious **Le Botanique** *(see p51)*. The botanical gardens are no longer located here, but the 19th-century glasshouse remains and the surrounding park is gorgeous in spring and summer.

Day 2
Morning Start your day with a look inside the **Notre-dame du Sablon** *(see p70)* before heading into the **Quartier Royal** *(see pp58–9)*, traditionally home to Belgium's kings and queens. The finest of the places built

Galleries St-Hubert in Brussels at sunrise

around the Parc de Bruxelles is the **Palais Royal** *(see pp60–61)*; do not miss the Throne Room with its superb chandeliers or the impressive Hall of Mirrors. Behind the palace are the **Musées Royaux des Beaux-Arts de Belgique** *(see pp64–9)*. Plan your time so as to see everything here. Choose which collection you want to see before entering; the Musée Magritte is particularly great.

Afternoon The finest church in the city is the **Cathédrale Sts Michel et Gudule** *(see pp72–3)*, first built as early as 1047. The window above the main entrance, depicting the Last Judgement, is a 16th-century treasure. From here, the metro at Parc makes it a short trip to Schumann, in the heart of the **Quartier Européen** *(see p74)*. The imposing Belaymont building, headquarters of the EU, is immediately recognizable. The equally bold Justus Lipsius

across the road is also worth a photo. Afterwards, take a walk around the majestic **Parc du Cinquantenaire** *(see pp76–7)*. Autombile fans should not miss Autoworld, while the Musée Royal de l'Armee warrants equal attention.

3 days in Brussels

Two adults allow at least €125

- Get to to know the hip world of the Sablon

- Climb the Atomium and see Europe in miniature

- Hunt for bargains on the Rue Neuve

Day 1
Morning Kick things off with a walk around **Le Botanique** *(see p51)* before exploring the **Quartier Royal** *(see pp58–9)*. Try to pack in as much of the **Musées Royaux des Beaux-Arts** *(see pp64–9)* as possible.

Afternoon Enjoy a casual lunch at one of the cafés on or around **Place du Grand Sablon** *(see p70)*, then head for the quirky boutiques and antique shops on the streets of the trendy Sablon area. Gawp at the splendour of the **Notre Dame du Sablon** *(see p70)* before making your way to the **Palais de Justice** *(see p71)*, one of the world's most impressive 19th-century buildings.

Day 2
Morning Pack a picnic of baguettes and ham and take the metro out to Stuyvenbergh

Majestic interior of Cathédrale Sts Michel et Gudule, Brussels

Triumphal Arch at the Parc du Cinquantenaire, Brussels

to escape the bustle of the city centre. Here lies the **Domaine de Laeken** (see pp88–9), the estate which surrounds the official residence of the Belgian monarch. Highlights include the Pavillon Chinois and the Serres Royales, the latter open to the public only in April.

Afternoon After an alfresco lunch at the beautiful estate, visitors can either walk or take the metro two stops to Heysel, and the iconic **Atomium** (see p89). In the shadow of the Atomium is Bruparck (see p89), where incredibly detailed scale replicas of the European Union's most famous buildings at Mini-Europe are the main attractions.

Day 3
Morning Take in the splendour of the **Grand Place** (see pp44 –5), not least the **Hôtel de Ville** (see pp46–7) and its exemplary guided tour. Don't forget the obligatory photo-op at the **Manneken Pis** (see pp46– 7) before getting immersed in the fantastic **Centre Belge de la Bande Dessinée** (see pp52–3). Later, shop at **Rue Nueve** (see p51), where the city's best selection of stores can be found on a lovely, fully-pedestrianized street.

Afternoon Having had lunch at one of the eateries in and around Rue Nueve, take the metro from de Brouckere to Schuman and explore the **Quartier Européen** (see p74) and the **Parc du Cinquantenaire** (see pp76–7). Don't miss the collection of pre-Columbian art in the Cinquantenaire Museum.

5 days in Brussels

Two adults allow at least €160

- Explore with ease the Centre Belge de la Bande Dessinée & the Musées Royaux des Beaux-Art
- Head to Bruges for a change of scenery
- Taste some of Belgium's best fries in Ghent

Day 1
Morning Begin your adventure at the **Grand Place** (see pp44–5), taking in the opulence of the **Hôtel de Ville** (see pp45 –6) before heading to the equally impressive **La Bourse** (see p49) and the city's landmark, the **Manneken Pis** (see pp46–7).

Afternoon Take the metro to Schuman to visit the **Parc du Cinquantenaire** (see pp76–7), home to many fine attractions, of which the Cinquantenaire Museum and Autworkd are not to be missed. Before heading back to the centre of town, have a good look around the **Quartier Européen** (see p74).

Day 2
Morning Start off with a stroll around **Le Botanique** (see p51) before heading to the **Centre Belge de la Bande Dessinée** (see pp52–3). After shopping on the **Rue Nueve** (see p51), pop into one of the many cafés in the area for lunch.

Afternoon The regal **Quartier Royal** (see pp58–9) is home to a wealth of palaces and parks, the

finest being the **Palais Royal** (see pp60–61) and the **Cathedrale Sts Michel et Gudule** (see pp72–3). Don't linger too long here however, as the treasures of the **Musées Royaux des Beaux-Arts** (see pp64–9) await.

Day 3
Morning Rise early to explore the fashionable **Place du Grand Sablon** (see p70). The area's parish church, the **Notre Dame du Sablon**, (see p70) is a must-see, as are the lavish gardens of the **Place du Petit Sablon** (see pp70–71). From here, it is a short walk to the exceptional **Palais de Justice** (see p71).

Afternoon Head out on the metro to Heysel to see the striking **Atomium** (see p89). Do not miss the Mini-Europe exhibition in the **Bruparck** (see p89). Spend time exploring **Domaine de Laeken** (see pp88–9), home to the Belgian royal family.

Day 4
Bruges is just an hour by train from Brussels Nord or Midi. Explore the picture-postcard city centre on foot – make sure you do not miss the **Stadhuis** (see p122) and the **Markt** (see p123), which still hosts a market every Wednesday. After lunch, climb the **Belfort** (see p123) for views over the entire ancient city. Reserve ample time for exploring **Gruuthuse Museum** (see pp124–5), whose Gothic façade is alone worth the trip.

Day 5
Jump on an early train for the half-hour ride to Ghent, once the centre of the European textile industry. Much of the city's rich history is documented in the **Design Museum** (see p117). Fabulous town houses line the **Graslei** and **Korenlei** (see p117) on either side of the River Leie, while around central Poeljemarkt are the **Stadhuis** (see p116), the 12th-century **St Baafskathedral** (see p116) and the **Belfort** (see p117). Don't leave without a cone of fries – Ghent does Belgium's best.

Putting Brussels on the Map

Brussels is the capital of Belgium and the centre of government for the European Union. Although one of Europe's smallest countries, covering 30,500 sq km (11,580 sq miles), Belgium has one of the highest population densities, with 11 million inhabitants (360 people for every square kilometre). Belgium is a trilingual country (Dutch, French and German). Although Brussels falls geographically in the Flemish (Dutch-speaking) half, it is largely French-speaking, and is Belgium's largest city, with more than one million inhabiting the region. Brussels is also the most visited, with around six million visitors a year, although 70 per cent of these come for business. Brussels' excellent communications make it an ideal place from which to explore Antwerp, Ghent and Bruges.

Key
▬▬ Motorway
▬▬ Major road
— Railway
▬▬ Regional border

Brussels and Environs

Amsterdam

Schiphol

Leiden

Den Haag

Hoek van Holland

Rotterdam

Gouda

Rotterdam

Dordrecht

NETHERLANDS

Bergen op Zoom

Breda

Eindhoven

Eindhoven

Venlo

Krefeld

Turnhout

Weert

Mönchengladbach

Antwerp

Antwerpen

Herentals

Niklaas

Lier

Erkelenz

GERMANY

Mechelen

FLANDERS

Demer

Genk

Aalst

See inset map above

Brussels

Hasselt

Maastricht

Maastricht

Aachen

BRUSSELS

Leuven

St-Truiden

Tongeren

Halle

Wavre

Liège

Liège

Eupen

Waterloo

Mébai

Vesdre

Verviers

BELGIUM

Namur

Huy

Spa

Malmedy

Brussels South Charleroi

Meuse

Ambléve

Mons

Binche

Charleroi

WALLONIA

St-Vith

Dinant

Ciney

Ourthe

Prüm

Maubeuge

La Roche-en-Ardenne

Sûre

Philippeville

N4

Alzette

Mosel

Chimay

Couvin

Bastogne

Wiltz

Vianden

Hirson

Libramont-Chevigny

Ettelbrück

LUXEMBOURG

Bouillon

Semois

Grevenmacher

Charleville-Mézières

Sedan

Arlon

FRANCE

Luxembourg

Luxembourg

Virton

Central Brussels

Central Brussels is divided into two main areas, each of which has its own chapter in the guide. Historically the poorer area where workers and immigrants lived, the Lower Town contains the exceptional 17th-century heart of the city, the Grand Place, as well as the cosmopolitan Place de Brouckère, and the historic workers' district, the Marolles. The Upper Town, traditional home of the aristocracy, is an elegant area which encircles the city's green oasis, the Parc de Bruxelles. Running up through the area is Rue Royale, which ends in the 18th-century Place Royale, home to the city's finest art museums, including the Musée Magritte.

Hôtel de Ville
The focus of the Grand Place, Brussels' historic Town Hall dates from the early 15th century. Its Gothic tracery façade features the famous needle-like crooked spire *(see pp46–7)*.

| 0 metres | 500 |
| 0 yards | 500 |

Key

▨ Major sight

La Bourse Façade
Just behind the Grand Place on busy Boulevard Anspach in the Lower Town, Brussels' Stock Exchange was built in 1873 in ornate style *(see p49)*.

For keys to symbols *see back flap*

Place du Petit Sablon
This square is a jewel of the Upper Town. Originally a horse market, the central area became a flower garden in 1890, surrounded by wrought-iron railings decorated with stone statuettes. Each figure represents a medieval trade or craft that brought prosperity to the capital *(see pp70–71)*.

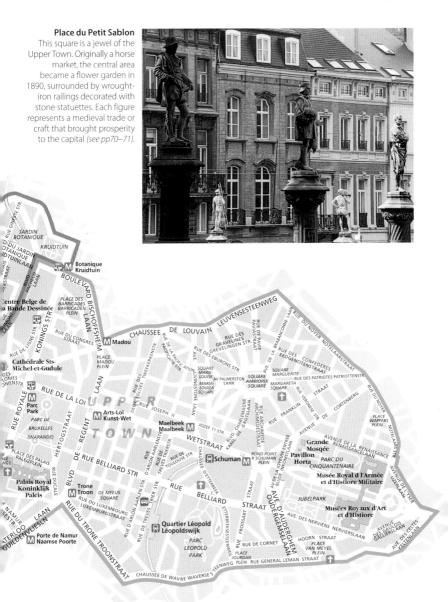

Palais Royal
The official work place of the Belgian monarch, this is one of the finest 18th-century buildings in the Upper Town. A highlight of Neo-Classical architecture, it overlooks Parc de Bruxelles *(see pp60–61)*.

Brussels' Best: Architecture

Reflecting Brussels' importance in the history of northern Europe, the city's architecture ranges from grand medieval towers to the glittering post-modern structures of European institutions. With a few examples of medieval Brabant Gothic still on show, the capital of Europe has the best Flemish Renaissance architecture in the world in the Baroque splendour of the Grand Place, as well as elegant Neo-Classical churches and houses. The quantity and quality of Art Nouveau *(see pp20–21)*, with its exquisite interiors and handmade features, are highlights of 19th- and 20th-century residential building. The cutting-edge designs in the Parliament Quarter, planned by committees of European architects, bring the tour up to date.

Basilique du Sacré-Coeur
Begun in 1905 and only completed in 1970, this huge Art Deco edifice is the world's fifth-largest church *(see p87)*.

Basilique du Sacré-Coeur 2km (1 mile)

Grand Place
Almost entirely rebuilt by merchants after French bombardment in 1695, this cobbled square is one of the world's best Baroque ensembles *(see pp44–5)*.

Palais de Justice
Bigger in area than St Peter's in Rome, the city's law courts were built in Neo-Classical style using the profits of colonialism, and completed in 1883 *(see p71)*.

THE LOWER TOWN

Porte de Hal
This imposing 14th-century tower is the only remaining trace of the city's solid, thick second perimeter wall. It owes its survival to its use as an 18th-century prison and latterly as a museum *(see p85)*.

0 metres		500
0 yards		500

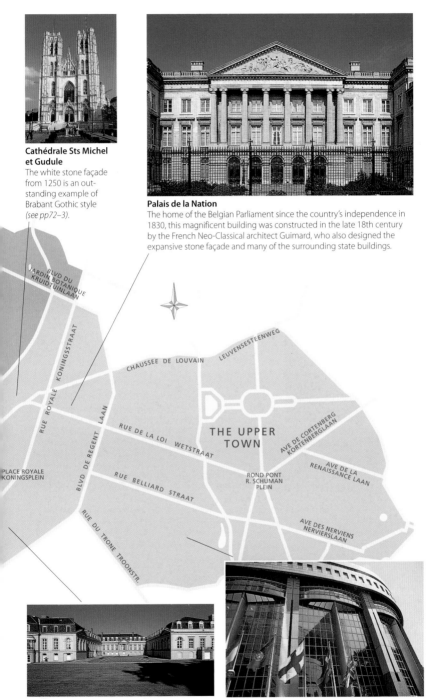

Cathédrale Sts Michel et Gudule
The white stone façade from 1250 is an outstanding example of Brabant Gothic style *(see pp72–3)*.

Palais de la Nation
The home of the Belgian Parliament since the country's independence in 1830, this magnificent building was constructed in the late 18th century by the French Neo-Classical architect Guimard, who also designed the expansive stone façade and many of the surrounding state buildings.

BLVD DU JARDIN BOTANIQUE KRUIDTUINLAAN

RUE ROYALE KONINGSSTRAAT

CHAUSSEE DE LOUVAIN   LEUVENSESTEENWEG

BLVD DE REGENT LAAN

RUE DE LA LOI   WETSTRAAT

THE UPPER TOWN

AVE DE CORTENBERG KORTENBERGLAAN

AVE DE LA RENAISSANCE LAAN

PLACE ROYALE KONINGSPLEIN

RUE BELLIARD STRAAT

ROND PONT R. SCHUMAN PLEIN

RUE DU TRONE TROONSTR.

AVE DES NERVIENS NERVIERSLAAN

Palais d'Egmont
This ducal mansion bears the name of a Flemish count executed for defending his countrymen's civil rights in 1568 *(see p71)*.

European Parliament
Nicknamed "Caprice des Dieux" ("Whim of the Gods"), this postmodern building serves more than 700 politicians.

Belgian Artists

Belgian art rose to the fore when the region came under Burgundian rule in the 15th century. Renaissance painters produced strong works in oil, characterized by intricate detail and lifelike, unidealized portraiture. The quest for realism and clarity of light was heavily influenced by the new Dutch schools of art. Yet, in contrast, Belgium's second golden artistic age, in the 20th century, abandoned reality for surrealism in the challenging work of artists such as René Magritte.

Belgium is justifiably proud of its long artistic tradition. Rubenshuis in Antwerp *(see pp104–105)*, Brussels' Musée Wiertz *(see p74)*, Musées Royaux des Beaux-Arts de Belgique and Musée Magritte *(see pp64–9)* are fine examples of the respect Belgium shows to its artists' homes and their works.

Portrait of Laurent Froimont by Rogier van der Weyden

The Flemish Primitives

Art in Brussels and Flanders first attracted European attention at the end of the Middle Ages. **Jan van Eyck** (c.1395–1441) is considered to be responsible for the major revolution in Flemish art. Widely credited as the creator of oil painting, van Eyck was the first artist to use the oil medium to fix longer-lasting glazes and to mix colour pigments for wood and canvas. As works could now be rendered more permanent, the innovation spread the Renaissance fashion for panel paintings. However, van Eyck was more than just a practical innovator, and can be seen as the forefather of the Flemish Primitive school with his lively depictions of human existence in an animated manner. Van Eyck is also responsible, with his brother, for the striking polyptych altarpiece *Adoration of the Mystic Lamb*, displayed in Ghent Cathedral *(see p116)*.

The trademarks of the Flemish Primitives are a lifelike vitality, enhanced by realism in portraiture, texture of clothes and furnishings and a clarity of light. The greatest interpreter of the style was Rogier de la Pasture (c.1400–64), better known as **Rogier van der Weyden**, the town painter of Brussels, who combined van Eyck's light and realism with work of religious intensity, as in *Lamentation (see p68)*.

Many in Belgium and across Europe were schooled and inspired by his work, continuing and expanding the new techniques. **Dirk Bouts** (1415–75) extended the style.

With his studies of bustling 15th-century Bruges, **Hans Memling** (c.1430–94) is considered the last Flemish Primitive. Moving towards the 16th century, landscape artist **Joachim Patinir** (c.1480–1524) produced the first European industrial scenes.

The Brueghel Dynasty

In the early years of the 16th century, Belgian art was strongly influenced by the Italians. Trained in Rome, **Jan Gossaert** (c.1478–1532) brought mythological themes to the art commissioned by the ruling Dukes of Brabant.

But it was the prolific Brueghel family who had the most influence on Flemish art throughout the 16th and 17th centuries. **Pieter Brueghel the Elder** (c.1525–69), one of the greatest Flemish artists, settled in Brussels in 1563. His earthy rustic landscapes of village life, peopled with comic peasants, are a social study of medieval life and remain his best-known work. **Pieter Brueghel the Younger** (1564–1636) produced religious works such as *The Enrolment of Bethlehem* (1610). In contrast, **Jan Brueghel the Elder** (1568–1625) painted intricate floral still lifes with a draped velvet backdrop, becoming known as "Velvet Brueghel". His son, **Jan Brueghel the Younger** (1601–78) also became a court painter in Brussels and a fine landscape artist of note.

The Fall of Icarus by Pieter Brueghel the Elder

Self-portrait by Rubens, one of many from his lifetime

The Antwerp Artists

In the 17th century, the main centre of Belgian art moved from the social capital, Brussels, to Antwerp, in the heart of Flanders. This move was largely influenced by **Pieter Paul Rubens** (1577–1640), who lived in Antwerp. He was one of the first Flemish artists to become known throughout Europe and Russia. A court painter, Rubens was also an accomplished landscape artist and interpreter of mythology, but is best known for his depiction of plump women, proud of their figures. Rubens was so popular in his own time that his bold and large-scale works were translated by Flemish weavers into series of tapestries.

Anthony van Dyck (1599–1641), a pupil of Rubens and court portraitist, was the second Antwerp artist to gain world renown. The Brueghel dynasty continued to produce notable figures: Jan Brueghel the Elder eventually settled in Antwerp to produce art with Rubens, while his son-in-law, **David Teniers II** (1610–90) founded the Antwerp Academy of Art in 1665.

The European Influence

The influence of Rubens was so great that little innovation took place in the Flemish art scene in the 18th century. In the early years of the 19th century, Belgian art was largely dominated by the influence of other European schools. **François-Joseph Navez** (1787–1869) introduced Neo-Classicism to Flemish art. Realism took off with **Constantin Meunier** (1831–1905) and Impressionism with **Guillaume Vogels** (1836–96). The Brussels-based **Antoine Wiertz** (1806–65) was considered a Romantic, but his distorted and occasionally disturbing works, such as *Inhumation précipitée* (c.1854) seem to have early Surrealist leanings. **Fernand Khnopff** (1858–1921) was influenced by the German Romantic Gustav Klimt. An early exponent of Belgian Symbolism, Khnopff's work is notable for his portraits of menacing and ambiguous women. Also on a journey from Naturalism to Surrealism, **James Ensor** (1860–1949) often used eerie skeletons in his work, reminiscent of Bosch. Between 1884 and 1894, the artists' cooperative **Les XX (Les Vingt)** reinvigorated the Brussels art scene with exhibitions of famous foreign and Avant Garde painters.

Sculpture by Rik Wouters

Surrealism

The 20th century began with the emergence of Fauvism led by **Rik Wouters** (1882–1916), whose bright sun-filled landscapes show the influence of Cézanne.

Surrealism began in Brussels in the mid-1920s, dominated from the start by **René Magritte** (1898–1967). The movement had its roots back in the 16th century, with the phantasmagoria of Bosch and Pieter Brueghel the Elder. Fuelled by the chaos of World War I, much of which took place on Flemish battlefields, Magritte defined his disorientating Surrealism as "[restoring] the familiar to the strange". More ostentatious and emotional, **Paul Delvaux** (1897–1994) produced elegant, freakish interiors occupied by ghostly figures. In 1948, the **COBRA Movement** promoted abstract art, which gave way in the 1960s to conceptual art, led by installationist **Marcel Broodthaers** (1924–76), who used daily objects, such as a casserole dish full of mussels, for his own interpretation.

Underground Art

Some 58 Brussels metro stations have been decorated with a combination of murals, sculptures and architecture by 54 Belgian artists. Although none but the most devoted visitor to the city is likely to see them all, there are several notable examples. **Anneessens** was decorated by the Belgian COBRA artists, Dotremont and Alechinsky. In the **Bourse**, surrealist Paul Delvaux's *Nos Vieux Trams Bruxellois* is still on show with *Moving Ceiling*, a series of 75 tubes that move in the breeze by sculptor Pol Bury. At **Horta** station, Art Nouveau wrought ironwork from Victor Horta's now destroyed People's Palace is displayed, and **Stockel** is a tribute to Hergé and his boy hero, Tintin *(see pp22–3)*.

Notre Temps (1976) by Expressionist Roger Somville at Hankar station

Brussels' Best: Art Nouveau

Among Europe's most important architectural movements at the start of the 20th century, Art Nouveau in Belgium was led by Brussels architect Victor Horta (1861–1947) and the Antwerp-born interior designer Henry van de Velde (1863–1957). The style evolved from the Arts and Crafts Movement in England and the fashion for Japanese simplicity, and is characterized by its sinuous decorative lines, stained glass, carved stone curves, floral frescoes and elaborately curled and twisted metalwork. As new suburbs rose up in the 1890s, over 2,000 new houses were built in the style. Although many were demolished, details can still be seen in almost every Brussels street.

Hôtel Métropole
The high-vaulted lobby and bar of this luxurious 1894 hotel recall the city's *fin-de-siècle* heyday *(see p51)*.

Old England
This former department store uses glass and steel rather than brick, with large windows and twisted metal turrets *(see p62)*.

Hôtel Ciamberlani
Architect Paul Hankar designed this red-brick house in rue Defacqz for the *sgraffiti* artist Albert Ciamberlani, with whom he worked.

Musée Horta
Curved window frames and elaborate metal balconies mark this out as the home and studio of Art Nouveau's best-known architect *(see p84)*.

Hôtel Hannon
This stylish 1902 town house was built by Jules Brunfaut (1852–1942). One of its metal-framed windows has striking stained-glass panes *(see p85)*.

BLVD DU
JARDIN BOTANIQUE
KRUIDTUINLAAN

BOULEVARD
E. JACQMAIN
LAAN

RUE A. DANSAERT STRAAT

THE LOWER
TOWN

GRAND PLACE
GROTE MARKT

BOULEVARD M.
LEMONNIER LAAN

RUE HAUTE HOOGSTRAAT

PLACE ROY
KONINGSPL

BLVD DE WATERLOO L

AVE LOUISE LOUIZAL

CH. DE CHARLEROI
CHARLEROISE STEENWEG

CH. DE WATERLOO WATERLOSE STEENWEG

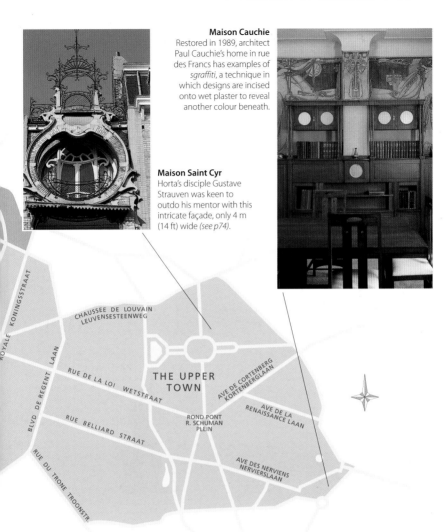

Maison Cauchie

Restored in 1989, architect Paul Cauchie's home in rue des Francs has examples of *sgraffiti*, a technique in which designs are incised onto wet plaster to reveal another colour beneath.

Maison Saint Cyr

Horta's disciple Gustave Strauven was keen to outdo his mentor with this intricate façade, only 4 m (14 ft) wide *(see p74)*.

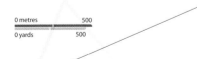

THE UPPER TOWN

ROYALE KONINGSSTRAAT

CHAUSSEE DE LOUVAIN
LEUVENSESTEENWEG

RUE DE LA LOI WETSTRAAT

BLVD DE REGENT LAAN

RUE BELLIARD STRAAT

RUE DU TRONE TROONSTR.

ROND PONT
R. SCHUMAN
PLEIN

AVE DE CORTENBERG
KORTENBERGLAAN

AVE DE LA
RENAISSANCE LAAN

AVE DES NERVIENS
NERVIERSLAAN

0 metres 500
0 yards 500

Hôtel Solvay

An early Horta creation of 1894, this home was built for a wealthy family. Horta designed every element of the building, from the ochre and yellow cast-iron façade columns and glass front door to the decorative but functional doorknobs *(see p85)*.

Belgian Comic Strip Art

Belgian comic strip art is as famous a part of Belgian culture as chocolates and beer. The seeds of this great passion were sown when the US comic strip Little Nemo was published in French in 1908 to huge popular acclaim in Belgium. The country's reputation for producing some of the best comic strip art in Europe was established after World War II. Before the war, Europe was awash with American comics, but the Nazis called a halt to the supply. Local artists took over, and found that there was a large audience who preferred homegrown comic heroes. This explosion in comic strip art was led by perhaps the most famous Belgian creation ever, Tintin, who, with his dog Snowy, is as recognizable across Europe as Mickey Mouse.

Hergé at work in his studio

Hergé and Tintin

Tintin's creator, Hergé, was born Georges Remi in Brussels in 1907. He began using his pen name (a phonetic spelling of his initials in reverse) in 1924. At the young age of 15, his drawings were published in the *Boy Scout Journal*. He became the protégé of a priest, Abbot Norbert Wallez, who also managed the Catholic journal *Le XXe Siècle*, and was swiftly given the responsibility of the children's supplement,

Le petit Vingtième. Eager to invent an original comic strip, Hergé came up with the character of Tintin the reporter, who first appeared in the story *Tintin au Pays des Soviets* on 10 January 1929. Over the next 10 years, the character developed and grew in popularity. Book-length stories began to appear from 1930.

During the Nazi occupation in the 1940s, *Tintin* continued to be published, with political references carefully omitted, in an approved paper *Le Soir*. This led to Hergé being accused of collaboration at the end of the war. He was called in for questioning but released later the same day without charge. Hergé's innocence was amply demonstrated by his work before and during the war,

where he expressed a strong sense of justice in such stories as *King Ottakar's Sceptre*, where a fascist army attempts to seize control of a central European state. Hergé took great care in researching his stories; for *Le Lotus Bleu* in 1934, which was set in China, he wrote: "I started… showing a real interest in the people and countries I was sending Tintin off to, concerned by a sense of honesty to my readers."

Spirou cover

Post-War Boom

Belgium's oldest comic strip journal *Spirou* was launched in April 1938 and, alongside the weekly *Journal de Tintin* begun in 1946, became a hothouse for the artistic talent that was to flourish after the war. Artists such as Morris, Jijé, Peyo and Roba worked on the journal. Morris (1923–2001) introduced the cowboy parody, *Lucky Luke* in *Spirou* in 1947, a character who went on to feature in live-action films and US television cartoons. Marc Sleen, another celebrated Belgian cartoonist, created the popular character *Nibbs* (or *Nero* in Flemish).

Statue of Tintin and Snowy

Comic Strip Characters

Some of the world's best-loved comic strip characters originated in Belgium. *Tintin* is the most famous, but *Lucky Luke* the cowboy, the cheeky children *Suske en Wiske* and *The Smurfs* have also been published worldwide, while modern artists such as Schueten break new ground.

Tintin by Hergé

Lucky Luke by Morris

During the 1960s, the idea of the comic strip being the Ninth Art (after the seventh and eighth, film and television) expanded to include adult themes in the form of the comic-strip graphic novel.

Peyo and The Smurfs

Best known for *The Smurfs*, Peyo (1928–92) was also a member of the team behind the *Spirou* journal which published his poetic medieval series *Johan et Pirlouit*, in 1952. *The Smurfs* first appeared as characters here – tiny blue people whose humorous foibles soon eclipsed any interest in the strip's supposed main characters. Reacting to their popularity, Peyo created a strip solely about them. Set in the Smurf village, the stories were infused with satirical social comment. *The Smurfs* were a popular craze between 1983 and 1985, featuring in advertising and merchandising of every type. They spawned a feature-length film, TV cartoons and popular music, and had several hit records in the 1980s.

Modern cover by Marvano

Willy Vandersteen

While *Spirou* and *Tintin* were French-language journals, Willy Vandersteen (1913–90) dominated the Flemish market. His popular creation, *Suske en*

Wiske has been translated into English and appears as *Bob and Bobette* in the UK, and *Willy and Wanda* in the US. The main characters are a pair of "ordinary" kids aged between 10 and 14 years who have extraordinary adventures all over the world, as well as travelling back and forth in time. Today, Vandersteen's books sell in their millions.

Comic Strip Art Today

Comic strips, known as *bandes dessinées* or *beeldverhaal*, continue to be published in Belgium in all their forms. In newspapers, children's comics and graphic novels the Ninth Art remains one of the country's biggest exports. The high standards and imaginative scope of a new generation of artists, such as Schueten and Marvano, have fed growing consumer demand for comic books. Both French and Flemish publishers issue over

Contemporary comic-strip artists at work in their studio

22 million comic books each year. Today, Belgian cartoons are sold in more than 30 countries, including the US.

Larger-than-life cartoon by Frank Pé adorning a Brussels building

Street Art

There are currently 18 large comic strip images decorating the sides of buildings around Brussels' city centre. This outdoor exhibition is known as the Comic Strip Route and is organized by the Centre Belge de la Bande Dessineé (the Belgian Comic Strip Centre) *(see pp52–3)* and the city of Brussels. Begun in 1991 as a tribute to Belgium's talent for comic strip art, this street art project continues to grow. A free map of the route is available from tourist information offices, as well as from the comic museum itself.

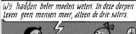

Suske en Wiske by Vandersteen

The Smurfs by Peyo

Contemporary cartoon strip by Schueten

Tapestry and Lace

For over six centuries, Belgian lace and tapestry have been highly prized luxury crafts. Originating in Flanders in the 12th century, tapestry has since been handmade in the centres of Tournai, Brussels, Arras, Mechelen and Oudenaarde, while the lace trade was practised from the 1500s onwards in all the Belgian provinces, with Bruges and Brussels particularly renowned for their delicate work. The makers often had aristocratic patrons; intricate lace and fine tapestries were status symbols of the nobility and staple exports throughout Europe from the 15th to 18th centuries. Today, Belgium remains home to the very best tapestry and lace studios in the world.

Tapestry weavers numbered over 50,000 in Flanders from 1450–1550. With the ruling Dukes of Burgundy as patrons, weavers prospered, and hangings grew more elaborate.

Tapestry designs involve weaver and artist working closely together. Painters, including Rubens, produced drawings for a series of weavings of six or more on grand themes (detail shown).

The texture of the weave was the finest ever achieved; often 12 threads to the inch (5 per cm).

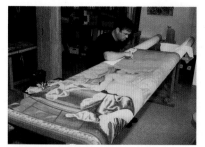

Weavers working today still use medieval techniques to produce contemporary tapestry, woven in Mechelen and Tournai to modern designs.

Tapestry

By 1200, the Flemish towns of Arras (now in France) and Tournai were Europe-wide known centres of weaving. Prized by the nobility, tapestries were portable and could be moved with the court as rulers travelled their estates. As trade grew, techniques were refined; real gold and silver were threaded into the fine wool, again increasing the value. Blending Italian idealism with Flemish realism, Bernard van Orley (1492–1542) revolutionized tapestry designs, as seen above in The Battle of Pavia 1525, *the first of a series. Flemish weavers were eventually lured across Europe, where ironically their skill led to the success of the Gobelins factory in Paris that finally stole Flanders' crown in the late 1700s.*

The lace trade rose to the fore during the early Renaissance. Emperor Charles V decreed that lace-making should be a compulsory skill for girls in convents and béguinages (see p55) throughout Flanders. Lace became fashionable on collars and cuffs for both sexes. Trade reached a peak in the 18th century.

Battles and classical myths were popular themes for tapestry series.

Lace makers are traditionally women. Although their numbers are dwindling, many craftswomen still work in Bruges and Brussels, centres of bobbin lace, creating intricate work by hand.

Victorian lace heralded a revival of the craft after its decline in the austere Neo-Classical period. Although men no longer wore it, the growth of the status of lace as a ladies' accessory and its use in soft furnishing led to its renewed popularity.

Belgian lace is bought today mainly as a souvenir, but despite the rise in machine-made lace from other countries, the quality here still remains as fine as it was in the Renaissance.

BRUSSELS THROUGH THE YEAR

The temperate climate of Brussels is typical of Northern Europe and means that a range of activities throughout the year take place both inside and out. Mild damp winters and gentle summers allow the city's strong artistic life to flourish in historic buildings and modern stadiums alike. The Belgians make the most of their seasonal changes. Theatre, dance and film start their season in January, with evening venues that range from ancient abbeys lit by the setting sun to drive-in cinemas. The city's flower festival launches the summer in highly colourful style, with the Grand Place literally carpeted in millions of blooms every other August. Through the year, festivals in Brussels range from energetic, exuberant historic processions that have taken place yearly since medieval times, to innovative European experimental art.

Spring

Brussels' lively cultural life takes off as the crisp spring days lengthen and visitors begin to arrive in the city. Music festivals take place in a wide variety of open-air venues. As the city's parks burst into bloom, the world-famous tropical greenhouses at Laeken are opened to the public and Brussels' chocolatiers produce delicious creations for Easter.

March
Eurantica *(mid-to end Mar)*. From archaeology to the modern arts, more than 150 antique dealers from all over Europe gather together for this large-scale fair.
Museum Night Fever *(early Mar)*. One night of exhibitions, music, dance, performances and DJs. Twenty museums take part.

April
BIFFF (Brussels International Fantastic Film Festival) *(early to mid-Apr)*. Two weeks of thrills, shivers and off-the-wall films. Over 150 cinemas open their doors for special festival screenings and a series of film-based discussions are held throughout the festival.
Brussels Short Film Festival *(third weekend)*. Cinephiles will love this festival showing 300 short movies from around the globe.
Sablon Baroque Spring *(third week)*. The Place du Grand Sablon hosts new classical ensembles in a gathering of young Belgian talent performing 17th-century music.

The Royal Glasshouse at Laeken, famed for its rare, exotic orchids

The Royal Greenhouses at Laeken *(late Apr to early May)*. The private greenhouses of the Belgian Royal family are opened to the public as their exotic plants and cacti start to flower. Breathtaking 19th-century glass and wrought ironwork shelters hundreds of rare species *(see pp88–9)*.
Flanders Festival *(mid-Apr to Oct)*. A celebration of all things musical, this classical medley offers more than 120 performances by internationally renowned choirs and orchestras.

May
Europe Day Festivities *(7–9 May)*. As the capital of Europe, Brussels celebrates its role in the European Union – even Manneken Pis is dressed as a Euro-supporter, in a suit of blue, decorated with yellow stars.

Kunsten FESTIVAL des Arts *(early to end May)*. This innovative theatre and dance festival provides a platform for new talent to perform.
Les Nuits Botaniques *(mid–May)*. Held in the former greenhouses of the Botanical gardens, now the French cultural centre, this series of musical events is a delight.
Queen Elisabeth Music Contest *(all month)*. Classical fans will flock to the prestigious musical competition, now in its fifth

Participants in the Brussels Twenty-Kilometre Race

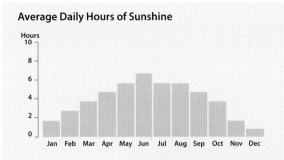

Average Daily Hours of Sunshine

Climate
Belgium has a fairly temperate Northern European climate. Winters are chilly and a heavy coat is required. Summers are warmer and much brighter, though you will still need a jersey for the evenings. Rainwear is always a necessity.

decade. Young singers, violinists and pianists gather in front of well-known conductors and soloists to determine the champion among Europe's finest student players.

Brussels Twenty-Kilometre Race *(either of the last two Sundays)*. As many as 20,000 keen professional and amateur runners race round the city, taking in its major landmarks.

Jazz Marathon *(last weekend)*. Bistros and cafés are the venues for myriad small jazz bands, with some well-known artists playing anonymously.

Summer

The season of pageantry arrives with Ommegang in July, one of Europe's oldest and best-known processions, which takes place in the Grand Place and the surrounding streets. Multicultural music runs throughout the summer, with classical, jazz and avant-garde US and European performers playing in venues ranging from tiny beer cafés to the great King Baudouin stadium in Heysel. Independence is celebrated on Belgian National Day. Families enjoy the Foire du Midi, the huge fairground over 2 km square (1 sq mile) covered with rides and stalls.

June

Brussels Rollers *(mid-Jun to end Aug)*. Rollerskaters dominate the streets of Brussels every Friday evening as they follow an exclusive skate route around the city.

African drummer performing at the Couleur Café Festival

City of Brussels Summer Festival *(mid-Jun to end Aug)*. Classical concerts take place in some of the city's best-known ancient buildings.

Brussels European Film Festival *(late Jun)*. Premières and film stars are adding weight to this European film showcase.

Couleur Café Festival *(last weekend)*. Spread over three summer evenings in the Tour et Taxis renovated warehouse, the fashionable and funky programme includes salsa, African drummers, acid jazz and multicultural music.

Fête de la Musique *(last weekend)*. Two days of concerts

and recitals featuring world music take place in the halls and museums of the city.

July

Ommegang *(first Thu in Jul and the Tue before)*. This festival has been celebrated in Brussels since 1549, and now draws crowds from around the world.

Translated as "a tour", the procession revolves around the Grand Place and the surrounding streets. Over 2,000 participants dress up and become members of a Renaissance town; jesters, courtiers, nobles and soldiers; they go on to parade before Belgian dignitaries. Tickets have to be booked months in advance.

Brosella Folk and Jazz Festival *(second weekend)*. Musicians from all over Europe play informal gigs in the Groentheater in the shadow of the Atomium.

The Ommegang pausing in front of dignitaries in the Grand Place

Average Monthly Rainfall

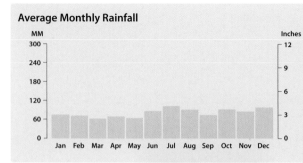

Rainfall chart
On the whole, Belgium is rather a rainy country, with Brussels experiencing constant low rainfall throughout the year. Spring is the driest season, but summers can be damp. In winter, rain may turn to snow and sleet.

Festival d'Eté de Bruxelles *(Jul–Aug)*. Classical concerts take place through the high summer in venues around the Upper and Lower Town.

Foire du Midi *(mid-Jul–mid-Aug)*. Brussels' main station, Gare du Midi, is host to this month-long funfair, which attracts people in their thousands. Especially popular with children, it is one of the biggest fairs in Europe, and includes an enormous Ferris wheel.

Belgian National Day *(21 Jul)*. The 1831 declaration of independence is commemorated annually with a military parade followed by a firework display in the Parc de Bruxelles.

Palais Royal Open Days *(last week in Jul–second week of Sep)*. The official residence of the Belgian Royal family, the opulent staterooms of the Palais Royal, including the huge throne room, are open to the public for six weeks during the summer *(see pp60–61)*.

August
Plantation du Meiboom *(9 Aug)*. This traditional festival dates from 1213. Parading crowds dressed in huge puppet costumes parade around the Lower Town and finally reach the Grand Place where a maypole is planted as a celebration of summer.

Tapis des Fleurs *(mid-Aug, biennially, for four days)*. Taking place on even-numbered years, this colourful celebration pays tribute to Brussels' long-established

Costumed revellers at the Plantation of the Meiboom

flower industry. The Grand Place is carpeted with millions of fresh flowers in patterns echoing historical scenes. The beautiful flower carpet measures 2,000 sq m (21,000 sq ft).

Autumn

Fresh autumn days are the cue for many indoor events; innovative jazz is performed in the city's cafés and the French cultural centre in Le Botanique. Architecture is celebrated in the heritage weekend where the public can tour many private houses and personal art collections.

September
The Birthday of Manneken Pis *(last weekend)*. Brussels' celebrated mascot is clothed in a new suit by a chosen dignitary from abroad.

International Comic Strip and Cartoon Festival *(early Sep)*. Artists and authors, both new and established, arrive for lectures and screenings in this city with its comic strip heritage.

The Grand Place, carpeted in millions of fresh flowers

Average Monthly Temperature

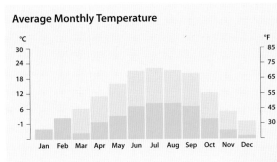

Temperature chart
This chart gives the average maximum and miminum temperatures for Brussels. Generally mild, Brussels' climate does produce chilly weather and cold winters from October to March. Spring sees milder temperatures and is followed by a warm summer.

Lucky Town Festival *(first weekend)*. Sixty concerts take place in over 30 of some of Brussels' best-known and atmospheric cafés.
Journées du Patrimoine/ Heritage Days *(second or third weekend)*. Private homes, listed buildings and art collections are opened for a rare public viewing to celebrate the city's architecture.

October
Skoda Jazz Festival *(early Oct–mid-Dec)*. All over Belgium, informal jazz concerts bring autumnal cheer to country towns and the capital. Performers are mainly local, but some European stars fly in for performances in Brussels' Palais des Beaux-Arts. Ray Charles and Herbie Hancock have appeared in past years.

Winter
Snow and rain typify Brussels' winter weather, and attractions move indoors. Art galleries launch world-class exhibitions and the Brussels Film Festival showcases new and established talent. As the festive season approaches, the ancient Lower Town is brightly lit and families gather for Christmas with traditional Belgian cuisine.

November
Ars Musica *(mid-Nov)*. This celebration of modern music is one of Europe's finest festivals, boasting famous performers and beautiful venues, often the Musée d'Art Ancien *(see pp64–5)*. The

festival is held biennially on even-number years and is a must for connoisseurs of the contemporary music world.
Nocturnes des Sablons *(last weekend)*. Shops and galleries stay open until 11pm around the Place du Grand Sablon. Horse-drawn carriages transport shoppers around the area, with mulled wine on offer in the festively decorated main square.

December
Fête de Saint Nicolas *(6 Dec)*. The original Santa Claus, the patron saint of Christmas, is alleged to arrive in the city on this day. Children throughout the country are given their presents, sweetmeats and chocolate.
Reveillon/Fête de Noel *(24–25 Dec)*. In common with the rest of mainland Europe, Christmas is celebrated over a feast on the evening of 24 December. Gifts are given by adults on this day, and 25 December is traditionally for visiting extended family. The city's Christmas decorations provide a lively sight until 6 January.

January
Fête des Rois *(6 Jan)*. Epiphany is celebrated with almond cake, the *galette des rois*, and the search for the bean inside that declares its finder king for the night.

Christmas market in the Grand Place around the traditional Christmas tree

February
Antiques Fair *(middle fortnight)*. Brussels' crossroads location is useful here as international dealers gather in the historic Palais des Beaux-Arts *(see p62)*.

Public Holidays

New Year's Day (1 Jan)
Easter Sunday (variable)
Easter Monday (variable)
Labour Day (1 May)
Ascension Day (variable)
Whit Sunday (variable)
Whit Monday (variable)
Belgian National Day (21 July)
Assumption Day (15 Aug)
All Saints' Day (1 Nov)
Armistice Day (11 Nov)
Christmas Day (25 Dec)

THE HISTORY OF BRUSSELS

As the cultural and civic heart of Belgium since the Middle Ages, Brussels has been the focus of much political upheaval over the centuries. But, from the battles of the 17th century to the warfare of the 20th century, it has always managed to re-create itself with vigour. Now, at the start of a new millennium, Belgium's capital is prospering as the political centre of Europe.

When Julius Caesar set out to conquer the Gauls of northern Europe in 58 BC, he encountered a fierce tribe known as the Belgae (the origins of the 19th-century name "Belgium"). Roman victory led to the establishment of the region they called Gallia Belgica. The earliest mention of Brussels itself is as "Broucsella", or "settlement in the marshes" and dates from a 7th-century manuscript.

Following the collapse of the Roman Empire in the 5th century, a Germanic race known as the Franks came to rule the region and established the Merovingian dynasty of kings, based in their capital at Tournai. They were followed by the Carolingian dynasty, which produced one of the most important figures of the Middle Ages – Charlemagne (AD 768–814). His noted military expertise ensured that invaders such as the Northern Saxons and the Lombards of Italy were repelled. He was also credited with establishing Christianity as the major religion across western Europe. The pope rewarded him by crowning him Emperor of the West in AD 800; effectively he was the first Holy Roman Emperor, ruling a vast area extending from Denmark to Italy. By the 10th century, the inheritance laws of the Franks meant that the empire was divided up among Charlemagne's grandsons, Louis, Charles the Bald and Lothair. Lothair's fortress, founded in 977, marks the official founding of Brussels. The period had brought a measure of stability to the area's volatile feudal fiefdoms, leading to a trading boom in the new towns of the low countries.

Industrial Beginnings

At the start of the 12th century, commerce became the guiding force in western Europe and the centres of trade quickly grew into powerful cities. Rivers and canals were the key to the growth of the area's trading towns. Ghent, Ypres, Antwerp and Bruges became the focus of the cloth trade plied across the North Sea between France, Germany, Italy and England. Brussels, with its skilled craftsmen, became a trade centre, and buildings such as the Cathédrale Sts Michel et Gudule (see pp72–3), started in 1225, demonstrated its stature.

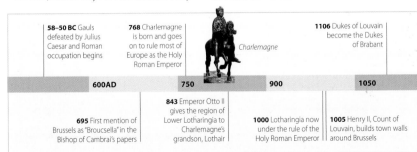

58–50 BC Gauls defeated by Julius Caesar and Roman occupation begins

768 Charlemagne is born and goes on to rule most of Europe as the Holy Roman Emperor

Charlemagne

1106 Dukes of Louvain become the Dukes of Brabant

600AD   **750**   **900**   **1050**

695 First mention of Brussels as "Broucsella" in the Bishop of Cambrai's papers

843 Emperor Otto II gives the region of Lower Lotharingia to Charlemagne's grandson, Lothair

1000 Lotharingia now under the rule of the Holy Roman Emperor

1005 Henry II, Count of Louvain, builds town walls around Brussels

◀ *Philip the Good, Duke of Burgundy (c.1500) by Rogier van der Weyden*

Nineteenth-century painting of the *Battle of the Golden Spurs*

The Craftsmen's Rebellion

Over the next two hundred years, Brussels became one of the foremost towns of the Duchy of Brabant. Trade here specialized in fine fabrics that were exported to lucrative markets in France, Italy and England. A handful of merchants became rich and exercised political power over the towns. However, conflict grew between the merchants, who wanted to maintain good relations with England, and their autocratic French rulers who relied upon tax revenue from the towns.

The 14th century witnessed a series of rebellions by the craftsmen of Bruges and Brussels against what they saw as the tyranny of the French lords. In May 1302, Flemish craftsmen, armed only with spears, defeated the French at the Battle of the Golden Spurs, named for the humiliating theft of the cavalry's spurs. Encouraged by this success, the Brussels craftsmen revolted against the aristocracy who controlled their trading economy in 1356. They were also angered by the Hundred Years' War between England and France, which began in 1337. The war threatened wool supplies from England which were crucial to their cloth-based economy. The subsequent depression marked the beginning of decades of conflict between the craftsmen and merchant classes. In 1356, Jeanne, Duchess of Louvain, gained control over Brussels, and instituted the workers' Charter of Liberties. Craftsmen were finally given some political powers in the city. Trade resumed, attracting new people to Brussels. As the population grew, new streets were built outside the city walls to accommodate them. Between 1357 and 1379, a second town wall was constructed around these new districts.

The House of Burgundy

The new town walls were also built in reply to the invasion of Brussels by the Count of Flanders. However, in 1369, Philip, Duke of Burgundy, married the daughter of the Count of Flanders, and when the count died in 1384, the Low Countries and eastern France came under the couple's Burgundian rule.

In the 1430s, Brussels became the capital of Burgundy, a situation that was to change the city forever. Brussels was now an administrative and cultural centre, famous

Richly detailed Brussels tapestries such as this *Allegory of Hope* (1525) were prized commodities

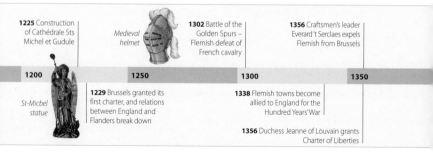

1225 Construction of Cathédrale Sts Michel et Gudule

Medieval helmet

1302 Battle of the Golden Spurs – Flemish defeat of French cavalry

1356 Craftsmen's leader Everard 't Serclaes expels Flemish from Brussels

1200　　　　　　**1250**　　　　　　**1300**　　　　　　**1350**

St-Michel statue

1229 Brussels granted its first charter, and relations between England and Flanders break down

1338 Flemish towns become allied to England for the Hundred Years' War

1356 Duchess Jeanne of Louvain grants Charter of Liberties

Painting of the family of the Hapsburg King of Austria, Maximillian I and Mary of Burgundy

for its grand architecture, in the form of mansions and churches, and its luxury crafts trade.

The Hapsburg Dynasty

In 1477, Mary of Burgundy, the last heir to the duchy, married Maximillian of Austria. Mary died in 1482, leaving Maximillian and the Hapsburg dynasty rulers of the city at a time when Brussels was experiencing serious economic depression. In 1488, Brussels and the rest of Flanders rebelled against this new power which had reinstated relations with France. The Austrians held on to power largely because of the plague of 1490 which halved Brussels' population. Maximillian passed his rule of the Low Countries to his son, Philip the Handsome in 1494, the year before he became Holy Roman Emperor. When Maximillian died, his daughter, Regent Empress Margaret of Austria, moved the

capital of Burgundy from Brussels to Mechelen, where she educated her nephew, the future emperor Charles V.

Spanish Rule

In 1515, at the age of 15, Charles became Sovereign of Burgundy. The following year he inherited the Spanish throne and, in 1519, became the Holy Roman Emperor. As he was born in Ghent, and considered Flanders his real home, he restored Brussels as the capital of Burgundy. Dutch officials arrived to run the three government councils that were now based here.

For the first time, the city had a court. Both aristocratic families and immigrants, eager to cash in on the city's expansion, were drawn to the heady mix of tolerance, intellectual sophistication and business. Brussels quickly emerged as the most powerful city in Flanders, overtaking its long-standing rivals Bruges and Antwerp. However, the Reformation, begun in Germany by Martin Luther, was to usher in a period of religious conflict. When Charles V abdicated in 1555, he fractured the empire's unity by leaving the Holy Roman Empire to his brother Ferdinand and all other dominions to his devoutly Catholic son, Philip II of Spain. His persecution of the Protestant movement finally sparked the Revolt of the Nether-lands led by the House of Orange. Brussels' Protestant rulers surren-dered to Philip in 1585. His power ended when the English defeated the Spanish Armada in 1588, by which time 8,000 Protestants had been put to death.

Portrait of Charles V, Holy Roman Emperor

1419 Philip the Good succeeds as Count of Burgundy	1506 Margaret of Austria moves the Burgundian capital from Brussels to Mechelen	1515 Charles Hapsburg becomes Sovereign of Burgundy	1555 Catholic Philip II succeeds Charles V as religious reformation comes to Brussels
1400	**1450**	**1500**	**1550**
1430 Under Burgundian control, Brussels becomes the major administrative centre of the region	1490 Plague decimates the city 1488 Civil war – Brussels joins Flanders against Maximillian of Austria	1566 Conseil des Troubles set up by Duke d'Alba. Prominent Counts Egmont and Hornes executed	Count Egmont

The armies of Louis XIV, the Sun King, bombard Brussels' city walls

The Counter-Reformation

From 1598, Archduchess Isabella and Archduke Albert were the Catholic rulers of the Spanish Netherlands, installing a Hapsburg governor in Brussels. They continued to persecute Protestants: all non-Catholics were barred from working. Many skilled workers moved to the Netherlands. But new trades like lace-making, diamond-cutting and silk-weaving flourished. Isabella and Albert were great patrons of the arts, and supported Rubens in Antwerp (see pp104–105).

Protestant prisoners paraded in Brussels during the Counter-Reformation under Albert and Isabella

Invasion of the Sun King

The 17th century was a time of of religious and political struggle all over Europe. The Thirty Years War (1618–48) divided western Europe along Catholic and Protestant lines. After 1648, France's Sun King, Louis XIV, was determined to add Flanders to his territory.

By 1633, both Albert and Isabella were dead and Philip IV of Spain passed control of the Spanish Netherlands to his weak brother, the Cardinal-Infant Ferdinand. Keen to pursue his ambitions, Louis XIV besieged Maastricht in the 1670s and took Luxembourg. Having failed to win the nearby enclave of Namur, the piqued Sun King moved his army to Brussels, whose defences were weaker.

On 13 August 1695, the French bombarded Brussels from a hill outside the city walls, destroying the Grand Place (see pp44–5) and much of its environs. The French withdrew, but their desire to rule the region was to cause conflict over subsequent decades.

A Phoenix from the Ashes

Brussels recovered quickly from the destruction caused by the bombardment. The guilds ensured that the Grand Place was rebuilt in a matter of years, with new guildhouses as a testament to the on-going success of the city's economic life.

The building of the Willebroek canal during the 17th century allowed access to the Rupel and Scheldt rivers, and thus to Antwerp and the North Sea. Large industries began to replace local market trading. Factories and mills grew up around the city's harbour, and Brussels became an export centre.

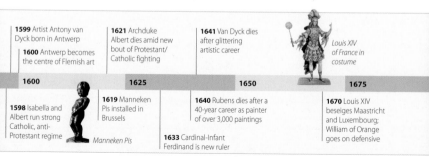

1599 Artist Antony van Dyck born in Antwerp

1600 Antwerp becomes the centre of Flemish art

1621 Archduke Albert dies amid new bout of Protestant/Catholic fighting

1641 Van Dyck dies after glittering artistic career

Louis XIV of France in costume

1600

1625

1650

1675

1598 Isabella and Albert run strong Catholic, anti-Protestant regime

1619 Manneken Pis installed in Brussels

Manneken Pis

1640 Rubens dies after a 40-year career as painter of over 3,000 paintings

1633 Cardinal-Infant Ferdinand is new ruler

1670 Louis XIV beseiges Maastricht and Luxembourg; William of Orange goes on defensive

Austrian Succession

Subsequent decades were dogged by war as Austria and England sought to stave off French ambitions. When Philip of Anjou succeeded to the Spanish throne, it looked as if the combined threat of Spain and France would overwhelm the rest of Europe. Emperor Leopold I of Austria, together with England and many German states, declared war on France. The resulting 14-year War of the Spanish Succession ended with the Treaty of Utrecht in 1713, which ceded the Netherlands, including Brussels, to Austria.

Governor of Brussels, Duke
Charles of Lorraine

The treaty did not end the conflict. Emperor Charles VI of Austria ruled after Leopold, but failed to produce a male heir. His death in 1731 sparked another 17 years of war – The War of the Austrian Succession over whether his daughter Maria Theresa should be allowed to inherit the crown. It was not until 1748, with the signing of the Treaty of Aix-la-Chapelle, that Maria Theresa gained control.

The Boom Period

The endless fighting took its toll, and Brussels was impoverished. The majority of the population were still ruled by feudal laws: they could not change jobs or move home without permission; and only three per cent were literate.

In the 1750s, Empress Maria Theresa of Austria installed her brother, Charles of Lorraine, in Brussels. Under the influence of the Enlightenment, his court attracted European artists and intellectuals, and Brussels became the most glamorous city in Europe. Industry also boomed with the construction of new roads and waterways. Brussels was transformed as the Place Royale and Parc de Bruxelles were laid out.

The Workers' Revolt

While the aristocracy and new middle-classes flourished, Brussels' workers were suffering. As the city's population grew, there were more workers than jobs: wages plummeted and factory conditions were harsh.

When Joseph II succeeded Maria Theresa in 1780, he enforced a series of reforms including freedom of religion. However, he also cancelled the 500-year-old Charter of Liberties. Influenced by the ideas of the French Revolution of 1789, the Belgians now demanded reform. Their rebellion was to result in an independent state.

French prince Philip of Anjou became Philip V of Spain, sparking the War of the Spanish Succession

1695 French Bombardment of Brussels	**1713–14** Treaties of Utrecht and Rastadt mark beginning of Austrian period	*Ceramic Delft plate*	**1760s** Brussels is cultural and artistic centre of Europe	**1788** Joseph II cancels Charter of Liberties which results in liberal opposition
1700	**1725**		**1750**	**1775**
1697 Willebroek Canal completed, links Brussels to the sea via Antwerp	**1731** Beginning of the 17-year-long war against Austrian rule	**1748** Treaty of Aix-la-Chapelle restores the Netherlands to Austrian rule	**1753** New roads and canals constructed, which boosts industry in Brussels	**1789** Belgian revolt for independence fired by French Revolution

The Fight for Independence

Belgium was again occupied by foreign powers between 1794 and 1830. First, by the French Republican armies, then, after Napoleon's defeat at Waterloo in 1815, by the Dutch. French radical reforms included the abolition of the guild system and fairer taxation laws. Although French rule was unpopular, their liberal ideas were to influence the Belgian drive for independence. William I of Orange was appointed King of the Netherlands (which included Belgium) after 1815. His autocratic style, together with a series of anti-Catholic measures, bred discontent, especially in Brussels and among the French-speaking Walloons in the south. The south was also angered when William refused to introduce tariffs to protect their trade – it was the last straw. The uprising of 1830 began in Brussels and Léopold I became king of the newly independent nation.

King William I of Orange
William's rule as King of the Netherlands after 1815 was unpopular.

A Cultural Revolution in Brussels
French ideas not only influenced the revolution, but also Belgian culture. Under Napoleon, the city walls were demolished and replaced by tree-lined boulevards.

Liberals joined workers already protesting in the square outside.

The Battle of Waterloo
Napoleon's influence came to an end after the battle of Waterloo on 18 June 1815. A Prussian army came to Wellington's aid, and by 5:30pm Napoleon faced his final defeat. This led to Dutch rule over Belgium.

Agricultural Workers
Harsh weather in the winter of 1829 caused hardship for both farmers and agricultural labourers, who also joined the protest.

The Revolution in Industry
Unemployment, low wages and factory closures during the early decades of the 19th century sparked unrest in 1830.

Le Théâtre de la Monnaie
A patriotic song, *L'Amour Sacré de la Patrie* led the audience on the night of 25 August 1830, to join demonstrators outside (see pp50–51).

Belgian Revolution

High unemployment, poor wages and a bad winter in 1829 provoked protests about living and working conditions. The revolution was ignited by a patriotic and radical opera at the Brussels' opera house, and the largely liberal audience rushed out into the street, raising the Brabant flag. Ten thousand troops were sent by William to quash the rebels, but the Belgian soldiers deserted and the Dutch were finally driven out of Belgium.

The initial list of demands asked for administrative independence from the Dutch, and for freedom of press.

King of Belgium, Léopold I
The crowning of German prince, Léopold of Saxe-Coburg, in Brussels in 1831 finally established Belgium's independence.

This symbolic illustration of the revolution shows both liberals and workers ready to die for their country.

1790 Republic of United Belgian States formed. Temporary end of Austrian rule

1799 Emperor Napoleon rules France
Wellington

1815 Battle of Waterloo. Napoleon defeated by army led by the Duke of Wellington

1830 Rebellion begins at the Théâtre de la Monnaie in Brussels

| 1790 | 1800 | 1810 | 1820 | 1830 |

1794 Brussels loses its importance to The Hague

1815 Belgium, allied with Holland under the United Kingdom of the Netherlands, is ruled by William I of Orange. Brussels becomes second capital

1831 State of Belgium formed on 21 July. Treaty of London grants independence

1790 War between France and Austria

1835 Continental railway built from Brussels to Mechelen

The Flemish and the Walloons: The Belgian Compromise

Linguistically and culturally, Belgium is divided. In the north, the Flemish have their roots in the Netherlands and Germany. In the south are the Walloons, the French-speaking Belgians, culturally connected to France. The "Linguistic Divide" of 1962 officially sanctioned this situation, dividing Belgium into

Bilingual road signs

Flemish- and French-speaking zones. The exception is Brussels, an officially bilingual city since the formation of Bruxelles-Capitale in 1963, and a national region by 1989 when it came to comprise 19 outlying districts. Conflicts still erupt over the issue, but the majority of Belgians seem to be in favour of a united country.

Consolidating the New State

During its early days as an independent nation, Brussels was a haven for free-thinkers, including the libertarian poet Baudelaire, and a refuge for exiles, such as Karl Marx and Victor Hugo. Belgium's industries also continued to expand throughout the 19th century. By 1870, there were no less than four main railway stations in Brussels able to export goods all over Europe. However, the population of Brussels had almost doubled, resulting in poor-quality housing and working conditions. Towards the end of the reign of Belgium's second monarch, Léopold II (r.1865–1909), industrial unrest led to new legislation which improved conditions, and all men over 25 gained the right to vote in 1893. But the king's principal concern was his colonialist policy in the Congo in Central Africa.

The German Occupations

Albert I succeeded Léopold II as Belgium's new king. He encouraged the nation's artists and architects, and was a keen supporter of Art Nouveau (see pp20–21). All of this ended as the country entered its bleakest period.

Despite its neutral status, Belgium was invaded by the German army in the summer of 1914. All of the country, except for the northern De Panne region, was occupied by the Germans. Some of the bloodiest battles of World War I were staged on Belgian soil. Flanders was the scene of brutal trench warfare, including the introduction of poison gas at Ypres (see p111). Today, Belgium contains several vast graveyards, which include the resting places of the tens of thousands of soldiers who died on the Western Front.

The Belgians conducted resistance from their stronghold in De Panne, cutting telephone wires and destroying train tracks. The Germans responded by confiscating property, deporting Belgians to German labour camps and murdering random hostages.

King Léopold III visits a goldmine in the Congo in Africa

1847 Opening of Europe's first shopping mall, the Galéries St Hubert

1871 Under Léopold II, the River Senne is reclaimed, and new districts built to cope with the growing city

1898 Flemish language given equal status to French in law

1914–18 World War I. Germany occupies Belgium

| 1840 | 1870 | 1900 | 1925 |

The Belgian Congo

1884 Léopold II is granted sovereignty over the Congo

1910 World Fair in Brussels promotes Belgium's industrial boom. Art Nouveau flourishes

1929–31 Great Depression and reduction in foreign trade

1839 Treaty of London grants neutrality to Belgium

German troops raising the flag of the Third Reich at the Royal Castle at Laeken, near Brussels

Belgium remained under German occupation until the last day of the war, 11 November 1918.

The 1919 Treaty of Versailles granted Belgium control of Eupen-Malmédy, the German-speaking area in the southeast. But by 1940, the country was again invaded by the Germans under Hitler. In May of that year, King Léopold III surrendered.

Despite national resistance to the Occupation, the King was interned at Laeken until 1944, after which he was moved to Germany until the end of the war. Rumours that Léopold had collaborated with the Nazis led to his abdication in 1951, in favour of his 20-year-old son, Baudouin.

International Status

Belgium's history in the latter half of the 20th century has been dominated by the ongoing language debate between the Flemish and the French-speaking Walloons. From 1970 to 1994, the constitution was redrawn, creating a federal state with three separate regions; the Flemish north, the Walloon south and bilingual Brussels. While this smoothed over conflicts, cultural divisions run deep. Today, all parliamentary speeches have to be delivered in both French and Flemish.

Like most of Europe, Belgium went from economic boom in the 1960s to recession and retrenchment in the 1970s and 1980s. Throughout these decades, Brussels' stature at the heart of Europe was consolidated. In 1958, the city became the headquarters for the European Economic Community (EEC), later the European Union. In 1967, NATO also moved to Brussels.

The European Capital

Modern Brussels is a multilingual and cosmopolitan city at the forefront of Europe. This historically industrial city now prospers as a base for many large corporations. Despite its flourishing status, the city has

The European Parliament, Brussels

had its fair share of disasters, including the deaths of 38 Italian football supporters at the Heysel stadium in 1985. Also, two tragic paedophile murder cases in the 1990s led many Belgians to protest against the apparent failures of the police system. However, Brussels' future as a city of world importance seems certain as it lies at the political centre of the European Union.

1939–45 World War II. Germany again occupies Belgium

1934 Albert I is killed in a climbing accident

1944 Benelux Unions with Holland and Luxembourg formed

1951 Abdication of Léopold III; Baudouin I succeeds

Baudouin I

1950

1960 The Belgian Congo is granted independence

European flag

1967 Brussels is new NATO HQ

1975

1985 Heysel Stadium disaster

1989 Brussels is officially a bilingual city with 19 outlying districts

1993 King Baudouin I dies; Albert II succeeds

2000

2001 Crown Prince Philippe and Princess Mathilde have a daughter, Elisabeth

2002 The euro becomes legal tender

2013 Albert II abdicates in favour of his son, Philippe I

2025

BRUSSELS AREA BY AREA

Sights at a Glance

Historic Buildings and Monuments
2 *Hôtel de Ville pp46–7*
3 Manneken Pis
7 La Bourse

Museums and Galleries
1 Musée du Costume et de la Dentelle
8 Bruxella 1238
14 *Centre Belge de la Bande Dessinée pp52–3*
21 Maison de la Bellone

Churches
4 Notre-Dame de la Chapelle
9 Eglise St-Nicolas
19 Eglise St-Jean-Baptiste
22 Eglise Ste-Catherine

Shopping
10 Galeries St-Hubert
16 Rue Neuve

Streets and Squares
11 Rue des Bouchers
18 Place de Brouckère

Theatres
12 Théâtre Marionnettes de Toone
13 Théâtre Royal de la Monnaie
20 Théâtre Royal Flamand

Cultural Centres
15 Le Botanique

Historic Districts
5 Quartier Marolles
6 Halles St-Géry

Hotels
17 Hôtel Métropole

A biblical scene beautifully depicted in stained glass at Kapellekerk, Brussels

THE LOWER TOWN

Most visits to Brussels begin with a stroll around the Lower Town, the ancient heart of the city and home to its most famous area, the Grand Place (see pp44–5). The original settlement of the city was located here and most of the streets surrounding this market square date from the Middle Ages up to the 18th century. The architecture is an eclectic blend of Gothic, Baroque and Flemish Renaissance. In and around the Place de

Brouckère and the busy Boulevard Anspach are the more recent additions to the city's history. These appeared in the 19th century when the slums around the River Senne were cleared to make way for ornate constructions such as the financial centre, La Bourse, and Europe's first shopping arcade, Galeries St-Hubert. With its many restaurants and cafés, the Lower Town is also popular at night.

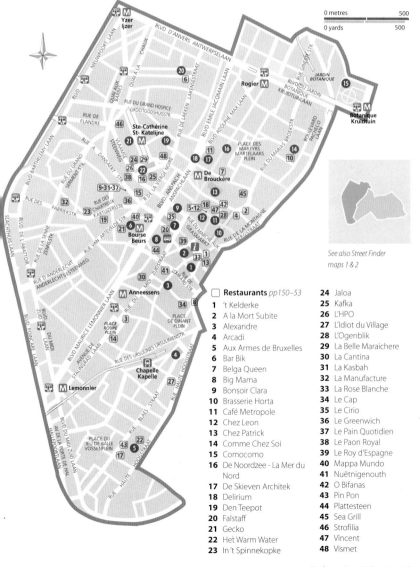

0 metres 500
0 yards 500

See also Street Finder
maps 1 & 2

Restaurants pp150–53

1 't Kelderke	24 Jaloa
2 A la Mort Subite	25 Kafka
3 Alexandre	26 L'HPO
4 Arcadi	27 L'Idiot du Village
5 Aux Armes de Bruxelles	28 L'Ogenblik
6 Bar Bik	29 La Belle Maraichere
7 Belga Queen	30 La Cantina
8 Big Mama	31 La Kasbah
9 Bonsoir Clara	32 La Manufacture
10 Brasserie Horta	33 La Rose Blanche
11 Café Metropole	34 Le Cap
12 Chez Leon	35 Le Cirio
13 Chez Patrick	36 Le Greenwich
14 Comme Chez Soi	37 Le Pain Quotidien
15 Comocomo	38 Le Paon Royal
16 De Noordzee - La Mer du Nord	39 Le Roy d'Espagne
17 De Skieven Architek	40 Mappa Mundo
18 Delirium	41 Nuëtnigenouth
19 Den Teepot	42 O Bifanas
20 Falstaff	43 Pin Pon
21 Gecko	44 Plattesteen
22 Het Warm Water	45 Sea Grill
23 In 't Spinnekopke	46 Strofilia
	47 Vincent
	48 Vismet

For keys to symbols see back flap

The Grand Place

The geographical, historical and commercial heart of the city, the Grand Place is the first port of call for most visitors to Brussels. The square remains the civic centre, centuries after its creation, and offers the finest surviving example in one area of Belgium's ornate 17th-century architecture. Open-air markets took place on or near this site as early as the 11th century, but by the end of the 15th century Brussels' town hall, the Hôtel de Ville, was built, and city traders added individual guildhouses in a medley of styles. In 1695, however, three days of cannon fire by the French destroyed all but the façades of the town hall and some of the guildhouses. Trade guilds were urged to rebuild their halls to styles approved by the Town Council, producing the harmonious unity of Flemish Baroque buildings here today.

The vibrant flower market in bloom in the Grand Place

The Maison du Roi was first built in 1536 but redesigned in 1873. Once used by the ruling Spanish monarchs, it is now home to the Musée de la Ville, which includes 16th-century paintings, tapestries, and the many tiny outfits of Manneken Pis.

① Northeast Corner

② Maison Du Roi

The Hôtel de Ville occupies the entire southwest side of the square. Still a functioning civic building, Brussels' town hall is the architectural masterpiece of the Grand Place (see pp46–7).

The spire was built by Jan van Ruysbroeck in 1449 and stands 96 m (315 ft) high; it is slightly crooked.

Ornate stone carvings

Everard 't Serclaes was murdered defending Brussels in the 14th century; touching the bronze arm of his statue is said to bring luck.

⑤ Everard 'T Serclaes

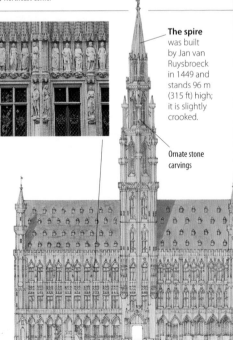

⑥ Hôtel De Ville

Le Pigeon was home to Victor Hugo, the exiled French novelist who chose the house as his Belgian residence in 1852. Some of the most complimentary comments about Brussels emerged later from his pen.

La Maison des Ducs de Brabant is a group of six guildhouses. Designed by the Controller of Public Works, Guillaume de Bruyn, the group looks like an Italian Baroque palazzo.

Locator Map
See Brussels Street Finder map 2

Stone busts of the ducal line along the façade gave this group of houses their name.

③ Le Pigeon

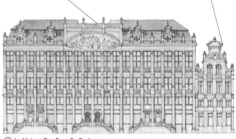

④ La Maison Des Ducs De Brabant

Le Renard was built in 1699 as the guildhouse of the haberdashers by the Flemish architects Marc de Vos and van Nerum. Façade details show St Nicolas, patron saint of merchants, and cherubs playing with haberdashery ribbons.

Le Cornet displays Italianate Flemish style. This Boatmen's Guildhouse (1697) is most notable for its gable, which is constructed in the form of a 17th-century frigate's bow.

La Maison des Boulangers, also known as "Le Roi d'Espagne", was a showpiece built by the wealthy and powerful guild of bakers. The 1697 octagonal copper dome is topped by a golden figure blowing a trumpet.

Le Roi d'Espagne now houses the Grand Place's finest bar with a view of the bustling square and its splendours above ground level. The gilt bust over the entrance represents Saint Aubert, patron saint of bakers. There is a vast bust of Charles II of Spain on the second floor.

⑦ Le Renard, Le Cornet and Le Roi D'Espagne

For keys to symbols *see back flap*

❶ Musée du Costume et de la Dentelle

Rue de la Violette 12, 1000 BRU.
Map 2 D3. 🚌 29, 38, 46, 48, 63, 71, 86, 95. 🚊 3, 4, 31, 32. **Tel** (02) 213 4450.
Ⓜ Gare Centrale. **Open** 10am–5pm Tue–Sun. **Closed** Mon, 1 May, 1 & 11 Nov, 25 Dec. 🅿 ♿ 📷 on request, call (02) 279 4355. 🅆 **museedu costumeetdeladentelle.be**

Found within two 17th-century gabled houses is the museum dedicated to one of Brussels' most successful exports, Belgian lace (see pp24–5). The intricate skill employed by Belgian lacemakers has contributed a vital economic role in the city since the 17th

A wedding dress at the Musée du Costume et de la Dentelle

century, and the collection explains and displays the history of this delicate craft. The second floor houses a small collection of antique

lace, carefully stored in drawers and demonstrating the various schools of lacemaking in France, Flanders and Italy. The museum displays temporary exhibitions of contemporary textiles and fashion.

❸ Manneken Pis

Rues de l'Etuve & du Chêne, 1000 BRU.
Map 1 C3. 🚌 29, 38, 46, 48, 63, 71, 86, 95. 🚊 3, 4, 31, 32. Ⓜ Gare Centrale.

An unlikely attraction, this tiny statue of a young boy barely 61 cm (2 ft) high relieving himself into a small pool is as much a part of Brussels as the Trevi Fountain is part of Rome

❷ Hôtel de Ville

The idea of having a town hall to reflect Brussels' growth as a major European trading centre had been under consideration since the end of the 13th century. It was not until 1401 that the first foundation stone was laid and the building was finally completed in 1455, emerging as the finest civic building in the country, a stature it still enjoys.

Jacques van Thienen was commissioned to design the left wing and belfry of the building, where he used ornate columns, sculptures, turrets and arcades. The tower and spire begun in 1449 by Jan van Ruysbroeck helped seal its reputation. In 1995, the 1455 statue of the city's patron saint, Michael, was restored and now resides inside the tower. A copy of the statue sits on top of the tower. Tours are available of the interior, which contains 18th-century tapestries and works of art.

A detail of the delicately carved façade with stone statues

137 statues adorn walls and many mullioned windows.

★ Aldermen's Room
Still in use today for the meetings of the aldermen and mayor of Brussels, this council chamber contains a series of 18th-century tapestries depicting the history of 6th-century King Clovis.

or Trafalgar Square's proud lions are of London.

The current statue of Manneken Pis by Jérôme Duquesnoy the Elder has been in place since 1619. However, there is evidence to suggest that a stone fountain depicting the same figure stood there before it, possibly as early as 1451. In its long history, the statuette has been the victim of several thefts. A particularly violent theft in 1965 left the statue broken in two pieces, leaving just the ankles and feet remaining. The missing body of

the statue reappeared a year later when it was found in a canal.

In 1698 the governor of the Netherlands, Maximilian Emmanuel, brought a gift to the city in the form of a blue woollen coat for the statue. This is a tradition that continues today, with visiting heads of state donating miniature versions of their national costume. The little boy has a collection of over 800 outfits which are housed in the Musée de la Ville de Bruxelles *(see p44)*, where 100 are on display at any one time. Among the collection is a miniature Samurai, Santa Claus and Elvis suit.

The Legends of Manneken Pis

The charm of this famous statue comes from the many rumours and fables behind it. One theory claims that in the 12th century the son of a duke was caught urinating against a tree in the midst of a battle and was thus commemorated in bronze as a symbol of military courage. The inspiration for the statue has been revealed as Cupid.

The belfry was built by architect Jan van Ruysbroeck. A statue of St Michael tops the 96 m (315 ft) spire.

Aldermen's Room

The gabled roof, like much of the town hall, was fully restored in 1837, and cleaned in the 1990s.

VISITORS' CHECKLIST

Practical Information
Grand Place, 1000 BRU
Map 2 D3. **Tel** (02) 279 2343 (general info); (02) 548 0447 (for visits). Hôtel de Ville: **Open** for guided tours. **Closed** pub hols, election days. 🎟 (tickets at Hôtel de Ville or Grand Place tourist office). 📷 Wed 3pm, Sun 10am & 2pm (in Eng).
🌐 visitbrussels.be

Transport
🚌 29, 38, 46, 48, 63, 66, 71, 86, 95.
🚊 3, 4, 31, 32. Ⓜ Gare Centrale.

★ Conference Room Council Chamber
The most splendid of all the public rooms, ancient tapestries and gilt mirrors line the walls above an inlaid floor.

Wedding Room
A Neo-Gothic style dominates this civil marriage office, with its many ornate carved timbers, including ancient ebony and mahogany.

Banqueting room

❹ Notre-Dame de la Chapelle

Place de la Chapelle 1, 1000 BRU.
Map 1 C4. **Tel** (02) 538 3087. 27,
48, 95. 3, 4, 31, 32. Anneessens,
Centrale. **Open** 9am–7pm daily;
Mass 4pm Sat, 8am, 9:30am, 11am,
5:30pm Sun.

In 1134, King Godefroid I
decided to build a chapel
outside the city walls. It
quickly became a market
church, serving the many
craftsmen living nearby. In
1210, its popularity was such
that it was made a parish
church, but it became really
famous in 1250, when a royal
donation of five pieces of the
True Cross turned the church
into a pilgrimage site.

Originally built in Romanesque style, the majority of the
church was destroyed by fire
in 1405. Rebuilding began in
1421 in a Gothic style typical
of 15th-century Brabant architecture, including gables
decorated with finials and
interior capitals decorated
with cabbage leaves at the
base. The Bishop of Cambrai
consecrated the new church
in 1434.

One of the most striking
features of the exterior are
the monstrously lifelike
gargoyles – a representation
of evil outside the sacred
interior. The Baroque bell
tower was added after the
1695 bombardment by the
French *(see p34)*. Another
moving feature is the carved
stone memorial to the

The elegant interior of
Notre-Dame de la Chapelle

Rue Haute in the Quartier Marolles, with old-style shops and cafés

16th-century Belgian artist
Pieter Brueghel the Elder *(see
p18)*, who is buried here.

❺ Quartier Marolles

Map 1 C5. 27, 48. 3, 4, 51, 92,
94, 97. Louise, Porte de Hal.

Known colloquially as "Les
Marolles", this quarter of Brussels
is traditionally working class.
Situated between the two city
walls, the area was home to
weavers and craftsmen. Street
names of the district, such as
Rue des Brodeurs (Embroiderers'
St) and Rue des Charpentiers
(Carpenters' St), reflect its
artisanal history.

Today, the area is best known
for its fine daily flea market,
held in the **Place du Jeu de
Balle**. The flea market has been
held on this site since 1640.
Between 7am and 2pm, with
the biggest and best markets
on Thursday and Sunday, almost
anything from junk to pre-war
collector's items can be found
among the stalls.

Shopping of a different kind
is on offer on nearby Rue Haute,
an ancient Roman road. A
shopping district since the 19th
century, it is still popular with
arty types with its specialist
stores, interior and antique
shops. The street has a long
artistic history, too – the elegant
red-brick house at No. 132 was
home to Pieter Brueghel the
Elder and the sculptor Auguste
Rodin had a studio at No. 224.

At the southern end of Rue
Haute is Porte de Hal, the

stone gateway of the now-
demolished outer city walls.
Looming over the Marolles is
the imposing Palais de Justice
(see p71), which has hilltop
views of the area west of the
city, including the 1958 Atomium *(see p89)* and the Basilique
Sacré-Coeur *(see p87)*.

Busy restaurants and cafés
outside Halles St-Géry

❻ Halles St-Géry

Place St-Géry 23, 1000 BRU. **Map** 1 C2.
46, 48, 86, 95. 3, 4, 31, 32.
De Brouckère.

In many ways, St-Géry can be
considered the birthplace of the
city. A chapel to Saint Géry was
built in the 6th century, then in
AD 977 a fortress took over the
site. A 16th-century church
followed and occupied the
location until the 18th century.
In 1881, a covered meat market
was erected in Neo-Renaissance

style. The glass and intricate ironwork was renovated in 1985, and the hall now serves as a cultural centre with an exhibition on local history.

❼ La Bourse

Palais de la Bourse, 1000 BRU. **Map** 1 C2. **Tel** (02) 509 1373. 🚌 29, 38, 46, 48, 63, 66, 71, 86, 95. 🚊 3, 4, 31, 32. Ⓜ De Brouckère. **Closed** to the public.

Brussels' Stock Exchange, La Bourse, is one of the city's most impressive buildings, dominating the square of the same name. Designed in Palladian style by architect Léon Suys, it was constructed from 1867 to 1873. Among the building's most notable features are the façade's ornate carvings. The great French sculptor, Auguste Rodin, is thought to have crafted the groups representing Africa and Asia, as well as four caryatids inside. Beneath the colonnade, two beautifully detailed winged figures representing Good and Evil were carved by sculptor Jacques de Haen. Once the scene of frantic trading, La Bourse now houses the offices of Euronext, owners of the Belgian Stock Exchange, and all trading is computerized. The building is no longer open to the public.

Detail of a Rodin statue, La Bourse

❽ Bruxella 1238

Rue de la Bourse, 1000 BRU. **Map** 1 C3. **Tel** (02) 279 4350. 🚌 29, 38, 46, 48, 63, 66, 71, 86, 88, 95. 🚊 3, 4, 31, 32. Ⓜ De Brouckère. **Open** 1st Wed of month: 10:15am (English), 11:15am (French), 2pm (Dutch); by appt only at other times. 🎧 📷 obligatory, starts from Maison du Roi, Grand Place.

Once home to a church and 13th-century Franciscan convent, in the early 19th century this site became a Butter Market until the building of the Bourse started in 1867. In 1988, municipal roadworks began alongside the Place de la Bourse. Medieval history must have been far from the minds of the city authorities but, in the course of working on the foundations, important relics were found, including 13th-century bones, pottery and the 1294 grave of Duke John I of Brabant. Visitors can see these and other pieces in a small museum built on the site.

❾ Eglise St-Nicolas

Rue au Beurre 1, 1000 BRU. **Map** 1 C2. **Tel** (02) 513 8022. 🚌 29, 38, 46, 48, 63, 66, 71, 86, 95. 🚊 3, 4, 31, 32. Ⓜ De Brouckère. **Open** 8am–6pm Mon–Fri, 9am–6pm Sat, 9am–7:30pm Sun & public hols.

At the end of the 12th century, a market church was built on this site, but, like much of the Lower Town, it was damaged in the 1695 French Bombardment. A cannon ball lodged itself into an interior pillar and the bell tower finally collapsed in 1714. Many restoration projects were planned but none came to fruition until 1956, when the west side of the building was given a new, Gothic-style façade. Named after St Nicolas, the patron saint of merchants, the church contains choir stalls dating from 1381 which display detailed medallions telling St Nicolas' story. Another interesting feature is the chapel, constructed at an angle, reputedly to avoid the flow of an old stream. Inside the church, works of art by Bernard van Orley and Peter Paul Rubens are well worth seeing.

The 19th-century domed glass roof of Galeries St-Hubert

❿ Galeries St-Hubert

Rue des Bouchers, 1000 BRU. **Map** 2 D2. 🚊 3, 4, 25, 31, 32, 94. Ⓜ Gare Centrale. ♿

Sixteen years after ascending the throne as the first king of Belgium, Léopold I inaugurated the opening of these grand arcades in 1847.

St-Hubert has the distinction of being the first shopping arcade in Europe, and one of the most elegant. Designed in Neo-Renaissance style by Jean-Pierre Cluysenaer, the vaulted glass roof covers its three sections, Galerie du Roi, Galerie de la Reine and Galerie des Princes, which house a range of luxury shops and cafés. The ornate interior and expensive goods on sale soon turned the galleries into a fashionable meeting place for 19th-century society, including resident literati – Victor Hugo and Alexandre Dumas attended lectures here. The arcades remain a popular venue, with shops, a cinema, theatre, cafés and restaurants.

Gothic-style façade of Eglise St-Nicolas

Outdoor seating at restaurants along Rue des Bouchers

⓫ Rue des Bouchers

Map 2 D2. 🚌 29, 38, 46, 48, 63, 66, 71, 86, 95. 🚊 3, 4, 31, 32, 33. Ⓜ De Brouckère, Gare Centrale.

Like many streets in this area of the city, Rue des Bouchers retains its medieval name, reminiscent of the time when this meandering, cobblestoned street was home to the butchers' trade. Aware of its historic importance and heeding the concerns of the public, the city council declared this area the Ilot Sacré (sacred islet) in 1960, forbidding any of the architectural façades to be altered or destroyed, and commanding those surviving to be restored. Hence Rue des Bouchers abounds with 17th-century stepped gables and decorated doorways.

Today, this pedestrianized thoroughfare is best known as the "belly of Brussels", a reference to its plethora of cafés and restaurants offering many types of cuisine. But the most impressive sights during an evening stroll along the street are the lavish pavement displays of seafood, piled high on mounds of ice, all romantically lit by an amber glow from the streetlamps.

At the end of the street, at the Impasse de la Fidélité, is an acknowledgement of sexual equality. Erected in 1987, Jeanneke Pis is a coy, cheeky female version of her "brother", the more famous Manneken Pis *(see p47)*.

⓬ Théâtre Marionettes de Toone

Impasse Ste Pétronille, 66 Rue du Marché aux Herbes, 1000 BRU. **Map** 2 D2. **Tel** (02) 511 7137. 🚌 29, 38, 46, 48, 63, 66, 71, 86, 95. 🚊 3, 4, 31, 32. Ⓜ Gare Centrale. **Open** bar: noon–midnight daily; theatre: performance times 4pm Sat, 8:30pm Thu–Sat. **Closed** Mon, Tue & pub hols. 🎭 📷 on request, for tour reservations **Tel** (02) 217 2753. Museum: **Open** intervals. 🌐 toone.be

A popular pub by day, at night the top floor of this tavern is home to a puppet theatre. During the time of the Spanish Netherlands *(see p34)*, all theatres were closed because of the satirical performances by actors aimed at their Latin rulers. This began a fashion for puppet shows, the vicious dialogue more easily forgiveable from inanimate dolls. In 1830, Antoine Toone opened his own theatre and

Harlequin puppet

it has been run by the Toone family ever since; the owner is the eighth generation, Toone VIII. The classics are enacted by these wooden marionettes in the local Bruxellois dialect, and occasionally in French, English, German or Dutch.

⓭ Théâtre Royal de la Monnaie

Place de la Monnaie, 1000 BRU. **Map** 2 D2. **Tel** (02) 229 1211. 🚌 29, 38, 46, 47, 48, 63, 66, 71, 86, 88, 95. 🚊 3, 4, 31, 32. Ⓜ De Brouckère. **Open** performance times, Tue–Sun; box office: noon–6pm Tue–Sat. **Closed** Sun, public hols. 🎭 📷 on written request. 🌐 lamonnaie.be

This theatre was first built in 1817 on the site of a 15th-century mint but, following a fire in 1855, only the front and pediment of the original Neo-Classical building remain. After the fire, the theatre was redesigned by the architect, Joseph Poelaert, also responsible for the imposing Palais de Justice *(see p71)*.

The original theatre made its historical mark before its destruction, however, when on 25 August 1830, a performance of *La Muette de Portici (The Mute Girl)* began a national rebellion. As the tenor began to sing the nationalist *Amour Sacré de la Patrie (Sacred love of the homeland)*, his words incited an already discontented city, fired by the libertarianism of the revolutions occurring in France, into revolt. The audience ran

The original Neo-Classical façade of Théâtre Royal de la Monnaie

The 19th-century glasshouse of Le Botanique in summer

into the street in a rampage that developed into the September Uprising *(see pp36–7)*. The theatre today remains the centre of Belgian performing arts; major renovations took place during the 1980s. The auditorium was raised 4 m (13 ft) to accommodate the elaborate stage designs, but the luxurious Louis XIV-style decor was carefully retained and blended with the new additions. The central dome is decorated with an allegory of Belgian arts.

⓮ Centre Belge de la Bande Dessinée

See pp52–53.

⓯ Le Botanique

Rue Royale 236, 1210 BRU. **Map** 2 E1. **Tel** (02) 218 3732. 🚌 61. 🚋 92, 93. Ⓜ Botanique. **Open** 11am–6pm Mon–Fri, noon–6pm Sat & Sun (till 10pm on concert nights. 🚹 🖳 🅦 botanique.be

In 1797, the city of Brussels created a botanical garden in the grounds of the Palais de Lorraine as a source of reference for botany students. The garden closed in 1826, and new gardens were relocated in Meise, 13 km (9 miles) from Brussels.

A grand glass-and-iron rotunda was designed at the centre of the gardens by the French architect Gineste. This iron glasshouse still stands, as does much of the 19th-century statuary by Constantin Meunier *(see p19)*, including depictions of the Four Seasons. The glasshouse is now home to the French Community Cultural Centre and offers concerts and contemporary art exhibitions.

⓰ Rue Neuve

Map 2 D2. 🚌 29, 38, 46, 47, 48, 58, 61, 63, 66, 71, 86, 88, 95. 🚋 3, 4, 25, 31, 32, 55. Ⓜ De Brouckère, Rogier.

Brussels shoppers have been flocking to the busy Rue Neuve since the 19th century for its reasonably priced goods and well-located stores. Similar to London's Oxford Street, but now pedestrianized, this is the heart

Rue Neuve, the longest pedestrian shopping street in the city

of commercial shopping. It houses well-known international chainstores and shopping malls, such as **City 2**, which has shops, cafés and the media store Fnac all under one roof. Inno department store was designed by Horta *(see p84)*, but after a fire in 1967 was entirely rebuilt.

To the east of Rue Neuve is Place des Martyrs, a peaceful square where a monument pays tribute to the 450 citizens killed during the 1830 uprising.

🏬 **City 2**
Rue Neuve 123, 1000 BRU. **Tel** (02) 211 4060. **Open** 10am–7pm Mon–Thu & Sat, 10am–8pm Fri. **Closed** Sun, public hols.

⓱ Hôtel Métropole

Place de Brouckère 31, 1000 BRU. **Map** 2 D2. **Tel** (02) 217 2300. 🚌 29, 38, 46, 47, 63, 66, 71, 86, 88. 🚋 3, 4, 31, 32. Ⓜ De Brouckère. 🅦 **metropolehotel.com**

The area lying between Place Rogier and Place de Brouckère is known as the hotel district of Brussels, and one of the oldest and grandest hotels in the area is the Métropole.

In 1891, the Wielemans Brewery bought the building and commissioned the architect Alban Chambon to redesign the interior, with money no object. The result was a fine Art Nouveau hotel which opened for business in 1895 and has since accommodated numerous acclaimed visitors, including actress Sarah Bernhardt. In 1911, the hotel was the location of the first science conference Conseil Physique Solvay, attended by the great scientists Marie Curie and Albert Einstein.

The Hôtel Métropole continues to welcome guests from all walks of life, at surprisingly reasonable cost given its beauty, history and location. It is particularly popular for drinks in its Café Métropole and heated pavement terrace, which are both open to non-residents to enjoy cocktails and coffees in elegant surroundings.

⓮ Centre Belge de la Bande Dessinée

Affectionately known as *cébébédé*, the Museum of Comic Strip Art pays tribute to the Belgian passion for comic strips or *bandes dessinées* and to many world-famous comic strip artists from Belgium and abroad.

Arranged over three levels, the collection is housed in a Horta-designed Art Nouveau building. One of the most popular permanent exhibitions is a tour of the great comic strip heroes, from *Tintin* to *The Smurfs*, both of whose creators were Belgian. Other displays detail the stages of putting together a comic strip, from examples of initial ideas and pencil sketches through to final publication. The museum regularly holds major exhibitions featuring the work of famous cartoonists and studios, and also houses some 8,000 original plates, displayed in rotation, as well as a valuable archive of photographs and artifacts.

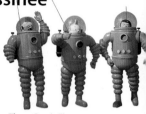

Three Comic Figures
Tintin, Professor Calculus and Captain Haddock greet visitors on the 1st floor.

The Smurfs
These tiny blue characters first appeared in the *Spirou* journal in 1958. By the 1980s, they had their own TV show and hit records.

A Suivre
Founded in 1978, A Suivre expanded the comic strip genre, and led to the new form of graphic novels: adult stories in cartoon form.

★ **Life-size Cartoon Sets**
A series of authentic comic scenes encourages children to enter the world of their favourite comic strip characters.

VISITORS' CHECKLIST

Practical Information
20 rue des Sables, 1000 BRU.
Map 2 E2.
Tel (02) 219 1980.
Open 10am– 6pm Tue–Sun.

Transport
🚌 29, 38, 46, 47, 61, 63,
66, 71, 86, 88. 🚋 3, 4, 31,
32, 92, 94. Ⓜ Botanique,
De Brouckère, Rogier.

★ **The Light Room**
This airy space designed
by Victor Horta features
stained glass and
wrought-ironwork.

Comic Library
The museum library
doubles as a study centre
for both art students and
enthusiasts of all ages.
This unique collection
includes a catalogue of
hundreds of old comic
strips, artists' equipment,
biographies, comic novels
and photographs.

A Horta-Designed Building

This beautiful building was constructed between
1903 and 1906 to the design of the Belgian
Art-Nouveau architect Victor Horta.
Originally built as a fabric warehouse, and
known as the Waucquez Building, it was one in a
series of department stores and warehouses in the
city designed by him. Saved from demolition by the
French Cultural Commission of Brussels, in 1989 the
building re-opened as a museum dedicated to the
comic strip, Belgium's so-called Ninth Art *(see pp22–
3)*. Carefully restored, the building has many classic
features of Art Nouveau design, including the use
of curves on structural iron pillars. In the
impressive entrance hall is a display of Horta's
architectural drawings for the building, and
on the right, the Brasserie Horta serves
traditional Belgian dishes in a charming glass
and marble Art Nouveau setting.

Cast-iron pillar

The Changing Face of Hergé's Tintin

*Perhaps the best-known Belgian comic
character, Tintin made his debut in a
children's paper in 1929. He began life as
a simple black line drawing, featuring the
famous quiff, but no mouth. By 1930 Hergé
began to produce Tintin in book-form and
gave him both a mouth and a more
complex character suggested by a greater
range of facial expressions. By the 1940s
Tintin was appearing in colour, alongside
such new characters as Captain Haddock,
the Thompsons and Professor Calculus.*

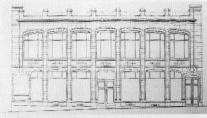

Horta's drawing of the CBBD building

Nineteenth-century building in Place de Brouckère

⓲ Place de Brouckère

Map 2 D2. 🚌 29, 38, 46, 47, 48, 63, 66, 71, 86, 88, 95. 🚋 3, 4, 31, 32. Ⓜ De Brouckère.

In 1872, a design competition was held to encourage the construction of buildings of architectural interest in de Brouckère. Twenty winning applicants were selected and commissioned to give prominence to this Brussels junction. The Parisian contractor Jean-Baptiste Mosnier was responsible for taking the original plans through to completion.

The French influence of Mosnier and his workers is still evident on the square. Many of the buildings were erected in stone, common in France at the end of the 19th century, whereas brickwork was more usual in Brussels. Several original façades survive today, including the 1874 Hôtel Continental by Eugene Carpentier.

One of the great hotels of Brussels, the Hôtel Métropole (*see p51*) is situated on the south side of the square. The 1900–10 interior is splendidly gilded and can be seen either through the doorway or by pretending to be a guest. Café Métropole next door is, however, open to the public; here, the lavishly ornate surroundings date from around 1890.

In the 20th century, architectural style was still at a premium in the district. In 1933, a Neo-Classical cinema was erected with an impressive Art Deco interior. During the 1960s, two imposing glass buildings blended the contemporary with the classical. Today, the varied historic architecture of Place de Brouckère enhances one of the city's busiest squares, despite the addition of advertising hoardings.

⓳ Eglise St-Jean-Baptiste-au-Béguinage

Place du Béguinage, 1000 BRU. **Map** 1 C1. **Tel** (02) 217 8742. 🚌 47, 88. Ⓜ Ste-Catherine. **Open** 10am–5pm Tue–Sat, 10am–8pm Sun. **Closed** Mon. ♿

This stone-clad church was consecrated in 1676 around the long-standing and largest béguine community in the country, established in 1250. Fields and orchards around the site contained cottages and houses for up to 1,200 béguine women, members of a lay religious order who took up charitable work and enclosed living after widowhood or failed marriages. In medieval times, the béguines ran a laundry, hospital and windmill for the people of the city. Still a popular place of worship,

the church is also notable for its Flemish Baroque details from the 17th century, especially the onion-shaped turrets and ornamental walls. The nave is also Baroque, decorated with ornate winged cherubs, angels and scrolls. The confessionals are carved with allegorical figures and saints. A more unusual feature are the aisles, which have been widened to allow more light in. In the apse is a statue of St John the Baptist. The 1757 pulpit is a fine example of Baroque woodcarving, showing St Dominic and a heretic.

⓴ Théâtre Royal Flamand

Quai au Pierre de Taille 9, 1000 BRU. **Map** 1 C1. **Tel** (02) 210 1112. 🚌 47, 48, 58, 61, 88. 🚋 3, 4, 25, 31, 32, 51, 55. Ⓜ Rogier, Yser. 🆆 kvs.be

The former quay area of Brussels, on the banks of the old River Senne, still survives as a reminder that the city was once a thriving port. In 1882, architect Jean Baes was commissioned to enlarge one of the former waterfront warehouses and then turn it into a theatre but was asked to retain the original 1780

The ornate façade of Eglise St-Jean-Baptiste-au-Béguinage

façade. Baes solved this problem by placing the façade directly behind the frontage of the new building. Other interesting design features are peculiar to the late 19th century. The four exterior metal terraces and a staircase leading to the ground were built for audience evacuation in the event of fire. Major renovations have restored the fabric of the original building and added a second building.

The 19th-century interior staircase of Théâtre Royal Flamand

㉑ Maison de la Bellone

Rue de Flandre 46, 1000 BRU. **Map** 1 C2. **Tel** (02) 513 3333. 🚌 47, 88. Ⓜ Ste-Catherine. **Open** 10am–6pm Mon–Fri. **Closed** Sat, Sun, Jul.

This 17th-century aristocratic residence, now shielded under a glass roof and no longer visible from the street, was once the headquarters of the Ommegang procession (see p27). The original façade is notable for its decoration. There is a statue of Bellona (goddess of war), after whom the house is named, above the central arch, and the window ledges have medallions of Roman emperors.

Today, the house, its exhibition centre and once-private theatre are open for dance and cinema shows, and temporary exhibitions of art and furniture.

Stonework on the Maison de la Bellone

The Béguine Movement

The béguine lifestyle swept across Western Europe from the 12th century, and Brussels once had a community of over 1,200 béguine women. The religious order is believed to have begun among widows of the Crusaders, who resorted to a pious life of sisterhood on the death of their husbands. The women were lay nuns, who opted for a secluded existence devoted to charitable deeds, but not bound by strict religious vows. Most béguine convents disappeared during the Protestant Reformation in much of Europe during the 16th century, but begijnhofs (béguinages) continued to thrive in Flanders. The grounds generally consisted of a church, a courtyard, communal rooms, homes for the women and extra rooms for work. The movement dissolved as female emancipation spread during the early 1800s, although 20 convents remain, including those in Bruges (see p125) and Ghent.

Béguine lay nun at prayer in a Brussels béguinage

㉒ Eglise Ste-Catherine

Place Ste-Catherine 50, 1000 BRU. **Map** 1 C2. **Tel** (02) 513 3481. 🚌 47, 88. Ⓜ Ste-Catherine, De Brouckère. **Open** 8am–5:30pm Mon–Sat, 10am–1:30pm Sun. ♿ on request.

Sadly, the only remnant of the first church here, built in the 15th century, is its Baroque tower, added in 1629. Inspired by the Eglise St-Eustache in Paris, the present church was redesigned in 1854–59 by Joseph Poelaert in a variety of styles. Notable features of the interior include a 14th-century statue of the Black Madonna and a portrait of St Catherine herself. A typically Flemish pulpit was installed at some stage; it may have come from the parish of Mechelen. Two impressive tombs were carved by Gilles-Lambert Godecharle. To the east of the church is the Tour Noire (Black Tower), a surviving remnant of the 12th-century stone city walls.

Although this area has been dedicated to the saint since the 13th century, the square of

Place Ste-Catherine was only laid in front of this large church after the basin once here was filled in. Paved in 1870, the square contrasts the peacefulness of the religious building with today's vigorous trade in good fish restaurants.

The central square was once the city's main fish market, and this is still the best place to indulge in a dish or two of Brussels' famous seafood, but prices are generally high. Flanking the square, Quai aux Briques and Quai au Bois à Brûler (Brick Quay and Timber Quay, named after their industrial past), contain lively parades of fish restaurants.

Eglise Ste-Catherine showing the spacious Victorian interior

Neo-Classical style architecture at the Justice Palace
(Palais de Justice), Brussels

Sights at a Glance

Historic Streets and Buildings
6 Hôtel Ravenstein
8 Palais de Charles de Lorraine
14 Palais d'Egmont
15 Palais de Justice
2 *Palais Royal pp60–61*
11 Place du Grand Sablon
13 Place du Petit Sablon
4 Place Royale
19 Square Ambiorix

Parks and Gardens
25 *Parc du Cinquantenaire pp76–7*
24 Parc Léopold

Museums and Galleries
1 BELvue Museum and the
  Coudenberg
23 Institut Royal des Sciences
  Naturelles
9 Musée Charlier

7 Musée des Instruments de Musique
21 Musée Wiertz
10 *Musées Royaux des Beaux-Arts de*
  Belgique pp64–9

Churches and Cathedrals
17 *Cathédrale Sts Michel et Gudule*
  pp72–3
18 Chapelle de la Madeleine
3 Eglise St-Jacques-
  sur-Coudenberg
12 Notre-Dame du Sablon

Theatres and Concert Halls
5 Palais des Beaux-Arts

Modern Architecture
20 Quartier Européen
22 Parliament Quarter

Shopping
16 Galérie Bortier

THE UPPER TOWN

Brussels' Upper Town is separated from the lower part of the city by an escarpment that runs roughly north-south from the far end of Rue Royale to the Palais de Justice. Modern developments are now scattered across the whole city, and the difference between the two areas is less distinct than in the past; traditionally, the Lower Town was mainly Flemish-speaking and a bustling centre for trade, while the Upper Town was home to French-speaking aristocrats and royalty. Today the Upper Town is known for its beautiful Gothic churches, modern architecture and fine museums. The late 18th-century elegance of the Parc de Bruxelles and Place Royale is complemented by "King of the Belgians" Leopold II's sweeping 19th-century boulevards that connect the Parc du Cinquantenaire to the centre.

See also Street Finder maps 2, 3 & 4

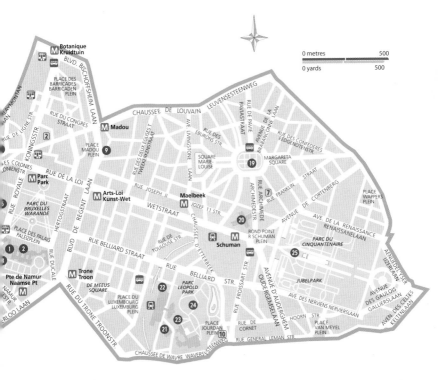

| 0 metres | 500 |
| 0 yards | 500 |

Street-by-Street: Quartier Royal

The Quartier Royal has traditionally been home to Brussels' nobility and rulers. Chosen because the air was purer on the hill than it was in the Lower Town, the area once known as Coudenberg Hill was occupied by the 15th-century Coudenberg Palace, home to the Dukes of Brabant and Renaissance rulers. In 1731, the palace was destroyed in just six hours by a fire. Slowly rebuilt during the 18th and 19th centuries, four new palaces and much of the park were designed in Neo-Classical style chosen by Charles de Lorraine (*see p35*). Today, the Royal quarter presents a peaceful elegance, with some of Europe's finest 18th-century buildings framing the tree-lined paths and fountains of Parc de Bruxelles.

Rue Royale runs for 2 km (1 mile) from the Quartier Royal to Jardin Botanique. In contrast to the 18th-century Neo-Classicism of its beginnings, along its route many fine examples of Victorian and Art Nouveau architecture stand out.

RUE ROYALE

❸ **Eglise St-Jacques-sur-Coudenberg**
One of Brussels' prettiest churches, St-Jacques' 18th-century façade was modelled exactly on a classical temple. The barrel-vaulted nave and half-domed apse are sprinkled with floral plasterwork and contain several fine Neo-Classical paintings

❹ ★ **Place Royale**
In the centre of this attractive, symmetrical square is a statue of Godefroi of Bouillon, a Brabant soldier who fought the first Catholic Crusades and died in Palestine

PLACE ROYALE

Key

— Suggested route

Place des Palais
divides Palais Royal and the park. In French, "Palais" refers to any large stately building, and does not necessarily have royal connotations.

★ Parc de Bruxelles
On the site of medieval hunting grounds once used by the Dukes of Brabant, the park was redesigned in the 1770s with fountains, statues and tree-lined walks.

Locator Map
See Street Finder map 2

Palais de la Nation
Designed by French architect Barnabé Guimard, the Palais de la Nation was built in 1783 and restored in 1883 after a fire. Since 1831, it has been the home of both chambers of the Belgian Parliament.

RUE DE LA LOI

RUE DUCALE

PLACE DES PALAIS

❷ ★ Palais Royal
The largest of the palaces, the low-rise Palais Royal is the official work place of the Belgian monarch and family. A flag flies to indicate when the king is in the country

Palais des Académies
Built in 1823 as the residence of the Crown Prince, this has been the private premises of the Académie Royale de Belgique since 1876.

0 metres	100
0 yards	100

❶ BELvue Museum and the Coudenberg

Place des Palais 7, 1000 BRU. **Map** 2 E4. **Tel** (070) 220 492. 🚌 27, 29, 34, 38, 54, 63, 64, 65, 66, 71, 80, 95. 🚋 92, 93. Ⓜ Trone, Parc, Porte de Namur. **Open** 9:30am–5pm Mon–Fri, 10am–6pm Sat & Sun. **Closed** 1 Jan, 21 Jul, 25 Dec. 🚻 ♿ ⧄ 🏠 **W belvue.be**

The BELvue Museum houses a wide collection of paintings, documents and other royal memorabilia charting the history of the Belgian monarchy from independence in 1830 to the present day. Since 1992, it has been housed in the former Hôtel Bellevue, an 18th-century Neo-Classical building lying adjacent to the Palais Royal. A permanent exhibition across nine rooms presents the history of Belgium through a collection of 1,500

The Neo-Classical façade of the BELvue Museum

unique historical documents, photographs, film extracts and objects. Complementary temporary exhibitions focus on a particular theme, era or perspective. The Coudenberg is a separate underground archeological site and museum that is within the grounds of the BELvue Museum.

❸ Eglise St-Jacques-sur-Coudenberg

Place Royale, 1000 BRU. **Map** 2 E4. **Tel** (02) 511 7836. 🚌 27, 29, 34, 38, 54, 63, 64, 65, 66, 71, 80, 95. 🚋 92, 93. Ⓜ Trone, Parc. **Open** Noon–2pm Mon, noon–5:45pm Tue–Fri, 1–6pm Sat, 8:30am–6:45pm Sun.

The prettiest building in the Place Royale, St-Jacques-sur-Coudenberg is the latest in a series of churches to have occupied this site. There has been a chapel here since the 12th century, when one was built to serve the Dukes of Brabant. On construction of the Coudenberg Palace in the 12th century, it became the ducal chapel. The chapel suffered over the years: it was ransacked in 1579 during conflict between Catholics and Protestants, and was so badly damaged in the

❷ Palais Royal

The Palais Royal is the most important of the palaces around the Parc de Bruxelles. An official residence of the Belgian monarchy, construction of the modern palace began in the 1820s on the site of the old Coudenberg Palace. Work continued under Léopold II (r.1865–1909), when much of the exterior was completed. Throughout the 20th century, the palace underwent interior improvements and restoration of its older sections. It is open only from late July to early September, but this is a fine opportunity to tour Belgium's lavish state reception rooms.

The Pilasters Room contains an original Franz Winterhalter portrait of the first Belgian king, Léopold I, dating from 1846.

★ Throne Room
One of Brussels' original state-rooms, the huge throne room is decorated in grand style, with huge pilastered columns, 11 large candelabras and 28 wall-mounted chandeliers.

The 19th-century cupola of Eglise St-Jacques-sur-Coudenberg

fire of 1731 that destroyed the Coudenberg Palace that it was demolished soon after. The present church was built in the Neo-Classical style and was consecrated in 1787, although it served several years as a Temple of Reason and Law during the French Revolution, returning to the Catholic Church in 1802. The cupola was completed in 1849. The interior is simple and elegant, with two large paintings by Jean Portaels on either side of the transept.

❹ Place Royale

Map 2 E4. 🚌 27, 29, 34, 38, 54, 63, 64, 65, 66, 71, 80, 95. 🚊 92, 93. Ⓜ Trone, Parc, Porte de Namur.

The influence of Charles de Lorraine is still keenly felt in the Place Royale. As Governor of Brussels from 1741 to 1780, he redeveloped the site once occupied by the Coudenberg Palace along Neo-Classical lines reminiscent of Vienna, a city he greatly admired.

When the area was being worked on, the ruins of the burnt-down palace were demolished and the entire site was rebuilt as two squares. However, in 1995, excavation work uncovered ruins of the 15th-century Aula Magna, the Great Hall of the former palace. This was part of the extension of the palace started under the Dukes of Brabant in the early 13th century and then developed under the rule of the Dukes of Burgundy, in particular Philip the Good. It was in this room that the Hapsburg emperor Charles V abdicated in favour of his son, Philip II. The ruins can now be seen as part of the BELvue Museum.

Although criss-crossed by tramlines and traffic, the Place Royale maintains a feeling of dignity with its tall, elegant, cream buildings symmetrically set around a cobbled square. Visitors can tour the area on foot, admiring the exceptional Neo-Classical buildings.

The Long Gallery features exquisite late 19th-century ceiling paintings representing Dawn, Day and Dusk.

Hall of Mirrors This large room is famous for its grandiose effect similar to the mirrored chamber at Versailles. The ceiling is decorated in green beetle and wing designs by sculptor Jan Fabre.

The Empire Room

★ **Small White Room**
Rows of 19th-century royal portraits dominate this gilt chamber with its large candle-lit chandeliers and late 18th-century furnishings.

The Victor Horta-designed façade of the Palais des Beaux-Arts

❺ Palais des Beaux-Arts

Rue Ravenstein 23, 1000 BRU. **Map** 2 E3. **Tel** (02) 507 8200. 27, 29, 38, 63, 65, 66, 71, 95. 92, 93. Gare Centrale, Parc. **Open** 11am–7pm Tue–Sat. **Closed** public hols. bozar.be

The Palais des Beaux-Arts owes its existence to Henri Le Boeuf, a music-loving financier who gave his name to the main auditorium. In 1922 he commissioned the architect Victor Horta (see p84) to design a cultural centre which would house concert halls and exhibition areas open to all visitors and embracing the artistic fields of music, art, theatre, cinema, architecture and literature. The centre was the first of its kind in Europe.

The complex has a fine reputation and has played a key role in the cultural life of Brussels for more than 80 years. It is the focus for the city's music, hosting 250 classical music concerts each year, and is home to the Belgian National Orchestra. The programme also includes about 50 concerts of rock, pop, jazz and world music.

The complex also houses the **CINEMATEK**, set up in 1962, with its fine archive and exhibition of old cameras and lenses. It screens classic films.

▥ CINEMATEK
Rue Baron Horta 9, 1000 BRU. **Tel** (02) 551 1919. **Open** 6:30–10pm Mon, Tue, 4:30–10pm Wed, Fri, Sat, 2:30–10pm Thu, Sun.

❻ Hôtel Ravenstein

Rue Ravenstein 3, 1000 BRU. **Map** 2 E3. 27, 29, 38, 63, 65, 66, 71, 95. 92, 93. Gare Centrale, Parc. **Open** restaurant only.

Over the centuries, the Hôtel Ravenstein has been the home of patrician families, soldiers and court officials, and, for the past 100 years, the Royal Society of Engineers. The building was designed at the end of the 15th century for Adolphe and Philip Cleves-Ravenstein; in 1515 it became the birthplace of Anne of Cleves. Consisting of two parts, joined by gardens and stables, it is the last remaining example of a Burgundian-style manor house. The Hôtel Ravenstein was acquired by the town in 1896 and used to store artworks.

The pretty open courtyard of the Hôtel Ravenstein

Sadly, it fell into disrepair and renovation took place in 1934. One half is now a Belgian restaurant, the other the Royal Society of Engineers' private HQ. However, the pretty, original inner courtyard can still be seen.

❼ Musée des Instruments de Musique

Rue Montagne de la Cour 2, 1000 BRU. **Map** 2 E4. **Tel** (02) 545 0130. 27, 29, 38, 63, 65, 66, 71, 95 92, 93. Gare Centrale, Parc. **Open** 9:30am–5pm Tue–Fri, 10am–5pm Sat & Sun. **Closed** 1 Jan, 1 May, 1 & 11 Nov, 25 Dec. mim.be

Once a department store, the building known as Old England is a striking showpiece of Art Nouveau architecture located by the Place Royale.

Architect Paul Saintenoy gave full rein to his imagination when he designed these shop premises for the Old England company in 1899. The façade is made entirely of glass and elaborate wrought iron. There is a domed gazebo on the roof, and a turret to one side. Surprisingly, it was only in the 1990s that a listed building policy was adopted in Brussels, which has secured treasures such as this. The building is now home to the Musée des Instruments de Musique, moved from the Sablon.

The façade of Old England

The collection of the Musée des Instruments de Musique began in the 19th century when the state bought 80 ancient and exotic instruments. It was doubled in 1876 when King Léopold II donated a gift of 97 Indian musical instruments presented to him by a maharajah. A museum displaying all of these artifacts opened in 1877, and by 1924 the museum boasted 3,300 pieces and was recognized as a leader in its field. Today the collection contains more than 6,000 items and includes many fine examples of wind, string and keyboard instruments from medieval times to the present. Chief attractions include prototype instruments by Adolphe Sax, the Belgian inventor of the saxophone, mini violins favoured by street musicians, and a violin maker's studio. In 2000, the museum moved to its specially designed home in the renovated Old England building, where there is much more room in which to display this world-class collection. Thanks to a clever infrared headset system, visitors can discover the sound of each instrument at their own pace.

Antique violin

❽ Palais de Charles de Lorraine

Place du Musée 1, 1000 BRU. **Map** 2 D4. **Tel** (02) 519 5311. 🚌 27, 29, 38, 63, 65, 66, 71, 95. Ⓜ Gare Centrale, Parc. **Open** 1–5pm Wed & Sat. **Closed** Sat in Jul & Aug, Tue–Sun, Thu & Fri, last week in Aug, last week in Dec. 🅿 🅾 for details **Tel** (02) 519 5786.

Hidden behind this Neo-Classical façade are the few rooms that remain of the palace of Charles de Lorraine, Governor

The state room with marble floor at the Palais de Charles de Lorraine

of Brussels during the mid-18th century. He was a keen patron of the arts, and the young Mozart is believed to have performed here. Few original features remain, as the palace was ransacked by marauding French troops in 1794. The bas-reliefs at the top of the stairway, representing air, earth, fire and water, reflect Charles de Lorraine's interest in alchemy. Most spectacular of all the original features is the 28-point star set in the floor of the circular drawing room. Each of the points is made of a different Belgian marble taken from Charles de Lorraine's personal mineral collection. The palace houses the Bibliothèque Royale (Royal Library) and the Musée du 18ème siècle.

❾ Musée Charlier

Avenue des Arts 16, 1210 BRU. **Map** 2 F2. **Tel** (02) 220 2691. 🚌 22, 29, 63, 65, 66. 🚋 29, 63. Ⓜ Madou, Arts-Loi. **Open** noon–5pm Mon–Thu, 10am–1pm Fri. **Closed** public hols. 🅿 🅾 French & Dutch only.

This quiet museum was once the home of Henri van Cutsem, a wealthy collector and patron of the arts. In 1890, he asked the young architect Victor Horta to re-design his house as an exhibition space for his extensive collections. When Van Cutsem died in 1904, his heir, the sculptor Charlier, took care of the house and the collections. On Charlier's death in 1925, the house and contents were left to the city as a museum.

The Musée Charlier opened in 1928. It contains paintings by a number of different artists, including portraits by Antoine Wiertz (see p74), landscapes by Hippolyte Boulenger and Guillaume Vogels, and impressionistic still lifes by James Ensor and Anna Boch. The collection also includes a large number of sculptures by Charlier and others by Rik Wouters, as well as glassware, porcelain, chinoiserie and silverware. Of special note are the tapestries, some from the Paris studios of Aubusson, on the staircases and the first floor, and the displays of Louis XV- and Louis XVI-style furniture on the first floor.

Musée Charlier, home to one of Belgium's finest individual collections of art and furnishings

⑩ Musées Royaux des Beaux-Arts: Musée d'Art Ancien

Officially known as the Musées Royaux des Beaux-Arts de Belgique, the Musée d'Art Ancien, Musée Fin de Siècle and Musée Magritte are Brussels' premier art museums. The museums' buildings are home to exhibits from two eras, *ancien* (15th–18th century) and *fin de siècle* (19th and 20th centuries). They house the world's largest collection of works by Belgian surrealist René Magritte (1898–1967). Housed in a Neo-Classical building, the Musée d'Art Ancien is the largest of the museum's sections and dates back to the 18th century when it consisted of the few valuable works left behind by the French Republican army. This small collection grew and the present gallery opened in 1887. The Musée d'Art Ancien is best known for the finest collection of Flemish art in the world, and many Old Masters, including van Dyck and Rubens, are also well represented.

Façade of Museum
Corinthian columns and busts of Flemish painters adorn the entrance.

The Census at Bethlehem *(1610)*
Pieter Brueghel the Younger (c.1564–1638) produced a version of this subject some 40 years after the original by his father. Shown together, the two works illustrate the development of Flemish painting in its peak period.

Ground level

Main Entrance

Entrance to The Museum Shop

Gallery Guide

The gallery is divided up into two different eras of art, as shown in the key. Two large auditoriums on the ground floor and lower levels are used for occasional lectures as well as presentations. Visitors can enter the Musée Magritte and from there, the Musée Fin de Siècle, via the escalator behind the museum's restaurant.

★ **The Annunciation** *(c.1406–7)*
The Master of Flémalle (c.1375–1444) sets the holy scene of the Archangel Gabriel announcing the impending birth of the Messiah in a homely, contemporary setting, with daily objects an apparent contrast to the momentous event.

Upper
level

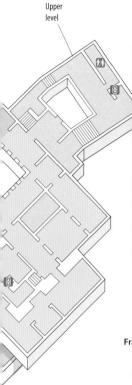

VISITORS' CHECKLIST

Practical Information
Rue de la Régence 3, 1000 BRU.
Map 2 D4. **Tel** (02) 508 3211.
Open 10am–5pm Tue–Sun.
Closed Mon, public hols.
♿ 📷 🎞 🖥 ✒
Ⓦ **fine-arts-museum.be**

Transport
🚌 27, 29, 38, 63, 65, 66, 71.
🚋 92, 93. Ⓜ Gare Centrale, Parc.

★ The Assumption of the Virgin
(c.1610)
Pieter Paul Rubens (1577–1640)
was the leading exponent of
Baroque art in Europe, combining
Flemish precision with Italian
flair. Here, Rubens suppresses
background colours to emphasize
the Virgin's blue robes.

**Madonna with
Saint Anne and a
Franciscan Donor** *(1470)*
Hugo van der Goes
(c.1430–82) was
commissioned to paint
this symbolic work for
the monk shown on the
right for his personal
devotional use.

To Musée
Magrite
→

Key
- 15th–16th century
- 17th–18th century
- Temporary exhibitions
- Non-exhibition space

Lower level

Auditorium

Interior of the Main Hall
Founded by Napoleon in 1801
to relieve the packed Louvre in
Paris, these are the oldest
museums in Belgium. More
than 2,500 works are exhibited
in the museums' buildings.

Musées Royaux des Beaux-Arts: Musée Magritte and Musée Fin de Siècle

The modern section of the museum is situated in a unique setting: eight levels of the building are underground, but a lightwell allows many of the works to be seen by natural daylight filtering in from the Place du Musée. The collection of art is varied, and includes many well-known 20th-century artists from 1900 to the present day, though works by the Belgian Surrealists are the most popular. Since the opening of the Musée Magritte in 2009, the Musées Royaux des Beaux-Arts has seen many changes, and construction work is ongoing behind the scenes.

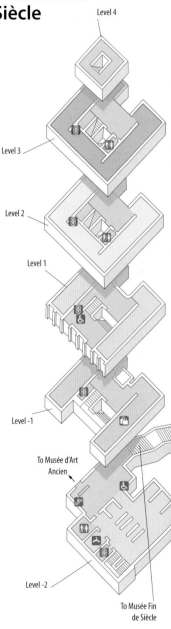

Level 4

Level 3

Level 2

Level 1

Level -1

To Musée d'Art Ancien

To Musée Fin de Siècle

Level -2

Le Joueur Secret *(1927)*
The museum owns this work, painted during Magritte's self-titled "Cavernous" period when he painted roughly a canvas each day.

★ The Domain of Arnheim
(1962)
The museum contains the world's largest collection of work by surrealist René Magritte (see p19). Here, an eagle-mountain rears over a small bird's nest. The inexplicable nature of the eerie composition draws its elements into question, but answers are made deliberately difficult.

Gallery Guide

Access to the museums is available through the main ticket hall of the Musées Royaux des Beaux-Arts de Belgique. The Musée Magritte is arranged in chronological order over six floors. Level -2 is a multimedia area, showing Magritte's films. From here, stairs lead further underground to the Musée Fin de Siècle. The area shaded in green is this permanent collection, which displays work from the 19th and 20th centuries.

★ **La Seine à la Grande-Jatte** *(1888)*
It was in this painting that Georges Seurat first
applied his pointilism technique on a large scale;
colour dots are juxtaposed and optically fuse in
the viewer's eye.

VISITORS' CHECKLIST

Practical Information
Place Royale 1, 1000 BRU.
Map 2 D4. **Tel** (02) 508 3211.
Open 10am–5pm Tue–Sun.
Closed Mon, public hols.
🦽 💾 📷 W **fine-arts-
museum.be.** Musée Magritte
W **musee-magritte-museum.be**

Transport
🚌 27, 29, 38, 63, 65, 66, 71.
🚊 92, 93. Ⓜ Gare Centrale, Parc.

La Nature *(1899–1900)*
Czech artist Alphonse
Mucha was best known for
his Art Nouveau poster
designs, but he also
created jewellery, stained
glass and sculptures like
this bronze, La Nature.

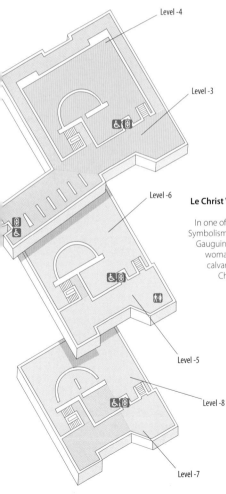

Level -4

Level -3

Level -6

Level -5

Level -8

Level -7

**Le Christ Vert ou Calvaire
Breton** *(1889)*
In one of the key works of
Symbolism in painting, Paul
Gauguin depicts a Breton
woman at the foot of a
calvary, or sculpture of
Christ's crucifixtion.

Key

🔲 Musée Fin de Siècle: 19th
and 20th century

🔲 Musée Magritte: 1898–1929

🔲 Musée Magritte: 1930–1950

🔲 Musée Magritte: 1951–1967

🔲 Musée Magritte: multimedia area

🔲 Temporary exhibitions

🔲 Non-exhibition space

Exploring the Musées Royaux des Beaux-Arts de Belgique

Six centuries of art, both Belgian and international, are displayed in the museums that make up the Musées Royaux des Beaux-Arts. The combination of the museums contains works from many artistic styles, from the religious paintings of the 15th-century Flemish Primitives to the graphic art of the 1960s and 1970s. Regular temporary exhibitions are staged at the museums, which are very well set out, guiding the visitor easily through the full collection or, if time is short, directly to the art era of special interest. Each section is highly accessible, with both main museums divided into different sections which relate to the art of each century, taking the visitor through galleries representing the varied schools of art by period.

Flemish still life, *Vase of Flowers* (1704) by Rachel Ruysch

Musée Old Masters

The Musée Old Masters exhibits works dating from the 15th to the 18th centuries. In the first few rooms are works by the renowned school of Flemish Primitives *(see p18)*. As is the case with most art from the Middle Ages, the paintings are chiefly religious in nature and depict biblical scenes and details from the lives of saints. Many of the works show deeds of horrific torture, martyrdom and violence, attended by the perplexing nonchalance of the elegantly attired bystanders. A typical example is the diptych *The Justice of Emperor Otto III* (c.1460) by Dirk Bouts, which includes a gory beheading (a famous miscarriage of justice in the 12th century) and an execution by burning at the stake. At the same time, the

detail is exquisite and provides a fascinating window on the textiles, architecture and faces of the 15th century. Also on display are works such as *Lamentation* (c.1441) by Rogier van der Weyden, the city painter to Brussels during the mid-15th century, and *The Martyrdom of Saint Sebastian* (c.1475) by Bruges artist, Hans Memling (c.1433–94).

Another unique aspect of the section is the extensive collection of paintings by the Brueghels, father and son. Both were renowned for their scenes of peasant life. On display are *The Fall of Icarus* (1558) by Brueghel the Elder and *The Struggle between Carnival and Lent* (c.1559) by his son, Pieter.

In the following rooms are works from the 17th and 18th centuries. A highlight of this section is the world-famous

collection of paintings by Baroque artist, Pieter Paul Rubens (1557–1640), which affords a fine overview of his art. As well as key examples of his religious works, there are some excellent portraits, such as *Hélène Fourment* (c.1614–73), of his young wife. Of special interest are the sketches made in preparation for Rubens's larger works, including *Four Negro Heads*, for his iconic *Adoration of the Magi* (1624).

Other works of note in this section are the paintings by Old Masters such as van Dyck's *Portrait of a Genoese Lady with her Daughter* from the 1620s and *Three Children with Goatcart* (c.1620) by Frans Hals. Representatives of the later Flemish schools include Jacob Jordaens and his depiction of myths such as *Pan and Syrinx* (c.1645) and *Satyr and Peasant*. Baroque and Flemish art are all well represented in the museum.

Also on display are some small sculptures that were studies of larger works by Laurent Delvaux, a leading sculptor of the 18th century. Most notably, *Hercules and Erymanthian Boar* is a study for the sculpture by the staircase in the Palais de Charles de Lorraine *(see p63)*. Works of the Italian, Spanish and French schools are also represented, notably the Classical landscape painter Claude Le Lorrain's poetic scene of *Aeneas Hunting the Stag on the Coast of Libya* (1672).

Other works on show include *Vase of Flowers* (1704) by Dutch artist Rachel Ruysch, who specialized in still-life paintings of flowers and fruits.

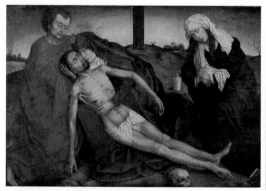

Lamentation (c.1441) by Rogier van der Weyden

Musée Fin de Siècle

The Musée Fin de Siècle showcases European and international art from the end of the 19th century and the beginning of the 20th century. This part of the museum has become a flagship cultural institution in the world of art thanks to the exhibits from the 31 different European art academies who, in 1868, created the Société Libre des Beaux-Arts. The Société introduced modernism and the avant-garde to Belgium.

The rediscovery of the Primitives, Impressionism, Symbolism and Art Nouveau are all represented by such artists as Khnopff, Seurat, Spilliaert, Gauguin, van de Velde, Mucha, Horta, Ensor and de Vlaminick.

There is an excellent collection of Symbolist art, such as the poetic and disturbing classics *Des Caresses* by Fernand Khnopff (1858–1921), which shows an androgynous figure nuzzling a human head on a cheetah's body. Léon Spilliaert (1881–1946) is included via his 1909 symbolist landscape, *The Dike*.

Many of the artists, such as Nice-born Henri Evenepoel (1872–99), who brought his distinctive post-Impressionist style to *The Orange Market in Blidah* (1898), deserve a close inspection. There are characteristically bizarre paintings by proto-Expressionist James Ensor (1860–1949), including his 1892 work *Singular Masks*.

Pointillism is represented by *La Seine à la Grand-Jatte* (1888) by Georges Seurat (1859–91), who developed the technique *(see p67)*, followed by Henry van de Velde's *Village Events VII. The*

The Orange Market at Blidah (1898) by Henri Evenepoel

Girl Mending (1890). Belgian van de Velde (1863–1957) went on to become one of the main founders of Art Nouveau in Belgium.

A highlight of the museum is the extraordinarily rich Gillion Crowet Collection of Art Nouveau, which includes Alphonse Mucha's *La Nature (see p67)* and Fernand Khnopff's *Acrasia The Faerie Queen* (1892).

Musée Magritte

The works of the Belgian Surrealist movement have long proved a popular highlight of the Musées Royaux des Beaux-Art's collection. The art of René Magritte (1898–1967) in particular has created an extraordinary public fascination since the increase in his popularity in the 1960s. The museum's collection of Magritte's work began in 1953. To reflect public demand, and to afford the best possible display, his work is now housed in this separate section of the museum.

Born the son of a wealthy manufacturer in Lessines,

Magritte entered the Brussels Academie des Beaux-Arts in 1916. A former poster and advertisement designer, he created visually striking work, frequently displaying a juxtaposition of familiar objects in unusual, sometimes unsettling, combinations and contexts. Many of the artist's best-known paintings are shown here in a striking collection of more than 200 works, including *L'Empire des Lumières* (1954), and *La Voleuse* (1927).

Of particular note are the paintings that date from Magritte's self-titled "Cavernous" period of 1927–30. At this time, while living in Paris, Magritte painted roughly a canvas a day. He then moved back to Brussels, where he lived for the rest of his life. Powerful, arresting paintings on display from this later period include the eerie *Domain of Arnheim (see p66)* and the melancholic *Saveur des Larmes* (1948). A cinema shows films dedicated to the artist and others who inspired his work.

Des Caresses (1896) by the symbolist artist, Fernand Khnopff.

Busy café scene at Place du Grand Sablon

⓫ Place du Grand Sablon

Map 2 D4. 🚌 27, 38, 48, 63, 65, 66, 71, 95. 🚋 92, 93, 94, 97. Ⓜ Gare Centrale, Louise, Parc.

Situated on the slope of the escarpment that divides Brussels in two, the Place du Grand Sablon is like a stepping stone between the upper and lower halves of the city. The name "sablon" derives from the French "*sable*" (sand) and the square is so-called because this old route down to the city centre once passed through an area of sandy marshes.

Today, the picture is very different. The square, more of a triangle in shape, stretches from a 1751 fountain by Jacques Berge at its base uphill to the Gothic church of Notre-Dame du Sablon. The fountain was a gift of the Englishman Lord Bruce, out of gratitude for the hospitality shown to him in Brussels. The square is surrounded by elegant town houses, some with Art Nouveau façades. This is a chic, wealthy and busy part of Brussels, an area of up-market antiques dealers, fashionable restaurants and trendy bars, which really come into their own in warm weather when people stay drinking outside until the early hours of the morning: a good place in which to soak up the atmosphere. Wittamer, at No. 12, is a

Notre-Dame du Sablon window

justifiably well-known *patisserie* and chocolate shop, which also has its own tea room on the first floor.

Every weekend the area near the church plays host to a lively and thriving, if rather expensive, antiques market.

⓬ Notre Dame du Sablon

Place du Grand Sablon, 1000 BRU. **Map** 2 D4. **Tel** (02) 213 0065. 🚌 27, 38, 48, 71, 95. 🚋 92, 93, 94, 97. Ⓜ Gare Centrale, Louise, Parc. **Open** 8am–6pm daily. ♿ 📷 on request.

Along with the Cathédrale Sts Michel et Gudule (*see p72–3*), this lovely church is one of the finest remaining examples of Brabant Gothic architecture in Belgium.

A church was first erected here when the guild of cross-bowmen was granted permission to build a chapel to Our Lady on this sandy hill. Legend has it that a young girl in Antwerp had a vision of the Virgin Mary who instructed her to take her statue to Brussels. The girl carried the statue of the Virgin to Brussels down the Senne river by boat and gave it to the crossbowmen's chapel, which rapidly became a place of pilgrimage. Work to enlarge the church began around 1400 but, due to lack of funds, was not completed until 1550. All that remains today are two

carvings depicting the young girl in a boat, since the statue was destroyed in 1565.

The interior of the church is simple but beautifully proportioned, with inter-connecting side chapels and an impressive pulpit dating from 1697. Of particular interest, however, are the 11 magnificent stained-glass windows, 14 m (45 ft) high, which dominate the inside of the church. As the church is lit from the inside, they shine out at night like welcoming beacons. Also worth a visit is the chapel of the Tour et Taxis family, whose mansion once stood near the Place du Petit Sablon. In 1517, the family had tapestries commissioned to commemorate the legend that led to the chapel becoming a place of pilgrimage. Some now hang in the Musées Royaux d'art et d'histoire in Parc du Cinquantenaire (*see p77*), but others were stolen by the French Revolutionary army in the 1790s.

The magnificent interior of the church of Notre-Dame du Sablon

⓭ Place du Petit Sablon

Map 2 D4. 🚌 27, 38, 48, 71, 95. 🚋 92, 93, 94, 97. Ⓜ Gare Centrale, Louise, Parc.

These pretty, formal gardens were laid out in 1890 and are a charming spot to stop for a rest. On top of the railings that enclose the gardens are 48 bronze statuettes by Art Nouveau artist Paul Hankar, each one representing a different medieval guild of the city.

One of the lavish fountains in the gardens of Petit Sablon

At the back of the gardens is a fountain built to commemorate Counts Egmont and Hornes, the martyrs who led a Dutch uprising against the tyrannical rule of the Spanish under Philip II, and were beheaded in the Grand Place in 1568 *(see p33)*. On either side of the fountain are 12 further statues of 15th- and 16th-century figures, including Bernard van Orley, whose stained-glass windows grace the city's cathedral, and the Flemish map-maker Gerhard Mercator, whose 16th-century projection of the world forms the basis of most modern maps.

Statue of Peter Pan in Palais d'Egmont gardens

palace has twice been rebuilt, in 1750 and again in 1891, following a fire. Today, it belongs to the Belgian Foreign Ministry. It was here that Great Britain, Denmark and Ireland signed as members of the EEC in 1972. Though the palace itself is closed to the public, the gardens, whose entrances are on the Rue du Grand Cerf and the Boulevard de Waterloo, are open. There is a statue of Peter Pan, a copy of one found in Kensington Gardens, in London. Many of the gardens' buildings are now run down, but the ancient orangery has been restored and has a restaurant.

⓮ Palais d'Egmont

Rue aux Laines, 1000 BRU. **Map** 2 E4. 🚌 27, 34, 38, 48, 63, 64, 65, 66, 71, 80, 95. 🚊 92, 93, 94, 97. Ⓜ Louise, Parc. 🚻

The Palais d'Egmont (also known as the Palais d'Arenberg) was originally built in the mid-16th century for Françoise of Luxembourg, mother of the 16th-century leader of the city's rebels, Count Egmont. This

⓯ Palais de Justice

Place Poelaert 1, 1000 BRU. **Map** 1 C5. **Tel** (02) 508 6578. 🚊 92, 93, 94, 97. Ⓜ Louise. **Open** 8am–5pm Mon–Fri. **Closed** Sat & Sun, public hols. 🚻 🎟 on request.

The Palais de Justice rules the Brussels skyline and can be seen from almost any vantage point in the city. Of all the ambitious projects of King Leopold II, this was perhaps the grandest. It occupies an area larger than St Peter's Basilica in Rome, and was one of the world's most impressive 19th-century buildings. It was built between 1866 and 1883 by architect Joseph Poelaert who looked for inspiration in classical temples, but sadly died mid-construction in 1879. The Palais de Justice is still home to the city's law courts.

Detail of a cornice at the Palais de Justice

⑯ Galérie Bortier

Rue de la Madeleine 55, 1000 BRU.
Map 2 D3. 🚌 29, 38, 63, 66, 71.
Ⓜ Gare Centrale. ♿

Galérie Bortier is the only shopping arcade in the city dedicated solely to book and map shops, and it has become the haunt of students, enthusiasts and researchers looking for secondhand French books and antiquarian finds.

The land on which the gallery stands was originally owned by a Monsieur Bortier, whose idea it was to have a covered arcade lined with shops on either side. He put 160,000 francs of his own money into the project,

quite a considerable sum in the 1840s. The 65-m (210-ft) long Galérie Bortier was built in 1848 and was designed by Jean-Pierre Cluysenaer, the architect of the Galéries St-Hubert nearby *(see p49)*. The Galérie Bortier opened along with the then-adjacent Marché de la Madeleine, but the latter was unfortunately destroyed by developers in 1958.

A complete restoration of Galérie Bortier was ordered by the Ville de Bruxelles in 1974. The new architects kept strictly to Cluysenaer's plans and installed a replacement glass and wrought-iron roof made to the original 19th-century

Parisian style. The Rue de la Madeleine itself also offers plenty of browsing material for bibliophiles and art lovers.

Crammed interior of a bookshop at the Galérie Bortier

⑰ Cathédrale Sts Michel et Gudule

The Cathédrale Sts Michel et Gudule is the national church of Belgium, although it was only granted cathedral status in 1962. It is the finest surviving example of Brabant Gothic architecture. There has been a church on the site of the cathedral since at least the 11th century. Work began on the Gothic cathedral in 1225 under Henry I, Duke of Brabant, and continued over a period of 300 years. It was finally completed with the construction of two front towers at the beginning of the 16th century under Charles V. The cathedral is made of a sandy limestone, brought from local quarries. It was fully restored and cleaned in the 1990s and now reveals its splendour. Of particular interest inside the cathedral are the Grenzig organ and the Baroque pulpit depicting Adam and Eve's expulsion from Paradise.

The twin towers rise above the city. Unusually, they were designed as a pair in the 1400s; Brabant architecture typically has only one.

★ Last Judgement Window
At the front of the cathedral, facing the altar, is a magnificent stained-glass window of 1528 depicting Christ awaiting saved souls. Its vivid reds, blues and yellows place it in the 16th-century style. The Renaissance panes are surrounded by later Baroque garlands of flowers.

Romanesque remains of the first church here, dating from 1047, were discovered during renovation work. They can be seen and toured in the crypt.

⑱ Chapelle de la Madeleine

Rue de la Madeleine, 1000 BRU.
Map 2 D3. **Tel** (02) 410 2957. 🚌 29, 38, 63, 66, 71. Ⓜ Gare Centrale.
🕐 9am– 8pm Mon–Fri, 9:30am–8pm Sat, 9:30–11:30am & 2–8pm Sun. ♿

This church once stood on the site now occupied by the Gare Centrale, but it was moved, stone by stone, further down the hill to make way for the construction of the Art Deco-style station in the early 1950s.

The 17th-century façade of the church has been restored. The original 15th-century interior has been replaced by a plain, modest decor, with simple stone pillars and modern stained-glass windows. Off the regular tourist track, the chapel is used by people as a quiet place for worship. The Baroque chapel which was once attached has now gone.

A view of the Chapelle de la Madeleine with restored brickwork

---

The transept windows represent the rulers of Belgium in 1537/38. Jan Haeck made the designs after Bernard van Orley's sketches.

The Lectern

Sainte Gudule
This 7th-century saint is very dear to the people of Brussels. Her relics were scattered to the winds by ransacking Protestants in 1579, but this only served to reinforce her cult.

Sainte Gudule

★ Baroque Pulpit
The flamboyantly carved pulpit in the central aisle is the work of an Antwerp-born sculptor, Henri-François Verbruggen. Designed in 1699, it was finally installed in 1776.

The Statue of St Michael is the cathedral's symbol of its links with the city. While the gilded plaster statue is not itself historically exceptional, its long heritage is; the patron saint of Brussels, the Archangel St Michael is shown killing the dragon, symbolic of his protection of the city.

The Art Nouveau façade of No. 11 Square Ambiorix

⓲ Square Ambiorix

Map 3 B2. 🚌 12, 21, 22, 29, 36, 60, 63, 64, 79. Ⓜ Schuman.

Close to the EU district, but totally different in style and spirit, lies the beautiful Square Ambiorix. Together with the Avenue Palmerston and the Square Marie-Louise below that, this marshland was transformed in the 1870s into one of the loveliest residential parts of Brussels, with a large central area of gardens, ponds and fountains.

The elegant houses have made this one of the truly sought-after suburbs in the city. The most spectacular Art Nouveau example is at No. 11. Known as the Maison Saint Cyr after the painter whose home it

once was, this wonderfully ornate house, with its curved wrought-iron balustrades and balconies, is a fine architectural feat considering that the man who designed it, Gustave Strauven, was only 22 years old when it was built at the turn of the 20th century.

⓳ Quartier Européen

Map 3 B3. 🚌 12, 21, 22, 27, 36, 60, 64, 79. Ⓜ Maelbeek, Schuman.

The area at the top of the Rue de la Loi and around the Schuman roundabout is where the main buildings of the European Union's administration are found.

The most recognizable of all the EU seats is the cross-shaped Berlaymont building, which has now reopened following the removal of large quantities of asbestos discovered in its structure. This is the headquarters of the European Commission, whose workers are, in effect, civil servants of the EU. The Council of Ministers, which comprises representatives of member-states' governments, now meets in the sprawling pink granite block across the road from the Berlaymont. This building is known as Justus Lipsius, after a Flemish philosopher.

Further down the road from the Justus Lipsius building is the Résidence Palace, a luxury 1920s housing complex that boasts a theatre, a pool and a roof garden as well as several floors of private flats. It now houses the International Press Centre. Only the theatre is open to the

public, but EU officials have access to the Art Deco pool.

This whole area is naturally full of life and bustle during the day, but much quieter in the evenings and can feel almost deserted at weekends. What is pleasant at any time, though, is the proximity of a number of the city's wonderful green spaces, which include Parc du Cinquantenaire (see pp76–7), Parc Léopold and the verdant Square Ambiorix.

Paintings and sculpture on show in the Musée Wiertz gallery

⓴ Musée Wiertz

Rue Vautier 62, 1050 BRU. **Map** 3 A4. **Tel** (02) 648 1718. 🚌 12, 21, 22, 27, 34, 36, 38, 54, 59, 60, 64, 71, 80, 95. Ⓜ Maelbeek, Schuman, Trone. **Open** 10am–noon & 1–5pm Tue–Fri. **Closed** Mon, weekends, public hols. 🖥 fine-arts-museum.be

Musée Wiertz houses some 160 works, including oil paintings, drawings and sculptures, that form the main body of Antoine Wiertz's (1806–65) artistic output. The collection fills the studio built for Wiertz by the Belgian state, where he lived and worked from 1850 until his death in 1865, when the studio became a museum.

The huge main room contains Wiertz's largest paintings, many depicting biblical and Homeric scenes, some in the style of Rubens. Also on display are sculptures and his death mask. The last of the six rooms contains his more gruesome efforts, one entitled Madness, Hunger and Crime.

The Justus Lipsius, the pink granite EU Council building

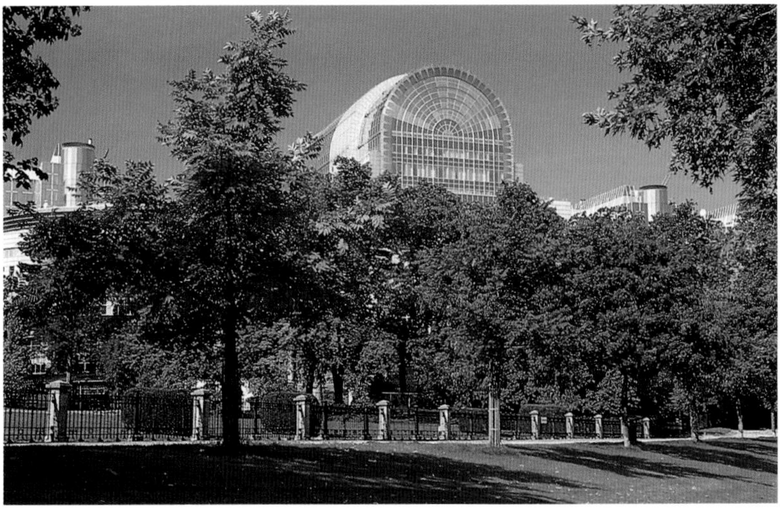

The tall European parliament building rising up behind the trees of Parc Léopold in the Parliament Quarter

㉒ Parliament Quarter

Map 3 A4. 12, 21, 22, 27, 36, 38, 54, 59, 60, 64, 80, 95. Ⓜ Maelbeek, Schuman.

The vast, modern, steel-and-glass complex, situated just behind Quartier Léopold train station, is one of three homes of the European Parliament, the elected body of the EU. Its permanent seat is in Strasbourg, France, where the plenary sessions are held once a month. The administrative centre is in Luxembourg and the committee meetings are held in Brussels.

This gleaming state-of-the-art building has many admirers, not least the parliamentary workers and MEPs themselves. But it also has its critics: the huge domed structure housing the hemicycle that seats the 700-plus MEPs has been dubbed the *"caprice des dieux"* ("whim of the gods"), which refers both to the shape of the building which is similar to a French cheese of the same name, and to its lofty aspirations. Many people also regret that, to make room for the new complex, a large part of Quartier Léopold has been lost. Though there are still plenty of restaurants and bars, a lot of the charm has gone. When the MEPs are absent, the building is often used for meetings of European Union committees.

㉓ Institut Royal des Sciences Naturelles

Rue Vautier 29, 1000 BRU. **Map** 3 A4. **Tel** (02) 627 4238. 12, 21, 22, 27, 34, 36, 38, 54, 59, 60, 64, 79, 80, 95. Ⓜ Maelbeek, Schuman, Trône. **Open** 9:30am–5pm Tue–Fri, 10am–6pm Sat & Sun. **Closed** Mon, 1 Jan, 1 May, 25 Dec.
Ⓦ **sciencesnaturelles.be**

The Institut Royal des Sciences Naturelles is best known for its fine collection of iguanadon skeletons dating back 250 million years. The museum also contains interactive and educational displays covering all eras of natural history.

㉔ Parc Léopold

Rue Belliard. **Map** 3 B4. 12, 21, 22, 27, 36, 59, 60, 64, 79, 80. Ⓜ Maelbeek, Schuman.

Parc Léopold occupies part of the grounds of an old estate and a walk around its lake follows the old path of the Maelbeek river.

At the end of the 19th century, scientist and industrialist Ernest Solvay put forward the idea of a science park development. Solvay was given the Parc Léopold, the site of a zoo since 1847, and set up five university centres here. Leading figures including Marie Curie and Albert Einstein met here to discuss new scientific issues. The park is still home to many scientific institutes, as well as a haven of peace in the heart of this busy political area.

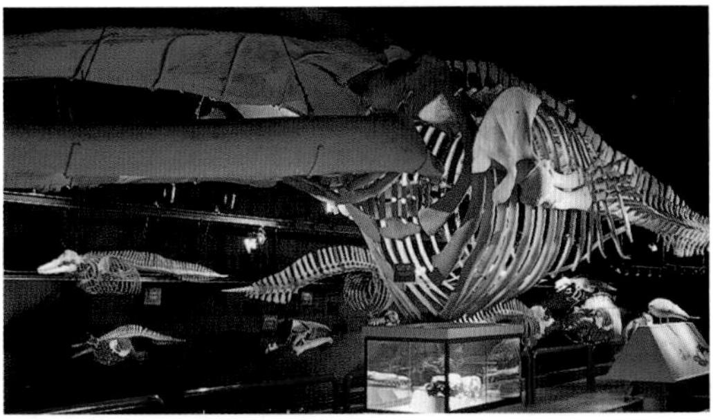

Whale skeleton inside the Institut Royal des Sciences Naturelles

⑳ Parc du Cinquantenaire

The finest of Leopold II's grand projects, the Parc and Palais du Cinquantenaire were built for the Golden Jubilee celebrations of Belgian independence in 1880. The park was laid out on unused town marshes. The palace, at its entrance, was to comprise a triumphal arch and two large exhibition areas, but by the time of the 1880 Art and Industry Expo, only the two side exhibition areas had been completed. Further funds were eventually found, and work continued for 50 years. Before being converted into museums, the large halls on either side of the central archway were used to hold trade fairs, the last of which was in 1935. They have also been used for horse races and to store homing pigeons. During World War II, the grounds of the park were used to grow vegetables to feed the people of Brussels.

★ **Musée de l'Armée**
Opened in 1923, the museum covers all aspects of Belgium's military history, and exhibits over 200 years of militaria. Historic aircraft are on display in the hall next door.

View of Park with Arch
Based on the Arc de Triomphe in Paris, the arch was not completed in time for the 50th Anniversary celebrations but was finished in 1905.

Tree-lined Avenue
In part formal garden, part forested walks, many of the plantations of elms and plane trees date from 1880.

0 metres   100
0 yards   100

KEY

① **Pavillon Horta**

② **The Grand Mosque** was built as the Oriental pavilion for the 1880 Exhibition. It became a mosque in 1978.

③ **Underpass**

④ **The park** is popular with Brussels' Eurocrats and families at lunchtimes and weekends.

The Central Archway
Conceived as a gateway into the city, the arch is crowned by the symbolic bronze sculpture *Brabant Raising the National Flag.*

VISITORS' CHECKLIST

Practical Information
Ave de Tervuren, 1040 BRU.
Map 3 C3. ♿ 🏛 Autoworld: (02) 736 4165. **Open** 10am–5pm (Sat, Sun & Apr–Sep: to 6pm). ♿ ♿
🕌 Grand Mosque: (02) 735 2173.
Open 9am–4pm Mon–Thu.
Please dress with respect.

Transport
🚌 12, 21, 22, 27, 36, 60, 61, 79, 80.
🚊 81, 83. Ⓜ Schuman, Mérode.

Cinquantenaire Museum
Parc du Cinquantenaire 10. **Tel** (02) 741 7211. **Open** 9:30am–5pm Tue–Fri (from 10am Sat, Sun and public hols). **Closed** 1 Jan, 1 May, 1 & 11 Nov, 25 Dec. 📷 ♿

Part of the Musées Royaux d'Art et d'Histoire, the Cinquantenaire Museum has occupied its present site since the early 1900s. It houses four main collections: Antiquity, National Archaeology, European Decorative Arts and Non-European Civilizations, which includes sections on Byzantium and Islam, China, South-East Asia and the Indian Subcontinent, and the Pre-Columbian civilizations of the Americas. There are decorative arts from all ages, with glassware, silverware and porcelain as well as a fine collection of tapestries. Religious sculptures and stained glass are displayed around a courtyard in the style of church cloisters.

Autoworld
Housed in the south wing of the Cinquantenaire Palace, Autoworld is one of the best collections of automobiles in the world. There are some 300 cars, including an 1886 motor, and a 1924 Model-T Ford that still runs.

The aircraft display at the Musée Royal de l'Armée

Musée Royal de l'Armée et d'Histoire Militaire
Parc du Cinquantenaire 3. **Tel** (02) 737 7833. **Open** 9am–5pm Tue–Fri, 10am–6pm Sat, Sun & school hols.. **Closed** Mon, 1 Jan, 1 May, 1 Nov, 25 Dec. ♿

Together with the section on aviation, displays cover the Belgian Army and its history from the late 1700s to today, including weapons, uniforms, decorations and paintings. There is a section covering the 1830 struggle for independence *(see pp36–7)*. Two other sections show both World Wars, including the activities of the Resistance.

★ Cinquantenaire Museum
Belgian architect Bordiau's plans for the two exhibition halls, later permanent showcases, were partly modelled on London's Victorian museums. The use of iron and glass in their construction was inspired by the Crystal Palace.

A 90-Minute Walk Around the Heart of Brussels

It is impossible to tire of the Grand Place, and there is no better place to start a walk that traces the history of the city. The route leads first to the island site where Brussels originated, and follows the watery landscape of the old, walled city before the river and canals disappeared. The walk then passes the opera house where Belgian independence was born *(see p50)*, leads to the cathedral, and then to the grand Galeries Royales de Saint-Hubert. Finally, it meanders through the Îlot Sacré, the web of medieval streets around the Grand Place.

The Grand Place, Brussels' theatrical centrepiece

Grand Place and Place St Géry
You could start with a quick wander around the Grand Place, to savour its magnificent gilded architecture *(see pp44–5)*. The fact that this was once the medieval trading centre is recorded in the names of the streets all around it: Rue des Harengs (herrings), Rue Chair et Pain (meat and bread), and so on. At No. 4 Grande Place is La Maison des Maîtres Chocolatiers Belges, which showcases ten artisans who create Belgian chocolate by

Tips for Walkers

Starting point: Grand Place
Length: 3.25 km (2 miles)
Getting there: The nearest Metro stop is Gare Centrale; numerous buses also go to the Bourse, and to De Brouckère/Place de la Monnaie a short walk away.
Stopping off points: This area is packed with places to eat and drink. The area around Place Ste-Catherine is famous for its fish restaurants. Among the many attractive yet average establishments in the Îlot Sacré, Aux Armes de Bruxelles stands out.

traditional methods. Leave the square on the Rue au Beurre (butter), an appropriate address of the Biscuiterie Dandoy ① at No. 31, famous for its traditional, buttery biscuits. On the opposite side of the road is the atmospheric Église St-Nicolas *(see p49)* ②, while ahead lies the Neo-Classical façade of the Stock Exchange, La Bourse ③. Go left; facing the Bourse on Rue Henri Maus is Falstaff ④, one of the few genuine Art Nouveau cafés in Brussels, dating from 1903. Ahead lies the Boulevard Anspach ⑤; this was once the route of Brussels' river, the Senne, which was canalized and covered over in around 1870. The Halles St-Géry *(see p48)* – the old meat market on Place St-Géry ⑥ – is now the hub of a trendy area of the city; this square was an island until the mid-19th century, and the site of one of Brussels' earliest chapels. The River Senne still runs beneath here; in the courtyard of renovated apartments at No. 23

Place St-Géry ⑦, some of the river can still be seen. Leave the square by the Rue Pont de la Carpe (carp bridge) and turn left at Rue Dansaert. ⑧

Place Ste-Catherine
The Rue du Vieux Marché aux Grains (old grain market) opens up into the Place Ste-Catherine ⑨, with the Église Ste-Catherine *(see p55)* ⑩ in its midst. Walk to the right of the church; at the far end, on the right, you will see

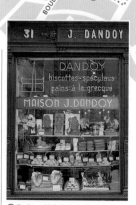

① Traditional Belgian butter biscuits at Biscuiterie Dandoy

the Tour Noire (Black Tower) ⑪. This is a rare remnant of the first ring of city walls built to protect Brussels in the 13th century. Loop round the eastern end of the Eglise Ste-Catherine to the broad, open space lined by the Quai au Bois à Brûler (firewood quay) and Quai aux Briques (brick quay) ⑫. The area between them – filled with pools and fountains – was once a canal; it was covered over in 1870, and the fish market was relocated here. This tradition is maintained by the numerous fish restaurants in these streets. The Rue du Peuplier leads to the Eglise St-Jean-Baptiste-au-Béguinage (see p54) ⑬; this beautiful Baroque church once stood at the heart of a *béguinage* (see p55) that occupied much of northwest Brussels in medieval times.

Place des Martyrs and La Monnaie

Via the Rue de Laeken, Rue des Hirondelles, and Boulevard Émile Jacqumain, you can reach the Place de Brouckère (see p54). On the opposite side is the Hôtel Métropole (see p51) ⑭, one of the city's grandest hotels. From the Boulevard Adolphe Max, turn right to walk through the Passage du Nord ⑮, a shopping arcade built in 1882. At the end lies Rue Neuve (see p51) ⑯, one of Brussels' main shopping streets. At one end you will find the Centre

⑭ The entrance to the Hôtel Métropole, one of Brussels' oldest Art Nouveau hotels

⑭ Marionettes de Toone puppet

Anspach, at the other City 2 (see p161). From here, the Rue St-Michel leads to the Place des Martyrs ⑰. In the middle is a marble statue of "Belga", under which is a mausoleum for the 450 "martyrs" killed in the 1830 Revolution that secured Belgium its independence. The building on the north of the square, decked with Flemish flags, is the seat of the Flemish government ⑱. Retrace your steps, then continue to the Place de la Monnaie ⑲, the site of the fine Neo-Classical opera house, the Théâtre Royal de la Monnaie (see p50) ⑳.

The Îlot Sacré

By walking some 200 m (220 yd) along the Rue de l'Écuyer, you come to the northern entrance of the Galeries St-Hubert (see p49) ㉑, a magnificent shopping arcade built in 1847. Walk through the arcade to the point, halfway along, where it is intersected by the pedestrianized Rue des Bouchers ㉒, the "butchers street" lined with colourful restaurants. You are now in the Îlot Sacré, a term that dates back to 1960 when this area was decreed a "sacred island" to be protected from development. Take the second left, the Petite Rue des Bouchers ㉓; halfway down, on the left-hand side, is an alley called the Impasse Schuddeveld, at the end of which is the Théâtre Marionettes de Toone (see p50) ㉔, the famous and historic puppet theatre. By continuing along the Petite Rue des Bouchers and the Rue Chair et Pain, you will return to the Grand Place.

㉑ Galeries St-Hubert, continental Europe's oldest shopping arcade

Key

• • • Walk Route

0 metres   100
0 yards   100

BLVD ADOLPHE MAX LAAN
RUE ST MICHEL ST MICHIELSTRAAT
R AUX CHOUX
KOOLSTR.
PLACE DES MARTYRS MARTELAARS PLEIN
RUE NEUVE NIEUW STR
RUE D'ARGENT ZILVERSTR
DE CKERE EIN
RUE DU FOSSE
AUX LOUPS WOLVENGRACHT
PLACE DE LA MONNAIE
RUE DE L'ECUYER SCHILDKNAAPSSTR
RUE D'ARENBERG ARENBERGSTRG
R D BOUCHERS BEENHOUWER STR
R D MARCHE AUX HERBES GRAS-MARKT
RUE DE LA MONTAGNE BERGSTRAAT
AND ACE OTE RKT

A 90-Minute Walk in the Sablons and Coudenberg

Brussels was historically divided into an Upper and Lower Town. The Upper Town, on the Coudenberg ("Cold Hill"), was the royal quarter, the site of a palace destroyed by fire in 1731. This walk climbs gently from the Grand Place in the Lower Town, past remnants of the old city walls and the working-class Marolles district, before entering the chic area of Sablon. On the Coudenberg, the route passes the elegant 18th-century palace of Charles of Lorraine before descending to Brussels' cathedral and returning to the Grand Place.

Cafés and restaurants in the Grand Place, or Grote Markt

Manneken Pis and the Marolles

Leave the Grand Place via the Rue Charles Buls, named after a Burgomaster of the 1890s who did much to preserve the historic face of Brussels. At the first crossroad is the Hôtel Amigo ①, on the site of a prison named the Amigo by the 16th-century rulers of the Spanish Netherlands. Opposite, on the wall of Rue des Brasseurs 1, is a plaque ② marking the hotel where, in 1873, the French poet Paul Verlaine shot fellow poet Arthur Rimbaud at the end of their affair. The next street, the Rue de la Violette,

contains the lace museum, the Musée du Costume et de la Dentelle *(see p46)* ③. Continue along Rue de l'Étuve ④, the site of a public bathhouse in the Middle Ages. At the corner with the Rue du Chêne is the famous statue of the Manneken Pis *(see pp46–7)* ⑤. Take the Rue du Chêne, then the Rue de Villers to reach the Tour de Villers ⑥, the remains of a tower and section of the 12th-century city walls. Across Boulevard de l'Empereur is the church of Notre-Dame de la Chapelle *(see p48)* ⑦, with its black bell tower. Rue Blaes and Rue Haute lead off to the south into the Quartier Marolles *(see p48)*. If you walk

along Rue Haute to the north, you reach the Tour d'Angle (or Tour d'Anneessens) ⑧, another remnant of the old city walls.

The Sablon

Walk up the picturesque Rue de Rollebeek ⑨. At the top, take a look down Rue Joseph Stevens to where the Maison du Peuple ⑩ once stood on the Place E. Vandervelde. Built for the Société Coopérative, it was one of Victor Horta's great Art Nouveau masterpieces, but it was demolished in 1965. The sloping triangular space

Musee du Costume et de la Dentelle ③

Tips for Walkers

Starting point: Grand Place
Length: 3.4 km (2.1 miles)
Getting there: The nearest Metro stop is Bourse; numerous buses also go to the Bourse, and to De Brouckère/Place de la Monnaie a short walk away.
Stopping off points: The Place du Grand Sablon has many fine restaurants, a branch of Le Pain Quotidien (No.14 in this walk), and the cafés of Wittamer (No.13). Near the Place Royale, Du Mim, within the Musée Instrumental, is recommended.

⑬ High-quality patisseries at renowned chocolatiers Wittamer

⑱ The Musées Royaux de Beaux-Arts de Belgique

nearby is the Place du Grand Sablon (*see p70*) ⑪. The fountain of Minerva ⑫, in the middle of the square, was erected in 1751 with funds from Thomas Bruce, an exiled friend of King James II of England. The Sablon still retains an upmarket air, and it is home to Wittamer ⑬, one of Brussels' most celebrated chocolate makers (shop and small café at No.12; café at No. 6). At Rue des Sablons 11 is a branch of Le Pain Quotidien ⑭, famed for its bread and pastries. At the upper end of the Place du Grand Sablon is the beautiful Notre-Dame du Sablon (*see p70*) ⑮. On the Rue de la Régence, look right for a view of the Palais de Justice (*see p71*) ⑯. Directly opposite you is the Place du Petit Sablon (*see pp70–71*) ⑰, a pretty garden with statues of medieval guildsmen.

Place Royale and Cathedral
Heading north along the Rue de la Régence, you reach the Musées Royaux des Beaux-Arts de Belgique (*see pp64–9*) ⑱, the city's most important art gallery, which houses the Musée Magritte. Beyond lies the Place Royale (*see p61*) on the top of the Coudenberg, the site of royal palaces since

medieval times. The present royal palace is just around the corner (*see pp59–61*), and is directly connected to the Eglise St-Jacques-sur-Coudenberg (*see pp60–61*) ⑲. On the opposite side of the square is the Musée des Instruments de Musique (*see pp62–3*) ⑳, which offers spectacular views from the terrace. Leave the Place Royale by the cobbled Rue du Musée, which leads to the Palais de Charles de Lorraine (*see p63*) ㉑. The Protestant Chapelle Royale ㉒, to the right, was where King Léopold I worshipped. At the top of Rue Ravenstein is the 15th-century Hôtel Ravenstein (*see p62*) ㉓. You can see the spire of the Hôtel de Ville (in the Grand Place) over the gardens on the Mont des Arts to the northeast. The modern building to the left of the gardens is the Bibliothèque Royale Albert I ㉔, the national library. Walk through the gardens to the equestrian statue of Albert I (r. 1909–34) ㉕, the "Soldier King" revered for leading Belgian troops in World War I. The arch at the lower end of the street called Mont des Arts has a carillon clock ㉖ on the side facing up the hill that includes figures from Belgian history that move on the hour. From here, a walk of 400 m (437 yd) leads to the Cathédrale Sts Michel et Gudule (*see pp72–3*) ㉗. On the route back to the Grand Place, stop in the Place Agora to admire Burgomaster Charles Buls and his dog, portrayed in a charming bronze statue ㉘.

㉖ The modern carillion clock on the arch in the Mont des Arts

Key

••• Walk route

0 metres 100
0 yards 100

GREATER BRUSSELS

Past the heart-shaped ring-road of Brussels city centre lie 19 suburbs *(communes)* which form the Bruxelles-Capitale region. While many are residential, a handful are definitely worth the short ride to sample outlying treasures of Brussels' fascinating history. For fans of early 20th-century architecture, the suburb of St-Gilles offers numerous original examples of striking Art Nouveau buildings, including Musée Horta. In Koekelberg and visible from the Upper Town is the huge Sacré-Coeur basilica, started in 1904. To the

north, Heysel offers attractions whose modernity contrasts with the historical city centre. The 1958 Atomium, now restored, stands next to the Bruparck theme park. To the east, the Central Africa Museum reflects Belgium's colonial past in the Congo, and the tram museum takes a journey through Brussels' urban past. Peace and tranquillity can be found close to the metropolis, in the orderly landscape of Royal Laeken and the lush green spaces of the Bois de la Cambre and the Fôret de Soignes.

Sights at a Glance

Churches and Cathedrals
❽ Basilique Nationale du Sacré-Coeur

Historic Monuments, Buildings and Districts
❼ Anderlecht
❷ Avenue Louise
❹ Ixelles
❸ St-Gilles
❻ Uccle

Parks and Gardens
❸ Bruparck
⓫ Domaine de Laeken *see pp88–9*
❺ Fôret de Soignes

Museums and Exhibition Areas
⓬ The Atomium
❶ Musée Horta *see p84*
❾ Musée du Tram
❿ Musée Royal de l'Afrique Centrale

Key
▦ Central Brussels
═ Motorway
▬ Major Road
═ Minor road
— Railway

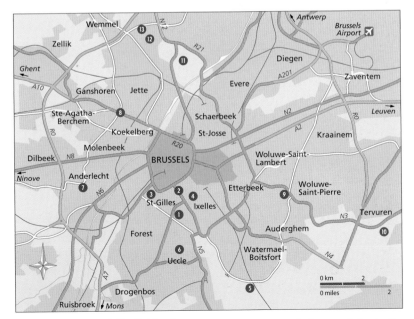

◀ The Atomium monument in the Heysel Park, Brussels

For keys to symbols *see back flap*

● Musée Horta

Architect Victor Horta (1861–1947) is considered by many to be the father of Art Nouveau, and his impact on Brussels architecture is unrivalled by any other designer of his time. A museum dedicated to his unique style is today housed in his restored family home, which he designed from 1898 to 1901. His skill lay not only in his grand, overall vision but in his equal talent as an interior designer, blending themes and materials into each detail. The airy interior of the building displays trademarks of the architect's style – iron, glass and curves – in every detail, while retaining a functional approach.

The bedroom features Art Nouveau furniture, including a wardrobe inlaid with pale and dark wood.

★ **Central Staircase**
Decorated with curved wrought iron, the stairs are enhanced further by mirrors and glass, bringing natural light into the house.

VISITORS' CHECKLIST

Practical Information
Rue Américaine 25, 1060 BRU.
Tel (02) 543 0490.
Open 2–5:30pm Tue–Sun.
Closed Mon, public hols. 🎫 📷

Transport
🚌 54. 🚊 33, 51, 81, 83, 92, 93, 94, 97. Ⓜ Louise.

Madame Horta's sitting-room features blue-and-cream wool rugs woven to Horta's design, and a marble fireplace.

★ **Dining Room**
White enamel tiles line the walls, rising to an ornate ceiling, decorated with the scrolled metalwork used in other rooms.

Living Room
The detail of Horta's work can be best seen here, from sculpted bannister ends to finely wrought door handles that echo larger forms.

Front Entrance

Exclusive boutique in the chic Avenue Louise

➋ Avenue Louise

Map 2 D5. 🚌 81, 83, 92, 93, 94, 97. Ⓜ Louise.

Most visitors to Brussels travelling by car will come across this busy thoroughfare, its various underpasses constructed in the 1950s and 1960s to link up the city centre with its suburbs. In fact, the avenue was constructed in 1864 to join the centre with the suburb of Ixelles. However, the north end of the avenue retains a chic atmosphere; by the Porte de Namur, fans of designer labels can indulge themselves in Gucci and Versace, as well as investigating the less expensive but no less chic boutiques.

The avenue also has its architectural treasures. The **Hôtel Solvay** at No. 224 was built by Victor Horta in 1894 for the industrialist Solvay family. Its ornate doorway, columns and balconies are a fine example of Art Nouveau style *(see pp20–21)*. The house is a private home, but visits can be arranged (www.hotel solvay.be). At No. 346, **Hôtel Max Hallet** is one of Horta's masterpieces, built in 1903. Continuing south leads to peaceful Ixelles.

➌ St-Gilles

🚌 27, 48. 🚋 3, 4, 51, 81, 83. Ⓜ Porte de Hal, Parvis St-Gilles.

Named after the patron saint of this district's main church, St-Gilles is traditionally one of Brussels' poorer areas. However, amid the low-quality functional housing are architectural survivors which make the suburb well worth a visit. Art Nouveau and *sgraffiti* gems *(see p21)* can be found in streets such as Avenue Jean Volders and Rue Vanderschrick. The **Hôtel Hannon** (1902), now a photography gallery, remains one of the city's most spectacular Art Nouveau structures. Restored in 1985, it has a stained-glass window and ornate statuary that take this architectural style to its peak *(see p20)*. Art Nouveau details can be seen in the nearby streets, particularly in Rue Felix Delhasse and in the nearby Rue Africaine.

One of the most striking features of St-Gilles is the **Porte de Hal**. Brussels' second set of town walls, built in the 14th century, originally included seven gateways, of which Porte de Hal is the only survivor *(see p16)*. Used as a prison from the 16th to 18th centuries, it was restored in 1870. Today, it houses a small museum dedicated to medieval and Renaissance Brussels, and is part of the Musées Royaux d'Art et d'Histoire.

Art Nouveau detail on façade in Rue Africaine

🏛 Hôtel Hannon
Ave de la Jonction 1, BRU 1060. **Tel** (02) 538 4220. Ⓜ Albert.

🏛 Porte de Hal
Blvd du Midi, BRU 1000. **Tel** (02) 534 1518. 🚌 27, 48, 134, 136, 137, 365. 🚋 3, 4, 51. Ⓜ Porte de Hal. **Open** 9:30am–5pm Tue–Fri, 10am–5pm Sat & Sun 🌐 ♿

➍ Ixelles

🚌 34, 54, 64, 71, 80. 🚋 7, 25, 81, 83, 93, 94. Ⓜ Porte de Namur.

Although one of Brussels' largest suburbs and a busy transport junction, the heart of Ixelles remains a peaceful oasis of lakes and woodland.

The idyllic **Abbaye de la Cambre** was founded in 1201, achieving fame and a degree of fortune in 1242, when Saint Boniface chose the site for his retirement. The abbey then endured a troubled history in the wars of religion during the 16th and 17th centuries. It finally closed as an operational abbey in 1796 and now houses a school of architecture. The abbey's pretty Gothic church can be toured and its grassy grounds and courtyards offer a peaceful walk.

South of the abbey, the Bois de la Cambre remains one of the city's most popular public parks. Created in 1860, it achieved popularity almost immediately when royalty promenaded its main route. Lakes, bridges and lush grass make it a favoured picnic site. **The Musée d'Ixelles** nearby has a fine collection of posters by 19th- and 20th-century greats, such as Toulouse Lautrec and Magritte, as well as sculptures by Rodin. The former home of one of Belgium's finest sculptors is now **Musée Constantin Meunier**, with 170 sculptures and 120 paintings by the artist, and his studio preserved in its turn-of-the-century style.

🏛 Abbaye de la Cambre
Ave de Général de Gaulle, BRU 1050. **Open** 9am–noon & 3–6pm Mon–Fri. **Closed** public hols.

🏛 Musée d'Ixelles
Rue J Van Volsem 71, BRU 1050. **Tel** (02) 515 6421. **Open** 9:30am–5pm Tue–Sun. **Closed** public hols. 📷

🏛 Musée Constantin Meunier
Rue de l'Abbaye 59, BRU 1050. **Tel** (02) 648 4449. **Open** 10am–noon & 1–5pm Tue–Fri. **Closed** public hols.

The Forêt de Soignes, once a royal hunting ground and now a park

❺ Forêt de Soignes

🚌 41, 72. 🚊 44, 94. Ⓜ Hermann Debroux. 🚶 guided walks 10am Thu & Sun. **Tel** (02) 215 1740.

The large forested area to the southeast of Brussels' city centre has a long history: thought to have had prehistoric beginnings, it was also here that the Gallic citizens suffered their defeat by the Romans *(see p31)*. However, the forest really gained renown in the 12th century when wild boar roamed the landscape, and local dukes enjoyed hunting trips in the woodland.

The density of the landscape has provided tranquillity over the ages. In the 14th and 15th centuries, it became a favoured location for monasteries and abbeys. Few have survived, but Abbaye de Rouge-Cloître is a rare example from this era.

In a former 18th-century priory is the **Groenendaal Arboretum**, in which more than 400 forest plants are housed, many of which are extinct elsewhere. The most common sight, however, is the locals enjoying a stroll.

🌳 **Groenendaal Arboretum**
Duboislaan 6, 1560 BRU. **Tel** (02) 657 5925. **Open** 1–5pm Wed–Sun. 🌐 **bosmuseum.be**

❻ Uccle

🚌 43, 60. 🚊 51.

Uccle is a smart residential district, nestling in its tree-lined avenues. Not immediately a tourist destination, it is worth-

while taking a trip to the **Musée David et Alice van Buuren**. The 1920s residence of this Dutch couple is now a small museum, displaying their eclectic acquisitions. Amid the Dutch Delftware and French Lalique lamps are great finds, such as original sketches by Van Gogh. Visitors will also enjoy the modern landscaped gardens at the rear.

Mirò-style drawings, Anderlecht

🏛 **Musée David et Alice van Buuren**
Ave Léo Errera 41, 1180 BRU. **Tel** (02) 343 4851. **Open** 2–5:30pm Wed–Mon. **Closed** Tue, 1 Jan, 25 Dec. 🎨

❼ Anderlecht

🚌 46, 49, 75. 🚊 31, 81. Ⓜ Bizet, Clemenceau, St-Guidon.

Considered to be Brussels' first genuine suburb (archaeological digs have uncovered remnants of Roman housing),

Anderlecht is now best known as an industrial area, for its meat market, and its successful football club of the same name. Despite this, the Modernist Spanish painter Joan Mirò added a unique artistic contribution inspiring bright cartoon-like murals on Rue Porcelaine.

Although only a few pockets of the suburb are now residential, during the 15th century this was a popular place of abode and some houses remain from that era. **Maison d'Erasme**, built in 1468, is now named after the great scholar and religious reformer, Erasmus (1466–1536), who lived here for five months in 1521. The house was restored in the 1930s. Now a museum dedicated to the most respected thinker of his generation, it displays a collection of 16th-century furniture and portraits of the great humanist by Holbein and van der Weyden.

Nearby is the huge edifice of **Eglise Sts-Pierre-et-Guidon**. This 14th-century Gothic church, completed with the addition of a tower in 1517, is notable for its sheer size and exterior gables, typical of Brabant architecture. The life of St Guidon, patron saint of peasants, is depicted on interior wall murals.

Illustrating a more recent history, the **Musée Gueuze** is a family brewery that has opened

Maison d'Erasme in Anderlecht, with its courtyard and fountain

The Basilique Nationale du Sacré-Coeur

its doors to the public to witness the production of classic Belgian beers.

🏛 Maison d'Érasme

Rue du Chapitre 31, 1070 BRU. **Tel** (02) 521 1383. **Open** 10am–6pm Tue–Sun. **Closed** Mon, 1 Jan, 25 Dec. 🅰

⛪ Eglise Sts-Pierre-et-Guidon

Place de la Vaillance, 1070 BRU. **Open** 2–5pm Mon–Fri. **Closed** Sat & Sun.

🏛 Musée Gueuze

Rue Gheude 56, 1070 BRU. **Tel** (02) 521 4928. **Open** 9am–5pm Mon–Fri, 10am–5pm Sat. **Closed** Sun, public hols. 🅰 including 1 free beer.

❽ Basilique Nationale du Sacré-Coeur

Parvis de la Basilique 1, Koekelberg, 1083 BRU. **Tel** (02) 421 1667. Ⓜ Simonis. 🚌 13, 14, 15, 20, 87. 🚋 19. **Open** summer: 9am–5pm daily; winter: 10am–4pm daily. 🅰 🅰 by appointment.

Although a small and popular suburb among Brussels' residents, there is little for the visitor to see in Koekelberg other than the striking Basilique Nationale du Sacré-Coeur, but this does make the journey worthwhile for those interested in Art Deco. King Léopold II was keen to build a church in the city which could accommodate vast congregations to reflect the burgeoning population of early 20th-century Brussels. He commissioned the church in 1904, although the building was not finished until 1970. Originally designed by Pierre Langerock, the final construction, which uses sandstone and terracotta, was the less expensive adaptation by Albert van Huffel. Very much a 20th-century church, in contrast to the many medieval religious buildings in the city centre, it is dedicated to those who died for Belgium, in particular the thousands of Belgian soldiers who were never to return from the two world wars, killed in battles fought on their own terrain.

The most dominating feature of the church is the vast green copper dome, rising 90 m (295 ft) above ground. For those who do not manage to visit the church itself, it is this central dome that is visible from many points in the city, including the Palais de Justice.

❾ Musée du Tram

Ave de Tervuren 364b, BRU 1150. **Tel** (02) 515 3108. 🚌 39, 44, 94. **Open** Apr–Sep: 1–7pm Sat & Sun, pub hols. Group tours possible. Every Sun and pub hol, the museum organizes a four-hour round tour to Heysel (10am). **Closed** Oct–Mar. 🅰

This museum traces the history of public transport in Belgium, with marvellous displays of heritage machinery. Horse-drawn trams are available to transport visitors round the site, which features fully-working early versions of the electric tram, buses and plenty of interactive exhibits.

❿ Musée Royal de l'Afrique Centrale

Leuvensesteenweg 13, Tervuren 3080. **Tel** (02) 769 5211. 🚌 44. **Open** 10am–5pm Tue–Fri, 10am–6pm Sat & Sun. **Closed** Mon, public hols. Closed till 2017 for renovations. 🅰 🅦 africamuseum.be

In the 19th century, the colony of the Belgian Congo was Belgium's only territorial possession. It was handed back to self-government in 1960 and eventually renamed Zaire (now the Democratic Republic of Congo). This museum, opened in 1899, is a collection gleaned from over 100 years of colonial rule. Galleries show ceremonial African dress and masks, and displays on colonial life.

Dugout canoes, pagan idols, weapons and stuffed wildlife, feature heavily. There is a horrifying collection of conserved giant African insects, much beloved by children. The museum hosts temporary exhibitions year round.

The Musée Royal de l'Afrique Centrale façade in Tervuren

⓫ Domaine de Laeken

In the 11th century Laeken, became popular among pilgrims after reported sightings of the Virgin Mary. Since the 19th century, however, it has been firmly associated in the minds of all Belgians with the nation's monarchy. A walk around the sedate and peaceful area reveals impressive buildings constructed in honour of the royal location, not least the sovereign's official residence and its beautifully landscaped parkland. More surprising is the sudden Oriental influence. The great builder, King Léopold II, wanted to create an architectural world tour; the Chinese and Japanese towers (currently closed for restoration) are the only two buildings that came to fruition, but show the scope of one monarch's vision.

★ **Pavillon Chinois**
Architect Alexandre Marcel designed this elaborate building (built 1901–09) that houses Oriental porcelain.

★ **Serres Royales**
These late 19th-century glasshouses are home to exotic trees, palms and camellias. Open to the public annually in April, they are the King's private property.

KEY

① **Parc Royal**

② **Monument Léopold** stands as the focus of the park complex and layout. It honours Léopold I, first king of the Belgians. Built in Neo-Gothic style, it has a filigree cast-iron canopy and tracery around the base.

③ **Place de la Dynastie** is part of the attractive park that was once the Royal Family's private hunting ground.

④ **Villa Belvedere** is home to King Albert II and Queen Paola, who stayed here instead of moving to the Château Royal on accession to the throne.

⑤ **Tour Japonais**

⑥ **Domaine Royale de Laeken** is the royal estate, adjacent to the Parc de Laeken in the city district of Laeken; the woodland features old magnolias and blooming hawthorns.

Château Royal
The Belgian royal residence was built in the late 18th century by architect-contractor Louis Montoyer following plans by renowned French architect Charles de Wailly.

VISITORS' CHECKLIST

Practical Information
Laeken, 1020 BRU. Château Royal:
Ave du Parc Royal. **Closed** to
public. Serres Royales: Ave de
Prince Royal. **Tel** (02) 551 2020.
Open mid-Apr–mid-May (phone
for details). 🚹 8–10pm Fri–Sun.
Pavillon Chinois: Ave J van Praet
44. **Tel** (02) 268 1608.
Open 9:30am–5pm Tue–Fri,
10am–5pm Sat & Sun. 🚹 Tour
Japonais: Avenue J van Praet 44.
Tel (02) 268 1608. **Open** 10am–
5pm Tue–Sun. 🚹 Eglise Notre
Dame de Laeken: Paris Notre
Dame. **Tel** (02) 479 2362.
Open 2–5pm Tue–Sun.

Transport
🚌 47, 49, 53, 57, 84, 88, 89.
🚊 3, 7, 19, 51, 62, 93.
Ⓜ Heysel, Bockstael.

The Atomium rising 102 m (335 ft) over the Bruparck at dusk

⑫ The Atomium

Square de l'Atomium, 1020 BRU.
Tel (02) 475 4775. 🚌 84, 88. 🚊 3, 7,
19, 51, 93. Ⓜ Heysel. **Open** 10am–
6pm daily. 🚹 ♿ Ⓦ **atomium.be**

Built for the 1958 World Fair *(see p37)*, the Atomium is probably the most identifiable symbol of Brussels. As the world moved into a new age of science and space travel at the end of the 1950s, so the design by André Waterkeyn reflected this with a structure of an iron crystal, magnified 165 billion times. Each of the nine spheres that make up the "atom" are 18 m (60 ft) in diameter, and linked by escalators and stairs. They include exhibition rooms and a smart restaurant at the top of the structure.

⑬ Bruparck

Boulevard du Centenaire, 1020 BRU.
Tel (02) 474 8383. 🚌 84, 88. 🚊 3, 7,
19, 51, 93. Ⓜ Heysel. Mini-Europe &
Océade: **Tel** (02) 478 0550 (Mini-
Europe); (02) 478 4320 (Océade).
Open Apr–Sep: 9:30am–6pm daily
(Jul–Aug: to 8pm); Oct–mid-Jan:
10am–6pm daily. **Closed** end Jan–
Mar. 🚹 Kinepolis: **Tel** (02) 474 2600.
Open perfomances. 🚹 for films. ♿
Ⓦ **minieurope.be**

Although nowhere near as large or as grand as many of the world's theme parks, Bruparck's sights and facilities are a popular family destination.

The first and favourite port of call for most visitors is Mini-Europe, where more than 300 miniature reconstructions take you around the landscapes of the European Union. Built at a scale of 1:25, the collection displays buildings of social or cultural importance, such as the Acropolis in Athens, the Brandenburg Gate of Berlin and the Houses of Parliament from London. Even at this scale, the detail is such that it can be second only to visiting the sights themselves.

For film fans, Kinepolis cannot be beaten. Large auditoriums show a range of popular films from different countries on 29 screens. The IMAX cinema features surround sound and a semi-circular 600 sq m (6,456 sq ft) widescreen.

If warmth and relaxation are what you are looking for, Océade is a tropically heated water park, complete with giant slides, wave machines, bars, cafés and even realistic re-created sandy beaches.

London's Houses of Parliament in small scale at Mini-Europe

| 0 metres | | 250 |
| 0 yards | | 250 |

View of the lively and colourful Bruges market ▶

BEYOND BRUSSELS

BEYOND BRUSSELS

Brussels is at the heart not only of Belgium, but also of Europe. The city marks the divide between the Flemish north and the French-speaking Walloon south. Its central position makes Brussels an ideal base for visitors: within easy reach are the ancient Flemish towns of Antwerp, Ghent and Bruges, each with their exquisite medieval architecture, superb museums and excellent restaurants.

Although Belgium is a small country, it has one of the highest population densities in Europe. An incredibly efficient road and rail network also means that large numbers of people move around the country every day, with around half the population employed in industry, particularly in textiles, metallurgy and chemicals. Despite this, parts of Belgium are still farmed. Stretching south from the defences of the North Sea is the plain of Flanders, a low-lying area which, like the Netherlands, has reclaimed land or *polders*, whose fertile soil is intensively cultivated with wheat and sugar beet. Bordering the Netherlands is the Kempenland, a sparsely populated area of peat moors, which in the 19th century was mined for coal. There

are small farms here today which cultivate mainly oats, rye and potatoes. Northeast Belgium also contains the large port of Antwerp, a major centre of European industry, with its shipbuilding yards and car factories. The towns of Leuven, Lier and Mechelen are noted for their medieval town centres. Ghent has an elegant grandeur and Bruges has superb medieval buildings and excellent museums.

Brussels itself is surrounded by both Flemish and Walloon Brabant, a fertile region famous for its wheat and beet farms and pasture for cows. Just a few kilometres south of the capital is Waterloo, the most visited battlefield in the world, where Napoleon was defeated by Wellington in 1815.

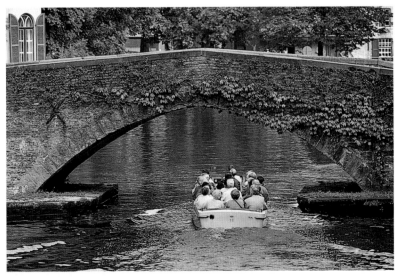

Visitors sail under the Blinde Ezelstraat Bridge on a tour of Bruges

◀ Tall spires of the Cathedral of Our Lady in Antwerp

Exploring Beyond Brussels

Belgium occupies one of the most densely populated parts of Europe, with a concentration of towns and villages across the flat landscapes of the Flemish plain. Along the North Sea coast, there are fewer settlements, set among fertile farmland. To the north and west of Brussels are the three easy-to-reach towns of Antwerp, Ghent and Bruges which, with their ancient buildings and vibrant cultural life, are attractive destinations. East of Brussels is the charming university town of Leuven, and to the south of the city is the site of Napoleon's defeat at the hands of the British army at Waterloo.

Bronze statue of Silvius Brabo in Antwerp's Grote Markt

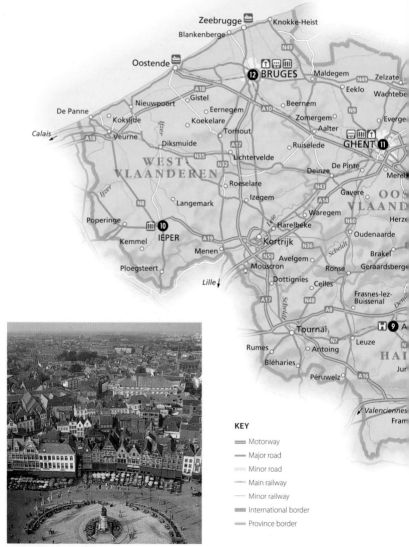

KEY

- Motorway
- Major road
- Minor road
- Main railway
- Minor railway
- International border
- Province border

View over Bruges from the Belfort

For keys to symbols *see back flap*

Getting Around

In Belgium, distances are short, with a wide choice of routes – even the tiniest village is easily reached. Brussels sits at the hub of several major highways such as the A10 and the A1 (which link the capital to the country's principal towns). The fully integrated public transport system has frequent train services and a comprehensive bus network.

The imposing walls of Ghent's Het Gravensteen

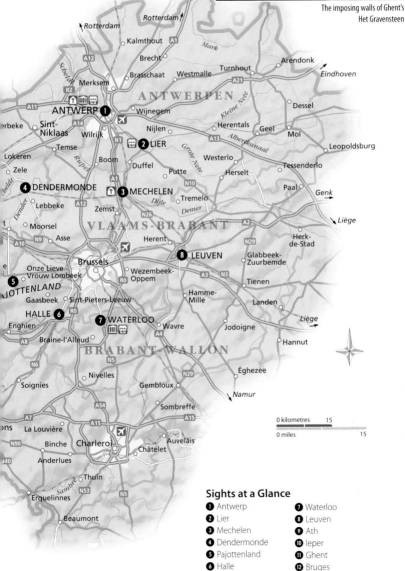

Sights at a Glance

1. Antwerp
2. Lier
3. Mechelen
4. Dendermonde
5. Pajottenland
6. Halle
7. Waterloo
8. Leuven
9. Ath
10. Ieper
11. Ghent
12. Bruges

❶ Antwerp

Antwerp is Belgium's second city and the largest city in Flanders, and it has one of Europe's busiest ports (its docks situated well to the north of the centre). Beginning as a settlement on the banks of the River Scheldt in the 2nd century, Antwerp became part of the Duchy of Brabant in 1106, and its main port. Within 200 years it was a thriving hub of the European cloth industry. But its golden age came during the era of Spanish rule *(see p33)*, when it was illuminated by the artistic genius of its most famous son, Pieter Paul Rubens (1577–1640). Today, mirroring this vigorous mercantile and cultural past, Antwerp is undergoing a spirited regeneration, seen in its widespread programme of rebuilding and renovation, and in its reputation as a key European source of cutting-edge fashion design.

Carvings above the cathedral door depicting the Last Judgement

of the Crossbowmen at number seven, on top of which is a statue of St George and the dragon. The central Brabo fountain is one of Antwerp's noted landmarks.

Key

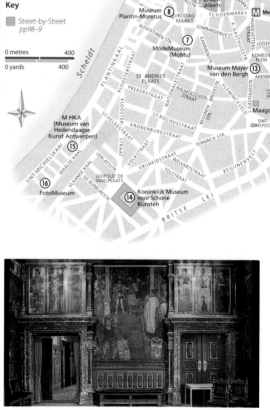

▨	Street-by-Street pp98–9

0 metres   400
0 yards   400

Visitors touring Antwerp on a horse-drawn bus in the summer

Getting Around

The best way to get around Antwerp is by using the public transport system. The excellent bus and tram network is focused on Centraal Station, where most visitors arrive. Fast and frequent trams and buses travel from here to the centre. Most of the city's main sights are within walking distance of the Grote Markt.

⊞ Grote Markt

Grote Markt. **Tel** (03) 232 0103 (tourist office). ♿

Antwerp's central square, or Grote Markt, is flanked by the ornately gabled Stadhuis (town hall), which was completed in 1564 by the architect and sculptor Cornelis Floris. The square's north side has a series of guildhouses, each of which is decorated with gilded figures. The tallest of these is the House

Fresco paintings of the dukes of Brabant in the Stadhuis, Grote Markt

⌂ Onze Lieve Vrouwe Kathedraal

Groenplaats 21 or Handschoenmarkt. **Tel** (03) 213 9951. **Open** 10am–5pm Mon–Fri, 10am–3pm Sat, 1–4pm Sun. 🌐 & 🚹 **dekathedraal.be**

The building of Antwerp's Onze Lieve Vrouwe Kathedraal (Cathedral of Our Lady) took almost two centuries, from 1352 to 1521. This magnificent structure has a graceful tiered spire that rises 123 m (404 ft) above the winding streets of the medieval city centre. Inside, the impression of light and space owes much to its seven-aisled nave and vaulted ceiling. The collection of paintings and sculpture includes three works by Rubens, of which two are triptychs – the *Raising of the Cross* (1610) and the *Descent from the Cross* (1612).

Sights at a Glance

① Grote Markt
② Onze Lieve Vrouwe Kathedraal
③ Antwerp Canals
④ Vleeshuis
⑤ Museum Aan De Stroom
⑥ Sint-Pauluskerk
⑦ ModeMuseum (MoMu)
⑧ Museum Plantin-Moretus
⑨ Sint-Carolus Borromeuskerk
⑩ Rockoxhuis
⑪ Sint Jacobskerk
⑫ Rubenshuis
⑬ Museum Mayer van den Bergh
⑭ Koninklijk Museum voor Schone Kunsten
⑮ MHKA
⑯ FotoMuseum
⑰ Red Star Line Museum

⊞ Antwerp Canals

Ruihuis, Suikerrui 21. **Tel** (03) 232 01 03. **Open** 10am–6pm Thu–Mon. **Closed** Tue, Wed. 🌐 🎧 10am, 2pm. 🔲 **visitantwerpen.be**

The Antwerp canals, or *ruien*, form the subterranean belly of the city and reveal a part of its history. It's possible to take a 15–20 minute walk along the canals without a guide, but there is also the "Long RUI" guided walk which takes three hours, (two hours underground and one hour above), during which you can ask the guide questions. Both walks include an exhibition on the history of the *ruien*, and you will be provided with a protective suit and boots (women are advised not to wear skirts).

⊞ Vleeshuis

Vleeshouwersstraat 38–40. **Tel** (03) 292 6100. **Open** 10am–5pm Thu–Sun, Easter Mon. **Closed** Mon, 1 & 2 Jan, 1 May, Ascension, 1 & 2 Nov, 25 & 26 Dec. 🌐

There has been a Vleeshuis (Meat Hall) on this site since 1250, but the existing hall was completed in 1504 to a design by architect Herman de Waghemakere. The structure features slender towers with five hexagonal turrets and rising gables, all built in alternate strips of stone and brick – giving the building a streaky bacon-like appearance.

The fine Gothic interior has been renovated to create a museum called "Sounds of the City", presenting 600 years of Antwerp's musical life.

⊞ Museum Aan De Stroom (MAS)

Hanzestedenplaats. **Tel** (03) 338 4400. **Open** 10am–5pm Tue–Fri, 10am–6pm Sat & Sun (10am–5pm in winter). **Closed** 1 Jan, 1 May, Ascension, 1 Nov, 25 Dec. 🌐 & 🎧 🔲 **mas.be**

Located in the old docks area just north of the historical centre is Antwerp's most innovative project, the Museum Aan De Stroom (MAS), meaning Museum on the River. This museum combines the best of the collections from the former

Maritime and Folklore Museums along with some of the Vleeshuis's collection. A broad range of objects on display cover everything from paintings and silverware to wood carvings, archaeological finds, folk art, maritime artifacts and model ships. These pieces span the prehistoric era through to the present day. The museum also features a cultural events space, and it will display highlights from the Koninklijk Museum voor Schone Kunsten while it is closed for refurbishment until 2017.

Imposing exterior of Antwerp's Sint Pauluskerk

⌂ Sint-Pauluskerk

St-Paulusstraat 22 or Veemarkt 14. **Tel** (03) 232 3267. **Open** Apr–Oct: 2–5pm daily. 🎧 3pm Sun & pub hols.

Completed in the early 17th century, this splendid church is distinguished by its combination of both Gothic and Baroque features. The exterior dates from about 1571, and has an added elaborate Baroque gateway. The interior is noted for its intricately carved wooden choir stalls. St Paulus also possesses a series of paintings illustrating the Fifteen Mysteries of the Rosary, one of which, *The Scourging of the Pillar*, is an exquisite canvas by Rubens. There are also paintings by van Dyck and Jordaens.

Street-by-Street: Around Grote Markt

Fanning out from the east bank of the River Scheldt, Antwerp was and is one of the leading trading cities of northern Europe. Today, the city's industries lie away from its medieval core whose narrow streets and fine buildings cluster around the cathedral and the Grote Markt. Packed with evidence of Antwerp's rich history, this is a delightful area to wander in. Most sites of interest are within easy walking distance of the Grote Markt, whose surrounding streets house museums, shops and exuberant cafés and bars.

To Koninklijk Museum voor Schone kunsten

The Vleeshuis
Occupied by the Butcher's Guild for three centuries, this beautiful 1504 building has striking layers of brick and stone that look like alternating strips of fat and lean meat.

Stadhuis
Flanking Antwerp's spectacular central square is the elegant 16th-century Stadhuis (town hall), designed by Cornelis Floris (1514–75).

Key

— Suggested route

0 metres	50
0 yards	50

The Brabo Fountain
This statue, in the centre of the Grote Markt, depicts the fearless soldier, Silvius Brabo. Said to be the nephew of Julius Caesar, Brabo is shown throwing the hand of the mythical giant, Antigonius, into the River Scheldt.

Sint-Pauluskerk

This imposing church was built in 1571, but has a magnificent Baroque gate and spire dating from the late 17th century. Inside, there is a noted collection of paintings, including one especially fine work by Rubens.

To Centraal Station

★ Grote Markt

Antwerp's golden age of trade in the 16th century is reflected in the square's cosmopolitan 1564 town hall, built by architects from all over Europe.

★ Onze-Lieve-Vrouwe Kathedraal

The largest Gothic cathedral in Belgium, this building occupies a 1-ha (2.5-acre)-site in Antwerp's centre. Work began on this elegant church in 1352 and took almost two centuries to complete.

To Rubenshuis

Groenplaats

The Groenplaats or Green Square is a pleasant open space with trees. Lined with cafés, bars and restaurants, the square is a popular spot with both locals and visitors for a peaceful stroll or meal.

Exploring Antwerp

Antwerp stretches out from its centre into its sprawling suburbs to a distance of some 7 km (4.3 miles). Badly damaged in both World Wars, the city has a broad mixture of architecture, ranging from the medieval to the ultra-modern. The old city centre is concentrated around the cathedral, Onze Lieve Vrouwe Kathedraal, and the Grote Markt *(see pp98–9)*. The area around the Centraal Station is the centre of the international diamond trade. The Zuid (South) district is an area of drained docks; now rejuvenated, this is a vibrant part of town, and the old dockland architecture of the Waalse Kaai and Vlaamse Kaai has become home to clubs, bars and museums. The area around the old, water-filled docks to the north of the city centre is now also undergoing rapid redevelopment. To the east of the cathedral – beyond Antwerp's pioneering 1930s skyscraper, the Boerentoren – lies the Meir, Antwerp's premier shopping street.

Printing press in the Museum Plantin-Moretus/Prentenkabinet

One of the changing exhibits at the ModeMuseum

Six in the 1980s, the city has entered the stratosphere of international haute-couture, and maintains a glowing reputation for nurturing new talent. This fashion museum provides the historical context to Antwerp's rise. Fashion items and accessories are shown in innovative ways in changing exhibitions, to serve as both an instructive resource and a fount of inspiration.

🏛 ModeMuseum (MoMu)
Nationalestraat 28. **Tel** (03) 470 27 70. **Open** 10am–6pm Tue–Sun; 10am–9pm first Sun of every month. **Closed** Mon. 🅿 🔲 **momu.be**

Following the rise to celebrity of the influential fashion designers called the Antwerp

🏛 Museum Plantin-Moretus/ Pretenkabinet
Vrijdagmarkt 22–23. **Tel** (03) 221 1450. **Open** 10am–5pm Tue–Sun, Easter Mon. **Closed** 1 Jan, 1 May, Ascension, 1 Nov, 25 Dec. 🅿 free last Wed of month. 🔲 **museumplantinmoretus.be**

This fascinating museum on the UNESCO World Heritage List occupies a large 16th-century house that belonged to the printer Christopher Plantin, who

moved here in 1576. The house's ancient rooms and narrow corridors resemble the types of interiors painted by Flemish and Dutch masters. The museum is devoted to the early years of printing, when Plantin and others began to produce books that bore no resemblance to earlier, illuminated manuscripts.

Antwerp was a centre for printing in the 15th and 16th centuries, and Plantin was its most successful printer. Today, his workshop displays several historic printing presses, as well as woodcuts and copper plates. Plantin's library is also on show. One of the gems here is an edition of the Gutenberg Bible – the first book to be printed using moveable type, a new technique invented by Johannes Gutenberg in 1455.

🏛 Sint-Carolus Borromeuskerk
Hendrik Conscienceplein. **Tel** (03) 231 3751. **Open** 10am–12:30pm & 2–5pm Mon–Sat.

This Jesuit church is celebrated for its elegant Baroque façade, which forms one flank of a charming 17th-century square. Rubens played a part in the design of both the exterior and interior when the church was built in 1615–21, and supplied 39 ceiling paintings, but sadly these were lost in a fire in 1718. The surviving parts of the interior indicate how lavish it once was – a triumphant showpiece of the Counter-Reformation.

The Baroque interior of Sint-Carolus Borromeuskerk

🏛 Rockoxhuis

Keizerstraat 12. **Tel** (03) 201 9250.
Open 10am–5pm Tue–Sun. **Closed**
Mon, 1 & 2 Jan, Ascension, 1 & 2 Nov,
25 & 26 Dec. 🅿 🆆 rockoxhuis.be

Nicolaas Rockox (1560–1640)
was mayor of Antwerp, a
humanist, philanthropist, and
a friend and patron of Rubens.
These attributes are reflected in
his beautifully renovated home
– a series of rooms set around a
formal courtyard garden. They
contain a fine collection of
contemporary furniture and
miscellaneous artifacts, all
interesting and well-
chosen. The paintings
and drawings
include work by
Rubens, Jordaens
and Van Dyck, as well
as work by Frans
Snyders (1579–1657),
who lived next door,
was much admired
by Rubens, and
painted flowers and
fruit in Rubens' work.

Detail from Fishmarket
Antwerp, by Frans
Snyders, at the Rockoxhuis

🏠 Sint Jacobskerk

Lange Nieuwstraat 73–75, Eikenstraat.
Tel (03) 225 0414. **Open** Apr–Oct:
2–5pm daily; Nov–Mar: 9am–noon,
Mon–Sat. 🅿

Noted as Rubens' burial place –
his tomb is in his family's chapel
behind the high altar – this sandstone church was built from
1491 to 1656. Sint Jacobskerk's
rich interior contains the
tombs of several other notable
Antwerp families, as well as
a collection of 17th-century
art, including sculptures by
Hendrik Verbruggen, and
paintings by van Dyck, Otto
Venius (Rubens' first master)
and Jacob Jordaens.

🏛 Rubenshuis

See pp104–5.

🏛 Museum Mayer van den Bergh

Lange Gasthuisstraat 19. **Tel** (03) 338
8188. **Open** 10am–5pm Tue–Sun,
Easter Mon. **Closed** Mon, 1 & 2 Jan, 1
May, Ascension, 1 Nov, 24 & 25 Dec.
🅿 🆆 museummayervan
denbergh.be

Fritz Mayer van den Bergh
(1858–1901) was the scion of
a wealthy trading family, but
instead of following in his
father's footsteps, he chose
to devote himself to
collecting art and curios.
After his death aged just
43, his mother created this
museum to display his
collections. Among
the many treasures
are tapestries,
furniture, ivories,
stained glass, medie-
val and Renaissance
sculpture and a
number of excellent
paintings, including
Dulle Griet (Mad Meg), a powerful image of a chaotic world by
Pieter Brueghel the Elder.

🏛 Koninklijk Museum voor Schone Kunsten

See pp102–103.

🏛 Museum van Hedendaagse Kunst Antwerpen (M HKA)

Leuvenstraat 32. **Tel** (03) 260 9999.
Open 11am–6pm Tue–Sun (to 9pm
Thu). **Closed** Mon, 1 Jan, 1 May,
Ascension & 25 Dec. 🅿 📷
🆆 muhka.be

This museum is what you might
expect from a city famed for its
sense of style and design. A

A room at the Museum Mayer van den Bergh

huge, sculptural building that
was once a 1920s dockside
grain silo and warehouse has
been transformed into a series
of unusual spaces to display
art from the front line of
international contemporary art
(1970–present). This includes
work by many of the artists who
have helped to place Belgium at
the forefront of the art scene,
such as Panamarenko, Luc
Tuymans, Jan Fabre and
Wim Delvoye.

🏛 FotoMuseum

Waalse Kaai 47. **Tel** (03) 242 9300.
Open 10am–6pm Tue–Sun.
Closed Mon, 25 & 26 Dec, 1 & 2
Jan. 🅿 🆆 fotomuseum.be

Antwerp's excellent museum
of photography, displaying a
wide range of historical artifacts
and images, has undergone a
complete makeover, and has
embraced the moving image
as well by incorporating the
Antwerp Film Museum (which
offers scheduled film viewings).
In addition to its extensive,
thematically organized
permanent collection, the
museum mounts regular
exhibitions of photography.

🏛 Red Star Line Museum

Montevideostraat 3. **Tel** (03) 298 2770.
Open 10am–5pm Tue–Fri, 10am–6pm
Sat–Sun. **Closed** Mon, 1 Jan, 1 May,
Ascension, 1 Nov, 25 Dec. ♿ 🅿
🆆 redstarline.be

Located in the old Red Star
Line terminal in the port area
of the city, this fascinating
museum tells the story of
Antwerp's historic shipping
company, and the over two
million people it took to a new
life in North America from the
late 19th century up to 1934.

A stained-glass window in Sint Jacobskerk

Koninklijk Museum voor Schone Kunsten

Antwerp's largest and most impressive fine art collection is exhibited in the Museum voor Schone Kunsten, which occupies a massive late 19th-century Neo-Classical building. The permanent collection contains both ancient and modern works. The earlier collection contains medieval Flemish painting and continues through the 19th century, with the "Antwerp Trio" of Rubens, van Dyck and Jordaens well represented. Modern exhibits include the work of Belgian artists Magritte, Ensor and Delvaux, as well as a major collection of work by Rik Wouters. Tissot and van Gogh are among the foreign artists on show. The museum is currently closed for renovations, however collection highlights can be found at the Cathedral of Our Lady and the Museum Aan De Stroom, MAS (*see p97*).

First Floor

Main Entrance

Façade of Gallery
Building began on this imposing structure in 1884. The Neo-Classical façade with its vast pillars has carved women charioteers atop each side. It was opened in 1890.

★ **Woman Ironing** *(1912)*
This peaceful domestic scene by Rik Wouters employs the muted colours of Impressionism. This was a productive period for Wouters who painted 60 canvases in 1912.

Madame Récamier *(1967)*
René Magritte's macabre version of the original painting by David is a classic Surrealist work.

Pink Bows *(1936)*
Paul Delvaux's dream-like style clearly shows the influence of Sigmund Freud's psychoanalytic theories on Surrealist painting.

★ **Saint Barbara** *(1437)*
Jan van Eyck's painting of Saint Barbara in several tones of grey shows the saint sitting in front of a huge Gothic cathedral tower still under construction, while a prayer book lies open on her lap.

Gallery Guide

The gallery is divided into two floors. Flemish Old Masters and 19th-century painters are housed on the first floor, while the ground floor focuses on James Ensor and the 20th century. Each room is lettered and visitors may view exhibits chronologically, starting in the entrance hall.

★ **Adoration of the Magi**
(1624)
One of Rubens' masterpieces, this painting displays a remarkable freedom of composition.

As the Old Sang, the Young Play Pipes *(1638)*
Jacob Jordaens' (1593–1678) joyous celebration of life in this painting of a family enjoying a musical evening contrasts with his religious paintings.

Ground Floor

Key
- 🟦 15th-century paintings
- 🟦 16th-century paintings
- 🟦 16th–18th-century sketches
- 🟦 17th-century paintings
- 🟦 19th-century sculpture
- 🟦 19th-century paintings
- 🟦 19th-century salon
- 🟦 20th-century paintings
- 🟦 Temporary exhibitions
- 🟦 Museum history
- 🟦 Non-exhibition space

Rubenshuis

Rubenshuis, on Wapper Square, was Pieter Paul Rubens' home and studio for the last 29 years of his life, from 1611 to 1640. The city bought the premises just before World War II, but by then the house was little more than a ruin, and what can be seen today is the result of careful restoration. It is divided into two sections. To the left of the entrance are the narrow rooms of the artist's living quarters, equipped with period furniture. Behind this part of the house is the kunstkamer, or art gallery, where Rubens exhibited both his own and other artists' work, and entertained his friends and wealthy patrons, such as the Archduke Albert and the Infanta Isabella. To the right of the entrance lies the main studio, a spacious salon where Rubens worked on – and showed – his works. A signposted route guides visitors through the house.

Façade of Rubenshuis
The older Flemish part of the house sits next to the later house, whose elegant early Baroque façade was designed by Rubens.

Formal Gardens
The small garden is laid out formally and its charming pavilion dates from Rubens' time. He was influenced by architects of the Italian Renaissance when he built the Italian Baroque addition to his house in the 1620s.

★ **Rubens' Studio**
It is estimated that Rubens produced some 2,500 paintings in this large, high-ceilinged room. In the Renaissance manner, Rubens designed the work which was usually completed by a team of other artists employed in his studio.

KEY

① **The Familiakamer**, or family sitting room, is cosy and has a pretty tiled floor. It overlooks Wapper Square.

② **Chequered mosaic tiled floor.**

Bedroom
The Rubens family lived in the Flemish section of the house, with its small rooms and narrow passages. The portrait by the bed is said to be of Rubens' second wife, Helena Fourment.

Dining Room
Intricately fashioned leather panels line the walls of this room, which also displays a noted work by Frans Snyders.

★ Kunstkamer
This art gallery contains a series of painted sketches by Rubens. At the far end is a semi-circular dome, modelled on Rome's Pantheon, displaying a number of marble busts.

Baroque Portico
One of the few remaining original features, this portico was designed by Rubens, and links the older house with the Baroque section. It is adorned with a frieze showing scenes from Greek mythology.

A 90-Minute Walk Across Antwerp

Antwerp handles 80 per cent of the world's entire trade in rough diamonds, yet this business is carried out in a distinctly unglamorous quarter in the east of the city; even the railway station is more elegant. This walk starts in the diamond district and heads west to the Meir, Antwerp's main shopping thoroughfare, before visiting the haunts of Rubens and his contemporaries at the Rubenshuis, Sint Jacobskerk and the Rockoxhuis. It then passes through medieval Antwerp to reach the broad sweep of the River Scheldt.

② The bar area in the impressive Radisson Blu Astrid Hotel

Diamond District and the Meir

Centraal Station ① is a palatial Neo-Classical building completed in 1905 that is worth visiting in its own right. It looks out over Koningin Astridplein, named after the hugely popular Queen Astrid (wife of Leopold III and grandmother of the present King Philippe I) who died tragically in a car accident, aged 29, in 1935. Behind the station, Antwerp Zoo ② is one of the oldest in the world, and its impressive entrance dates from 1843, the year the zoo opened. On the far side of the square is the Radisson Blu Astrid Hotel ③, a bold example of post-modern architecture. For a flavour of Antwerp's connection with diamonds, go to the diamond district. You can get a feel for this distinctively Jewish neighbourhood by walking down Pelikaanstraat ④ and Vestingstraat ⑤. By continuing along De Keyserlei and Leysstraat, you enter the Meir ⑥, a broad, pedestrianized high street packed with large shops.

③ Zebras at the Antwerp Zoo

Rubenshuis and Rockoxhuis

Turn left off the Meir into the broad street called the Wapper ⑦. On the left-hand side of the street is the Rubenshuis *(see pp104–105)* ⑧, the impressive mansion that Rubens bought as his home and studio in 1610. At the end of the Wapper, at Hopland 2, is the Grand Café Horta ⑨, a dynamic café-restaurant built in 2000 around structural remnants salvaged from Victor Horta's classic Art Nouveau building, the Maison du Peuple, in Brussels *(see p80)*. Returning

to the Meir, look left – the tallest building is the KBC Tower ⑩. Complete with Art Deco detailing, it was Europe's highest skyscraper when topped out in 1931. By walking up Lange Klarenstraat, you can reach the Sint Jacobskerk *(see p101)* ⑪ on Lange Nieuwstraat. This richly decorated church is famous as the burial place of Rubens. St-Jacobsstraat and Keizerstraat lead to the Rockoxhuis *(see p101)* ⑫, which offers an insight into how the homes of the rich looked in the time of Rubens. Wijngaardstraat will bring you to the little square called Hendrik Conscienceplein ⑬, named after the Flemish author who wrote the novel *The Lion of Flanders* (1838), a stirring tale about the Battle of the Golden Spurs of 1302; the book was a landmark in the resurgence of Flemish national pride.

⑫ One of the rooms inside the Rockoxhuis

Overlooking the square is the fine Baroque façade of the Sint-Carolus Borromeuskerk (see p100) ⑭.

The Cathedral and the Scheldt

Continue along Wijngaardstraat to reach Lijnwaadmarkt (Linen Market) ⑮. The street names here recall the specialist markets that once clustered around the cathedral. Note how buildings have been constructed right up against the cathedral walls, such as the restaurant Het Vermoeide Model ("The Artist's Sleepy Model") ⑯. The bar on the corner on the other side of the street called Het Elfde Gebod ⑰,

⑲ The Grote Markt and its elegant 16th-century Stadhuis (town hall)

at Torfbrug 10, is packed with religious statuary and the walls adorned with paintings of saints – the name means "The Eleventh Commandment". Continue to the Handschoenmarkt (Glove Market) from where there is a magnificent view of Onze Lieve Vrouwe Kathedraal (see p97) ⑱.

Antwerp's spectacular main square, where you will see the more famous version of Brabo, by the noted Antwerp sculptor Jef Lambeaux, and the town hall. Head down the Oude Koornmarkt (Old Cornmarket) and Pelgrimsstraat. On the corner with Reyndersstraat is the pub called De Vagant ⑳, which specializes in jenever gin. De Groote Witte Arend (The Great White Eagle) ㉑, at Reyndersstraat 18, is an old and celebrated tavern with a courtyard. On Vrijdagmarkt (Friday Market) you will find the Museum Plantin-Moretus (see p100) ㉒, a museum of early printing, set in the 16th-century house of the printer who gave us the typeface called Plantin. From here, walk down Steenhouwersvest to the square called St-Jansvliet, with the River Scheldt beyond. For the most part, Antwerp turns its back on its wide and windy river, but not the café-restaurant Zuiderterras ㉓ – an award-winning modern building with fine views across the water.

Key

••• Walk route

Tips for Walkers

Starting point: Centraal Station
Length: 3.2 km (2 miles)
Getting there: Centraal Station is served by bus and tram routes from all over the city.
Stopping-off points: There are plenty of welcoming refreshment stops along the way. For a touch of class, try the Grand Café Horta (No. 9 on this walk). The walk also passes other noted watering holes, such as Het Vermoeide Model (No. 16), Het Elfde Gebod (No. 17), De Vagant (No. 20), and De Groote Witte Arend (No. 21). Or save yourself for the spectacular Zuiderterras (No. 23) overlooking the River Scheldt.

0 metres 200
0 yards 200

There is a well in the square decorated with metalwork foliage and a figure; this is said to have been forged by the painter Quentin Metsys in around 1495. The figure depicts the Roman soldier Silvius Brabo, throwing the hand of the evil giant Antigonius into the River Scheldt – the folkloric origin of the name Antwerp (handwerpen means "hand-throw"). Now go to the Grote Markt (see p96) ⑲,

Boats moored on the busy dockside of the River Scheldt

For keys to symbols see back flap

The Centenary Clock on Lier's Zimmertoren or watchtower

❷ Lier

🏙 34,000. 🚉 🚌 ℹ Grote Markt 57, (03) 800 0555. 🌐 **toerismelier.be**

Lier is an attractive small town, just 20 km (12 miles) southeast of Antwerp. The Grote Markt is a spacious cobbled square framed by handsome historic buildings. The Stadhuis (town hall) was built in 1740, and its elegant dimensions contrast strongly with the square, turreted 14th-century Belfort (belfry) adjoining. Nearby is the **Stedelijk Museum Wuyts**, with its collection of paintings by Flemish masters including Jan Steen, Brueghel and Rubens. East of here, the church of St Gummaruserk, with its soaring stone pillars and vaulted roof, evokes medieval times, and the carved altarpiece is notable for its intricate biblical scenes. The stained-glass windows are among the finest in Belgium and were a gift from Emperor Maximillian I in 1516.

One of Lier's highlights is the **Zimmertoren**, a 14th-century watchtower that now houses the clocks of Lodewijk Zimmer (1888–1970). This Lier merchant wanted to share his knowledge of timepieces.

🏛 **Stedelijk Museum Wuyts**
Florent van Cauwenberg Straat 14. **Tel** (03) 800 0396. **Open** 10am–midday 1–5pm Tue–Sun. **Closed** Mon, public hols. 🚫

🚏 **Zimmertoren**
Zimmerplein 18. **Tel** (03) 800 0395. **Open** Tue–Sun. 🚫

❸ Mechelen

🏙 77,000. 🚉 🚌 ℹ Hallestraat 2, Grote Markt, (070) 22 00 08.

The seat of the Catholic Archbishop of Belgium, Mechelen was the administrative capital of the country under the Burgundian prince, Charles the Bold, in 1473. Today, it is an appealing town whose expansive main square is flanked by pleasant cafés and bars. To the west of the square is the main attraction, **St Romboutskathedraal**, a huge cathedral that took some 300 years to complete. The building might never have been finished but for a deal with the Vatican: the cathedral was allowed to sell special indulgences (which absolved the purchaser of their sins) to raise funds, on condition that the pope received a percentage. Completed in 1546, the cathedral's tower has Belgium's finest carillon, a set of 49 bells, whose peals ring out at weekends and on public holidays. The church also contains *The Crucifixion* by Antony van Dyck (1599–1641). Less well-known in Mechelen are three 16th-century houses by the River Dilje. They are not open to visitors, but their exteriors are delightful. The "House of the Little Devils" is adorned with carved demons. Mechelen is famous for its local beers, and visitors should try the Gouden Carolus, a dark brew, which is said to have been the favourite tipple of the Emperor Charles V.

🏛 **St Romboutskathedraal**
St Romboutskerkhof. **Tel** (015) 29 7655. 📷 obligatory for tower. **Open** Apr–Oct: 9am–5:30pm daily; Nov–Mar: 9am–4:30pm daily. Tours depart Tourist Office.

Mechelen's main square, the Grote Markt, on market day

❹ Dendermonde

🏙 40,000. 🚉 🚌 ℹ Stadhuis, Grote Markt, (052) 21 3956.

A quiet, industrial town, Dendermonde is about 20 km (12 miles) southeast of Ghent. Its strategic position, at the confluence of the Scheldt and Dender rivers, has attracted the attention of a string of invaders over the centuries, including

Vleeshuis façade on the Grote Markt in Dendermonde

Wood panelled walls and paintings in the hall at Gaasbeek Castle

the Germans who shelled Dendermonde in 1914. But the town is perhaps best-known as the site of the Steed Bayard, a carnival held every ten years at the end of August.

Today, the town's spacious main square is framed by the quaint turrets and towers of the Vleeshuis or Meat Hall. The Town Hall is an elegant 14th-century building which was extensively restored in 1920. Dendermonde also possesses two exquisite early religious paintings by Anthony van Dyck which are on display in the Onze Lieve Vrouwekerk (Church of Our Lady).

➎ Pajottenland

🏔 113,000. 🛈 Grote Markt 1, Halle, (02) 356 4259. 🆆 **toerisme-pajottenland.be**

The Pajottenland forms part of the Brabant province to the southwest of Brussels, and is bordered in the west by the Dender River. The gentle rolling hills of the landscape contain many farms, some of which date back to the 17th century. The village of Onze Lieve Vrouw Lombeek, just 12 km (7 miles) west of Brussels, is named after its church, an outstanding example of 14th-century Gothic architecture.

Just a short distance south of the village lies the area's main attraction, the castle and grounds of **Gaasbeek**. The castle was remodelled in the 19th century, but actually dates from the 13th century, and boasts a moat and a thick curtain wall, strengthened by huge semi-circular towers. The castle's interior holds an excellent collection of fine and applied arts. Among the treasures are rich tapestries, 15th-century alabaster reliefs from England, silverware and a delightful ivory and copper hunting horn which belonged to the Protestant martyr Count Egmont in the 16th century. The Pajottenland is also known for its beers, especially lambic and gueuze. Lambic is one of the most popular types of beer in Belgium (see pp148–9).

🏛 **Gaasbeek**
Kasteelstraat 40. **Tel** (02) 531 0130. **Open** Apr–Nov: 10am–6pm Tue–Sun. **Closed** Dec–Mar. (Park open all year.) 🅿

➏ Halle

🏔 36,800. 🚉 🚌 🛈 Stadhuis, Grote Markt, (02) 363 2211. 🆆 **toerisme-halle.be**

Located on the outskirts of Brussels, in the province of Brabant, Halle is a peaceful little town. It has been a major religious centre since the 13th century because of the cult of the Black Virgin, an effigy in the Onze Lieve Vrouwebasiliek, the town's main church. The holy statue's blackness is due to its stained colour, which is said to have occurred through contact with gunpowder during the religious wars of the 17th century.

The virgin has long been one of Belgium's most venerated icons and each year, on Whit Sunday, the statue is paraded through the town.

The Steed Bayard

Dendermonde's famous carnival of the Steed Bayard occurs every ten years at the end of August – the next one is in 2020. The focus of the festival is a horse, the Steed Bayard itself, represented in the carnival by a giant model. It takes 34 bearers to carry the horse which weighs 700 kg (1,540 lb) and is 5.8 m (19 ft) high. A procession of locals dressed in medieval costume re-enact the Steed Bayard legend – a complex tale of chivalry and treachery, family loyalty and betrayal. The four Aymon brothers (who were said to be the nephews of Emperor Charlemagne) ride the horse, and it is their behaviour towards the animal which serves to demonstrate their moral worth.

❼ Waterloo

The Battle of Waterloo was fought on 18 June 1815. It pitted Napoleon and his French army against the Duke of Wellington, who was in command of troops mostly drawn from Britain, Germany and the Netherlands. The two armies met outside the hamlet of Waterloo, to the south of Brussels. The result was decisive. The battle began at 11:30am and just nine hours later the French were in full retreat. Napoleon abdicated and was subsequently exiled to the island of St Helena, where he died in mysterious circumstances six years later. Today, the battlefield is one of the biggest European historical and cultural sites, and one of the best preserved. The best place to start a visit is at the Musée Wellington, some 5 km (3 miles) from the battlefield, in the centre of Waterloo.

the Netherlands, the Prince of Orange, was wounded during the battle. Steps lead to the top, which is guarded by a huge cast-iron lion, and from here, there is a great view over the battlefield. The French army approached from the south and fought up the slope across farmland that became

The Butte du Lion viewed from the Waterloo battlefield

🏛 Musée Wellington

Chaussée de Bruxelles 147. **Tel** (02) 357 2860. **Open** Apr–Sep: 9:30am–6pm daily; Oct–Mar: 10am–5pm daily. **Closed** 1 Jan, 25 Dec. 🦽 🔲

W museewellington.be

The Waterloo Inn, where the Duke of Wellington spent the night before the battle, has been turned into a museum, its rooms packed with curios alongside plans and models of the actual battle. One of the more quirky exhibits is the artificial leg of Lord Uxbridge, one of Wellington's commanders. His leg was blown off during the battle and buried in Waterloo. After his death, the leg was sent to join the rest of him in England and, as recompense, his relatives sent his artificial one back to Waterloo.

⛪ Eglise St-Joseph

Chaussée de Bruxelles. **Tel** (02) 352 0910.

Across the road from the Musée Wellington is the church of St-Joseph, which was originally built as a royal chapel at the end of the 17th century. Its dainty, elegant cupola pre-dates the battle, after which it was extended, with the newer portions containing dozens of memorial plaques and flagstones dedicated to those British soldiers who died at Waterloo. Several of these plaques were paid for by voluntary contributions from ordinary soldiers in honour of their officers.

🦁 Butte du Lion

315 Route du Lion, Ring Ouest exit 25, 5 km (3 miles) S of Waterloo. **Tel** (02) 385 1912. **Open** daily. 🦽

Dating from 1826, the Butte du Lion is a 45-m- (148-ft-) high earthen mound built on the spot where the future King of

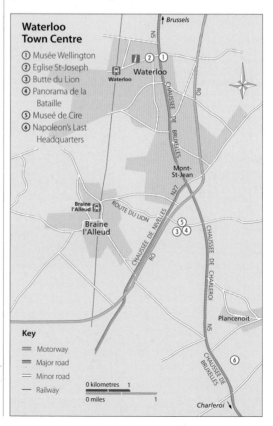

Waterloo Town Centre

① Musée Wellington
② Eglise St-Joseph
③ Butte du Lion
④ Panorama de la Bataille
⑤ Musée de Cire
⑥ Napoleon's Last Headquarters

Brussels

Waterloo

Mont-St-Jean

Braine l'Alleud

Plancenoit

Charleroi

Key

▬▬ Motorway
▬▬ Major road
— Minor road
— Railway

0 kilometres   1
0 miles   1

increasingly marshy as the day went on, while their opponents had the drier ridge at the foot of the mound. A plan of the battle is displayed at the top.

🎦 Panorama de la Bataille

252–254 Route du Lion, Braine-L'Alleud. N5, 5 km (3 miles) S of Waterloo. **Tel** (02) 385 1912. **Open** 10am–5pm daily. 🎦

This is perhaps the most fascinating of the several attractions beneath the Butte du Lion. This circular painting of the battle by artist Louis Demoulin was erected in 1912. It is 110 m (360 ft) long and stretches right round a circular, purpose-built gallery. This is one of the few late 19th-century panoramic, circular paintings that remain intact.

🏛 Musée de Cire

315 Route du Lion, N5, 5 km (3 miles) S of Waterloo. **Tel** (02) 384 6740. **Open** Apr–Oct: daily; Nov–Mar: pub hols, Sat & Sun. 🎦

The Musée de Cire is a wax museum where pride of place goes to the models of soldiers dressed in the military regalia of 1815. It seems strange today that the various armies dressed their men in such vivid colours, which made them easy targets. Indeed, many commanders paid for the uniforms of their men themselves.

🏛 Napoleon's Last Headquarters

66 Chaussée de Bruxelles, Vieux-Genappe, N5, 7 km (4.5 miles) S of Waterloo. **Tel** (02) 384 2424. **Open** daily. **Closed** 1 Jan, 25 Dec. 🎦

Napoleon spent the eve of the battle in a farmhouse, Le Caillou. This is now a museum that is often referred to as the Caillou Museum, containing a number of artifacts from Napoleon's army, a bronze death mask of the Emperor, and his army-issue bed. A building in the garden contains the bones of some of the soldiers from the battle.

❽ Leuven

See pp112–13.

The summer drawing room in the 18th-century Château d'Attre, near Ath

❾ Ath

🏙 28,500. 🚆 🚌 ℹ Rue de Pintamont 18, (068) 26 5170.

This quiet town is known for its festival – the Ducasse – which occurs every year on the fourth weekend in August. It features the "Parade of the Giants", a procession of gaily decorated giant figures representing characters from local folklore and the Bible.

A few kilometres northeast is one of the most popular attractions in the region, the **Château d'Attre**. This handsome 18th-century palace was built in 1752 by the Count of Gomegnies, chamberlain to the Hapsburg Emperor Joseph II.

🏠 Château d'Attre

Attre. **Tel** (068) 45 4460. 🚆 to Attre. **Open** Jul–Aug: 1–5pm Sat & Sun; Apr–Jun & Sep–Oct: 2–5pm Sun. **Closed** Nov–Mar.

❿ Ieper

🏙 35,000. 🚆 🚌 ℹ 34 Market Square, (057) 23 9220.

Ieper is the Flemish name of the town familiar to British soldiers as Ypres. During World War I, this town was used as a supply depot for the British army. The Germans shelled Ieper to pieces, but after the war, the town was rebuilt to its earlier design, complete with a replica of its 13th-century Lakenhalle (cloth hall). Part of its interior has been turned into the "In Flander's Fields" Museum, a thoughtfully laid-out series of displays that attempt to conjure the full horrors of World War I.

There is also the Menin Gate memorial, inscribed with the names of over 50,000 British and Commonwealth troops who died in the area but have no known resting place.

The Ypres Salient

The Ypres Salient was the name given to a bulge in the line of trenches that both the German and British armies felt was a good place to break through each others' lines. This led to large concentrations of men and four major battles including Passchendaele in July 1917, in which more than 500,000 men died. Today, visitors can choose to view the site with its vast cemeteries and monuments by car or guided tour.

View of the battlefield at Passchendaele Ridge in 1917

⑧ Leuven

Within easy striking distance of Brussels, the historic Flemish town of Leuven traces its origins to a fortified camp constructed here by Julius Caesar. In medieval times, the town became an important centre of the cloth trade, but it was as a seat of learning that it achieved international prominence. In 1425, Pope Martin V and Count John of Brabant founded Leuven's university, and by the mid-1500s it was one of Europe's most prestigious academic institutions, the home of such famous scholars as Erasmus and Mercator. Even today, the university exercises a dominant influence over the town, and its students give Leuven a vibrant atmosphere. The bars and cafés flanking the Oude Markt, a large square in the centre of town, are especially popular. Adjoining the square is the medieval Grote Markt, and near the centre is the Stella Artois Brewery, part of the world's largest brewery group.

Huge buttresses supporting the tower of St Pieterskerk

Lively café society in the Oude Markt

🍺 Oude Markt

This handsome, cobble-stoned square is flanked by a tasteful ensemble of high-gabled brick buildings. Some of these date from the 18th century; others are comparatively new. At ground level, these buildings house the largest concentration of bars and cafés in town, and as such attract the town's university students in their droves.

🏛 Stadhuis

Grote Markt. **Tel** (016) 20 3020. **Open** daily. 🖼 🎫 obligatory. At 3pm daily (Apr–Sep: also at 11am Mon–Fri).

Built between 1439 and 1463 from the profits of the cloth trade, Leuven's town hall, the Stadhuis, was designed to demonstrate the wealth of the city's merchants. This distinctive, tall building is renowned for its lavishly carved and decorated façade. A line of narrow windows rise up over three floors beneath a steeply pitched roof adorned with dormer windows and pencil-thin turrets. It is,

however, in the fine quality of its stonework that the building excels, with delicately carved tracery and detailed medieval figures beneath 300 niche bases. There are grotesques of every description as well as representations of folktales and biblical stories, all carved in exuberant late-Gothic style. Within the niche alcoves is a series of 19th-century statues depicting local dignitaries and politicians. Guided tours of the interior are available, and include three lavishly decorated reception rooms.

Stone carvings of medieval figures decorate the Stadhuis façade

🏛 St Pieterskerk and Museum Schatkamer van St Pieter

Grote Markt. **Tel** (016) 29 5133. **Open** Mar–Oct: daily, Nov–Feb: Tue–Sun. 🖼 to museum.

Across the square from the Stadhuis rises St Pieterskerk, a massive church built over a period of two hundred years from the 1420s.

Inside the church, the sweeping lines of the nave are intercepted by an impressive 1499 rood screen and a Baroque wooden pulpit.

The church also houses the Museum Schatkamer van St Pieter (Treasury), which has three paintings by Dirk Bouts (1415–75). Born in the Netherlands, Bouts spent most of his working life in Leuven, becoming its official artist.

🍺 Stella Artois Brewery

Vuurkruisenlaan. **Open** May–Oct: Sat & Sun. 🖼 🎫 obligatory. Tour with beer tasting in Dutch at 2pm and in English at 3:30pm; tour without beer tasting in Dutch at 1pm and in English at 2:30pm Sat & Sun.

With brewing being an important part of Leuven's history since the 16th century, a visit to Belgium's beer capital would not be complete without a brewery tour. The Stella Artois Brewery offers a variety of tours on weekends from May to October. All tours take place in the brewing hall, covering local beer-making history and the secrets of the brewing process, with the option to finish with a beer in the bar.

Fochplein

Adjacent to the Grote Markt is the Fochplein, a narrow triangular square containing some of Leuven's most popular shops, selling everything from fashion to food. In the middle is the Fons Sapienza, a modern fountain that shows a student pouring water through his empty head – a pithy view of the town's student population.

M-Museum Leuven

Leopold Vanderkelenstraat 28.
Tel (016) 27 2929. **Open** 11am–6pm Fri–Tue (to 10pm Thu).
mleuven.be

The former Museum Vander Kelen-Mertens has been revamped as "M" and provides a dynamic space for high profile art exhibitions. It also gives credance to Leuven's claim as a major city of the arts. The original collection still remains in the 17th–18th century mansion, which was owned by the Vander Kelen-Mertens family until it was donated to the city in 1918. The rooms were refurbished in a variety of styles, ranging from a Renaissance salon to a Rococo dining room, each with the appropriate antique furniture, silverware and ceramics. Much of the art on permanent display is by the early Flemish Masters, including the work of Quentin Metsys (1465–1530), who was born in Leuven and introduced Italian style to northern European art.

St Michielskerk

Naamsestraat. **Open** Jun–Sep: 1:30–4:30pm Tue–Sun.

One of Leuven's most impressive churches, St Michielskerk was built for the Jesuits in the middle of the 17th century. The church was badly damaged during World War II, but has since been carefully restored. Its graceful façade with its flowing lines is an excellent illustration of the Baroque style. The interior is regularly open to visitors for three afternoons during the summer months. The stunning 1660 carved woodwork around the altar and choir are well worth seeing.

Groot Begijnhof

Schapenstraat. **Open** daily, for street access only.

Founded around 1230, the Groot Begijnhof, now a World Heritage Site, was once one of the largest béguinages in Belgium, home to several hundred béguines *(see p55)*. The complex of 72 charming red-brick cottages (dating mostly from the 17th century) is set around the grassy squares and cobbled streets near the River Dilje. Leuven university bought the complex in 1961 and converted the cottages into student accommodation.

VISITORS' CHECKLIST

Practical Information
97,300. Naamsestraat 1, 3000 Leuven, (016) 20 3020.

Transport
Bondgenotenlaan. Grote Markt 9.

The red-brick houses of Leuven's Groot Begijnhof

Leuven Town Centre

① Oude Markt
② Stadhuis
③ St Pieterskerk and Museum Schatkamer van St Pieter
④ Stella Artois Brewery
⑤ Fochplein
⑥ M-Museum Leuven
⑦ St Michielskerk
⑧ Groot Begijnhof

0 metres 300
0 yards 300

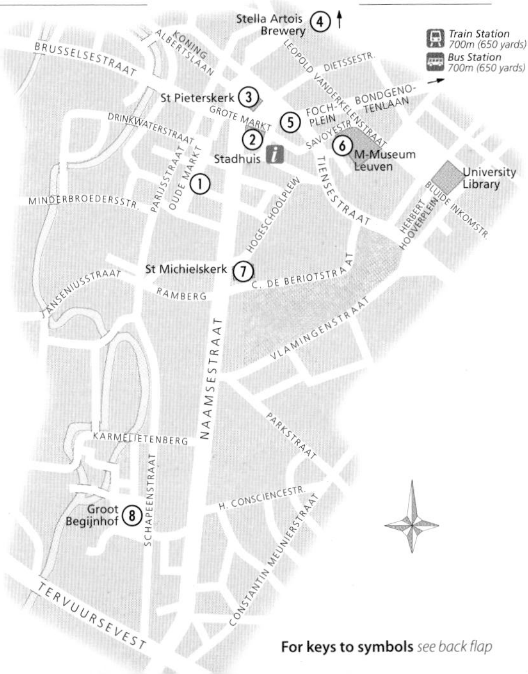
Stella Artois Brewery
Train Station 700m (650 yards)
Bus Station 700m (650 yards)
BRUSSELSESTRAAT
KONING ALBERTSLAAN
LEOPOLD VANDERKELENSTRAAT
DIETSSESTR.
St Pieterskerk
GROTE MARKT
FOCH-PLEIN
BONDGENOTENLAAN
DRINKWATERSTRAAT
SAVOYESTR.
M-Museum Leuven
Stadhuis
PARIJSSTRAAT
OUDE MARKT
TIENSESTRAAT
University Library
MINDERBROEDERSSTR.
HOGESCHOOLPLEIN
HERBERT HOOVERPLEIN
BLIJDE INKOMSTR.
St Michielskerk
JANSENIUSSTRAAT
C. DE BERIOTSTRAAT
RAMBERG
NAAMSESTRAAT
VLAMINGENSTRAAT
PARKSTRAAT
KARMELIETENBERG
SCHAPENSTRAAT
Groot Begijnhof
H. CONSCIENCESTR.
CONSTANTIN MEUNIERSTRAAT
TERVUURSEVEST

For keys to symbols *see back flap*

⓫ Street-by-Street: Ghent

As a tourist destination, the Flemish city of Ghent has long been over-shadowed by its neighbour, Bruges. In part this reflects their divergent histories. The success of the cloth trade during the Middle Ages was followed by a period of stagnation for Bruges, while Ghent became a major industrial centre in the 18th and 19th centuries. The resulting pollution coated the city's antique buildings in layers of grime from its many factories. In the 1980s, Ghent initiated a restoration programme. The city's medieval buildings were cleaned, industrial sites were tidied up and the canals were cleared. Today, it is the intricately carved stonework of its churches and antique buildings, as well as the city's excellent museums and stern, forbidding castle that give the centre its character.

★ Het Gravensteen
Ghent's centre is dominated by the thick stone walls and imposing gatehouse of its ancient Castle of the Counts.

★ Design Museum Ghent
This elegant 19th-century dining room is just one of many charming period rooms in the decorative arts museum. The collection is housed in an 18th-century mansion and covers art and design from the 1600s to the present.

Graslei
One of Ghent's most picturesque streets, the Graslei overlooks the River Leie on the site of the city's medieval harbour. It is lined with perfectly preserved guildhouses; some date from the 12th century.

Korenmarkt
This busy square was once the corn market; the commercial centre of the city since the Middle Ages. Today, it is lined with popular cafés.

To Ghent St-Pieters and Stadsmuseum

Key

— Suggested route

Het Huis van Alijn

A row of humble whitewashed cottages house this excellent folk museum. Exhibits here include everyday objects from the late 19th century.

VISITORS' CHECKLIST

Practical Information

250,000.

Oude Vismijn, (09) 266 5660.

w **visitgent.be**

Transport

St-Pieters. St-Pieters.

Korenmarkt.

Stadhuis

Visitors can view this throne room in the town hall, which displays the 1780 coronation throne of Joseph II.

★ St Baafskathedraal
Dating from the 1200s, this magnificent Gothic cathedral was built over several hundred years.

LANGE MUNT

VRIJDAG MARKT

KAMERSTRAAT

ONDERSTRAAT

HOOGPOORT

BELFORTSTRAAT

POELJEMARKT

KAPITTELSTRAAT

St. Niklaaskerk

The Belfort is one of the city's great landmarks and, together with the adjacent Lakenhalle (Cloth Hall), was a centre of medieval trade.

0 metres 50
0 yards 50

Exploring Ghent

The heart of Ghent's historic centre was originally built during the 13th and 14th centuries when the city prospered as a result of the cloth trade. Ghent was founded in the 9th century when Baldwin Iron-Arm, the first Count of Flanders, built a castle to protect two abbeys from Viking raids. Despite many religious and dynastic conflicts, Ghent continued to flourish throughout the 16th and early 17th centuries. After 1648, the Dutch sealed the Scheldt estuary near Antwerp, closing vital canal links, which led to a decline in the fortunes of both cities. The 19th-century boom in cotton spinning reinvigorated Ghent and led to the building of wide boulevards in the south of the city. Today, textiles still feature in Ghent's industry, while its university lends a youthful vibrancy to city life.

Tiled flooring forms a maze in the Pacification Hall in Ghent's Stadhuis

Getting Around

Ghent is a large city with an excellent bus and tram system. The main rail station, Ghent St-Pieters, adjoins the bus station from where several trams travel to the centre every few minutes. However, many of Ghent's main sights are within walking distance of each other. Canal boat trips are also available.

⬆ St Baafskathedraal

Sint Baafsplein. **Map** F2. **Tel** (09) 269 2045. **Open** daily. Adoration of the Mystic Lamb: **Open** daily.

Built in several stages, St Baafskathedraal (St Bavo's Cathedral) has features representing every phase of Gothic style, from the early chancel through to the later cavernous nave, which is supported by slender columns and is the cathedral's architectural highlight. In a small side chapel is one of Europe's most remarkable paintings, Jan van Eyck's polyptych *Adoration of the Mystic Lamb* (1432). St Bavo (or Bavon) was Ghent's own 7th-century saint, who abandoned the life of a wealthy degenerate to become a missionary in France and Flanders and then a hermit. He was buried in about AD 653.

Stadhuis

Botermarkt 1. **Map** F2. **Tel** (09) 266 5111. May–Oct: 3pm Mon–Thu. Tours depart 2:30pm from the Tourist Office.

The Stadhuis façade displays two different architectural styles. Overlooking Hoogstraat, the older half dates from the early 16th century, its tracery in the elaborate Flamboyant Gothic style. The plainer, newer part, which flanks the Botermarkt, is

The Adoration of the Mystic Lamb

The 12 panels of the painting, with the main image at the centre

In a side-chapel of Sint Baafskathedraal, in the centre of Ghent, is one of the greatest cultural treasures of Northern Europe. *The Adoration of the Mystic Lamb* is a monumental, multi-panelled painting by the first of the great early Flemish artists, Jan van Eyck, and his lesser-known brother, Hubrecht.

Completed in 1432, it is not only exquisitely painted; it is also an expression of the deepest beliefs of Christianity – that human salvation lies in the sacrifice of Christ, the Lamb of God. What you see today is almost entirely original; only the lower left panel is a modern copy, following its theft in 1934. This is a remarkable achievement, given the painting's history. It was rescued from Protestant church-wreckers in 1566 and from fire in 1822; parts of it were removed by French soldiers in 1794, and other parts were sold in 1816. Audioguides to the painting (included in the price of the entry ticket) explain the significance of the 12 panels.

a characteristic example of post-Reformation architecture. The statues in the niches on the façade were added in the 1890s. Among this group of figures it is possible to spot the original architect, Rombout Keldermans, who is shown studying his plans.

The building is still the city's administrative centre. Guided tours pass through a series of rooms, the most fascinating of which is the Pacification Hall. This was once the Court of Justice and the site of the signing of the Pacification of Ghent (a treaty between Catholics and Protestants against Hapsburg rule) in 1576.

🔲 Belfort
Sint Baafsplein. **Map** F2. **Tel** (09) 233 3954. **Open** Open daily 10am–6pm 15 Mar–15 Nov. 🔲 🔲 in Dutch and English at 3:30pm, May–Oct.

Ghent's belfry, a prominent landmark rising 91 m (299 ft) to the gilded-copper dragon on the tip of its spire, is situated between the cathedral and the town hall. A lift to its parapet at 65 m (213 ft) offers magnificent views over the city. Originally built in 1313, the Belfort was restored in the 19th and 20th centuries. Its bells today include a 54-bell carillon, which plays tunes to accompany the clock chimes every 15 minutes, and for keyboard concerts every Sunday around noon and evenings on the first Friday of the month. Below the Belfort is the *Lakenhalle* (Cloth Hall), a fine Flemish-Gothic building from 1425, where the city's cloth-trade was carried out (guided tours only, on request). The building also incorporates a small prison.

🔲 St Niklaaskerk
Cataloniëstraat. **Map** E2. **Open** daily. This merchants' church, built in the 13th–15th centuries, was dedicated to their patron saint, St Nicholas, Bishop of Myra (and Santa Claus). The church is a fine example of the distinctive and austere style called Scheldt Gothic. The interior was once packed full of guild shrines and chapels, until Protestant church-wreckers destroyed them in 1566; today it is remarkable for

its pure architectural forms, with soaring columns brightly lit by high windows. The space is punctuated by a massive and extravagantly Baroque altar screen, a clarion call to the Counter-Reformation; unusually for such latter-day alterations, it harmonizes with the rest of the church to exhilarating effect.

🔲 Graslei and Korenlei
Map E2.
These are two embankments that face each other across the Tusschen Brugghen, once Ghent's main medieval harbour. The Graslei, on the eastern side, possesses a fine set of guildhouses. Among them, at No. 14, the sandstone façade of the Guildhouse of the Free Boatmen is decorated with finely detailed nautical scenes, while the Corn Measurers' guildhouse next door is adorned by bunches of fruit and cartouches. The earliest building here is the 12th-century *Spijker* (Staple House) at No. 10. This simple Romanesque structure stored the city's grain supply for hundreds of years until a fire destroyed its interior. The gabled buildings of the Korenlei, facing the Graslei across the water, date from later centuries, but gracefully complement the Graslei. The views from the St Michielsbrug, the bridge at the southern end, are among the most beautiful in Ghent.

Views of Graslei and 16th-century guildhouses along the River Leie

🔲 Design Museum Ghent
Jan Breydelstraat 5. **Map** E1. **Tel** (09) 267 9999. **Open** 10am–6pm Tue–Sun. **Closed** 1 Jan, 24, 25 & 31 Dec. 🔲 🔲 designmuseumgent.be

This decorative arts museum has a large collection contained within an elegant 18th-century town house. The displays are arranged in two sections, beginning at the front with a series of lavishly furnished period rooms that feature textiles, furniture and artifacts from the 17th to the 19th centuries. At the back, an extension completed in 1992 focuses on modern design from Art Nouveau to contemporary works, and includes furniture by Victor Horta (*see p84*), Marcel Breuer and Ludwig Mies van der Rohe.

Sofa at Design Museum

Gothic turrets of Sint-Niklaaskerk seen from St Michael's Bridge

🏛 Groot Vleeshuis

Groentenmarkt 7. **Map** E1.
Tel (09) 223 23 24. **Open** 10am–6pm
Tue–Sun. **Closed** Mon. 📷 🚫
🌐 grootvleeshuis.be

The "Great Meat Hall" was built in 1407–19, and its long, low interior space still reflects its basic, original purpose as a covered butchers' market, complete with ancient beams and wonky flooring. Into this space a large, modern glass box has been ingeniously inserted to serves as a centre to promote East Flemish food: on the one side, a small restaurant serves interesting and good-value Flemish dishes; on the other is a delicatessen.

The original covered butchers' market of the Groot Vleeshuis

🏛 Dulle Griet

Groot Kanonplein (off Vrijdagmarkt).
Map F1.

This giant cannon, sitting on the embankment of the River Leie, is famous in the folklore of Ghent. Cast in about 1450, 5 m (16 ft 5 in) long and weighing 16

The Dulle Griet cannon

tonnes, it could fire stone cannonballs the size of a beachball; it was brought to Ghent in 1578, during an era of Calvinist government in defiance of Spain. The name Dulle Griet means "Mad Meg", a legendary medieval character who embodied mad, violent frenzy and disorder. It was recently repainted its original red, reflecting its other nickname "Groten Rooden Duyvele" (Great Red Devil).

🏠 Het Gravensteen

Sint-Veerleplein. **Map** E1. **Tel** (09) 225 9306. **Open** Apr–Sep: 9am–6pm daily; Oct–Mar: 9am–5pm daily.
Closed 1 Jan, 24, 25 & 31 Dec. 📷

Once the seat of the counts of Flanders, the imposing stone walls of Het Gravensteen (or the Castle of the Counts) eloquently recall the unsettled and violent context of Ghent's early medieval past. Parts of the castle date back to the late 1100s, but most are later additions. Up to the 14th century, the castle was Ghent's main military stronghold, and from then until the late 1700s, it was used as the city's jail. Later, it became a cotton mill.

From the gatehouse, a long and heavily fortified tunnel leads up to the courtyard, which is overseen by two large buildings, the count's medieval residence and the earlier keep. Arrows guide visitors round the interior of both buildings, and in the upper rooms, there is a spine-chilling collection of medieval torture instruments.

🏛 Het Huis van Alijn

Kraanlei 65. **Map** E1. **Tel** (09) 269 23 50. **Open** 11am–5pm Tue–Sat, 10am–5:30pm Sun. **Closed** Mon, 1 Jan, 25 Dec. 📷 🏠 🌐 huisvanalijn.be

This is one of Belgium's best folk museums, graphically evoking daily life in the past through a huge collection of fascinating artifacts – dolls and other toys, games, clothes, furniture, kitchenware, funerary mementoes, as well as complete shops and craftsmen's workshops. There is also a puppet theatre, which presents plays (in Dutch) throughout the year. The museum is set out in a sequence of rooms in a

Het Gravensteen, a classic medieval castle complete with turrets and torture instruments

pretty group of whitewashed almshouses, "The House of Alijn", surrounding a grassy courtyard. Although mainly 16th-century, the almshouses were originally founded in 1363 as a children's hospital – not out of philanthropy, but as an act of penance by the Rijm family for the murder of two members of the rival Alijn family.

🏛 The Patershol

Map E1.

North of the Kraanlei are the quaint little lanes and low brick houses of the Patershol, a district that developed in the 17th century to house the city's weavers. This once down-at-heel area underwent extensive refurbishment in the 1980s and is now one of the trendiest parts of town, with upmarket restaurants, cafés and shops.

The Patershol's 17th-century buildings which now house shops and cafés

⊡ Vlaamse Opera

Schouwburgstraat 3. **Map** E3. **Tel** (09) 268 1011. **Open** for performances; guided tours third Saturday of the month. 🅿 🆆 vlaamseopera.be

This classic opera house was built in 1837–40; it has been restored to reclaim its reputation as one of the most spectacular theatres in Europe, with an auditorium and adjoining salons encrusted with gilding, chandeliers and sculptural decorations. The resident company is the much-respected Vlaamse Opera (Flemish Opera), which formed when the opera companies of Ghent and Antwerp merged.

The grand, Neo-Classical façade of the Museum voor Schone Kunsten

The stunning interior of the Vlaamse Opera building

⊡ Klein Begijnhof

Lange Violettestraat 205.
Open 6:30am–9:30pm daily.
The Klein Begijnhof (Small Béguinage) is the prettiest of Ghent's three béguinages (see p55). Rows of step-gabled, whitewashed houses – most dating from the 17th century –

enclose a small park and Baroque church, creating a tranquil refuge. This Begijnhof was founded as a community of single women in about 1235. It has been occupied ever since, but the residents today are no longer béguines.

🏛 STAM

Bijlokesite, Godshuizenlaan 2. **Map** E4. **Tel** (09) 267 1400. **Open** 10am–6pm Tue–Sun. **Closed** Mon, 1 Jan, 24, 25 & 31 Dec. ♿ 🅿 ✏ 🆆 stamgent.be

Located on a site that brings together a 14th-century Gothic abbey, a 17th-century monastery and the latest in 21st-century architecture, STAM is Ghent's excellent city museum. It provides an introduction to the city's history and cultural heritage, tracing its evolution to the present day. Visitors staying in Ghent for 2–3 days will find the CityCard Gent an economical way of seeing the city's main museums.

🏛 Stedelijk Museum voor Actuele Kunst (SMAK)

Citadelpark. **Map** E5. **Tel** (09) 240 7601. **Open** 10am–6pm, Tue–Sun. **Closed** Mon. 🅿 📷 ✏ 🆆 smak.be

SMAK is one of Europe's most dynamic modern art galleries, a force in the art world that has helped to bring the spotlight to the Belgian art scene. Its extensive and challenging permanent collection includes work by artists such as Bacon, Beuys, Broodthaers, Long, Muñoz, Nauman, Panamarenko, Tuymans and Warhol, while temporary exhibitions feature international artists at the cutting edge of contemporary art. The airy and attractive building dates from 1949 but was remodelled in the 1990s.

🏛 Museum voor Schone Kunsten

Ferdinand Scribedreef, Citadelpark. **Map** F5. **Tel** (09) 240 0700. **Open** 10am–6pm Tue–Sun. 🅿 🆆 mskgent.be

Ghent's largest collection of fine art is displayed in this Neo-Classical building. Inside, a rotunda divides the works, with the older exhibits in a series of rooms on the right and 19th- and 20th-century art to the left. Medieval paintings include the *Bearing of the Cross* by Hieronymus Bosch (1450–1516). There are also works by Rubens (see p19), Anthony van Dyck (1599–1641) and Jacob Jordaens (1593–1678).

Visitors planning to also visit the Royal Museum of Fine Arts in Antwerp and the Groeninge Museum in Bruges should invest in the Flemish Art Collection combiticket.

A small garden surrounded by step-gabled houses in the Klein Begijnhof

⑫ Street-by-Street: Bruges

With good reason, Bruges is one of the most popular tourist destinations in Belgium. An unspoilt medieval town, Bruges' winding streets pass by picturesque canals lined with fine buildings. The centre of Bruges is amazingly well preserved. The town's trade was badly affected when the River Zwin silted up at the end of the 15th century. It was never heavily industrialized and has retained most of its medieval buildings. As a further bonus, Bruges also escaped major damage in both world wars.

Today, the streets are well maintained: there are no billboards or high rises, and traffic is heavily regulated. All the major attractions are located within the circle of boulevards that marks the line of the old medieval walls.

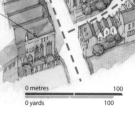

View of the Rozenhoedkaai
A charming introduction to Bruges is provided by the boat trips along the city's canal network.

Onze Lieve Vrouwekerk
The Church of Our Lady employs many architectural styles. It took around 200 years to build, and its spire is Belgium's tallest in brick.

Memling in Sint-Janshospitaal
Six of the artist's works are shown in the small chapel of the 12th-century Sint-Janshospitaal, a city hospital that was still operating until 1976.

MARKT

ST. NIKLAASS

STEENSTRAAT

LOPPEM STRAAT

SIMON

OUDE BUR

STEVINPLEIN

NIEUWSTRAAT

ST. SALVATORSKERKHOF

MARIASTRAAT

0 metres   100
0 yards   100

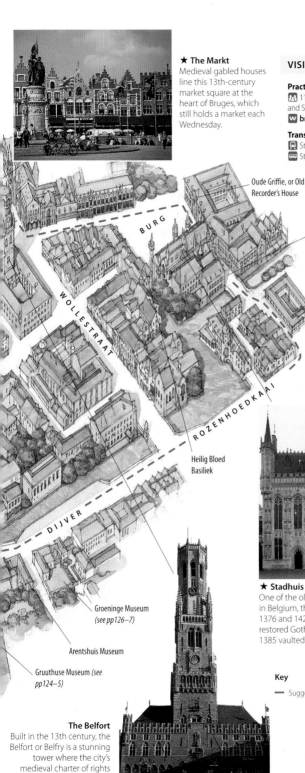

★ **The Markt**
Medieval gabled houses line this 13th-century market square at the heart of Bruges, which still holds a market each Wednesday.

VISITORS' CHECKLIST

Practical Information
🗺 119,000. 🛈 T'Zand, Markt 1, and Stationsplein. (050) 44 4646.
Ⓦ **brugge.be**

Transport
🚉 Stationsplein.
🚌 Stationsplein, Markt.

Oude Griffie, or Old Recorder's House

Blind Donkey Alley
This narrow, arched alley leads from the Burg to the 19th-century Vismarkt.

BURG

WOLLESTRAAT

ROZENHOEDKAAI

Heilig Bloed Basiliek

DIJVER

★ **Stadhuis**
One of the oldest and finest town halls in Belgium, this was built between 1376 and 1420. Inside, the beautifully restored Gothic hall is noted for its 1385 vaulted ceiling.

Groeninge Museum
(see pp126–7)

Arentshuis Museum

Gruuthuse Museum *(see pp124–5)*

Key

— Suggested route

The Belfort
Built in the 13th century, the Belfort or Belfry is a stunning tower where the city's medieval charter of rights were held.

Exploring Central Bruges

Bruges developed around a 9th-century fortress, built to defend the coast against the Vikings. Despite the vagaries of successive invasions by the French, between the 14th and 16th centuries, Bruges became one of northern Europe's most sophisticated cities. Today, it owes its pre-eminent position to the beauty of its historic centre, whose narrow cobbled lanes and meandering canals are lined by an ensemble of medieval buildings. These are mostly the legacy of the town's heyday as a centre of the international cloth trade, which flourished for 200 years from the 13th century. During this golden age, Bruges' merchants lavished their fortunes on fine mansions, churches and a set of civic buildings of such extravagance that they were the wonder of northern Europe.

Bruges' medieval buildings reflected in the Dijver

Getting Around
The centre of Bruges is compact, and it is easiest to walk around. However, the bus service is useful for getting from the railway station to the centre. Half-hour boat trips along the canals leave from several jetties. From March to November, boats depart twice every hour.

The Vismarkt
Braambergstraat. **Map** B3.
Open 8am–1pm Tue–Sat.

From the Burg, an attractive arched path called the Alley of the Blind Donkey (Blinde Ezelstraat) leads to the open-air fish market with its elegant 19th-century colonnades. Fish is still sold here early each morning and business is brisk.

The Burg
Map B3.
This pleasant cobbled square a few metres from the Markt was once the political and religious focus of Bruges. It is also the site of the original fort around which the city grew. Some of the most imposing civic buildings are located here. The beautiful sandstone Stadhuis or town hall has a façade dating from 1375, and is adorned with turrets and statues. In contrast, the Proostdij or Provost's House was built of grey stone in 1662 in the Baroque style and boasts an ornate entrance.

Stadhuis
Burg 12. **Map** B3. **Tel** (050) 44 8711.
Open 9:30am–5pm daily. **Closed** 1 Jan, 25 Dec.

The intricately carved façade of the Stadhuis was completed in 1375, but the niche statues are modern effigies of the counts and countesses of Flanders. These were added in the 1960s to replace those destroyed by the French army over a century before. The building is still used as a town hall. It is also a popular venue for weddings. Inside, a staircase leads up from the spacious foyer to the beautiful Gothic Hall, which is open to visitors year round. This magnificent parliamentary chamber was built around 1400. The ceiling boasts some lavish woodcarvings including 16 beautiful corbels (brackets) bearing representations of the seasons and the elements. A series of paintings around the hall was completed in 1895, each portraying a key event in the city's history.

Next door to the Stadhuis is the Brugse Vrije museum, which houses a massive wood, marble and alabaster chimney designed by Lanceloot Blondeel. The chimney is one of the best sculptural works of 16th-century Flanders.

Heilig Bloed Basiliek
Burg 15. **Map** B3. **Tel** (050) 33 6792, 33 3767. **Open** 10am–noon, 2–5pm daily (opens at 9:30am in summer).

The Basilica of the Holy Blood holds one of the most sacred reliquaries in Europe. The basilica divides into two distinct sections, the lower part being the evocative St Basil's chapel with its plain stone-pillared entrance and arches. The upper chapel was rebuilt in the 19th century after the French destroyed it in the 1790s. Here, brightly coloured decorations surround a silver tabernacle of 1611 which houses a sacred phial, supposed to contain a few drops of blood and water washed from the body of Christ by Joseph of Arimathea. The phial was brought here from Jerusalem in 1150, and is still the object of great veneration. The church also has a museum of paintings, vestments and other artifacts.

🖼 The Markt
Map A3.

A market has been held on Bruges' main square since the 10th century. It is an impressive open space lined with 17th-century houses and overlooked by the Belfort on one side. The oldest façade on the square (dating from the 15th century) belongs to the Huis Bouchoute, which was the home of Charles II of England during part of his exile from 1656–7.

In the middle is a statue of Pieter de Coninck and Jan Breydel, two 14th-century guildsmen who led a rebellion against the French in 1302. Known as the *Bruges Matin*, they led Flemish soldiers to attack the French at dawn on May 18 1302, killing almost all of them. This bloody uprising paved the way for a form of independence for the Low Countries' major towns. Rights such as the freedom to trade were subsequently enshrined in the towns' charters until the 15th century.

🖼 The Belfort
Markt. **Map** B3. **Open** 9:30am–5pm daily. 🖼

The Markt is dominated by the belfry, whose octagonal belltower rises 83 m (272 ft) above the square. Built between the 13th and 15th centuries, the belfry is Bruges' most celebrated landmark as it was used to store the town's charter, and is therefore a constant reminder of the city's past as a centre of trade. Inside the tower, a winding staircase leads up, past the chamber where the town's rights and

Bruges' Belfort or bell tower overlooking the Markt

privileges were stored, to the roof, where the views across Bruges are delightful.

Gruuthuse Museum
See pp124–5.

🏛 Arentshuis Museum
Dijver 16. **Map** B4. **Tel** (050) 44 8763. **Open** 9:30am–5pm daily. **Closed** Mon (except Easter Mon and Whit Mon). 🖼

The Arentshuis Museum is housed in an 18th-century mansion overlooking the Dijver Canal. The interior is divided into two sections, with the ground floor devoted to temporary art exhibitions. These are often focused on a single theme or artist and draw on the archives of the Groeninge Museum, offering the chance to see some of the museum's more rarely-seen works. Upstairs is the work of Frank Brangwyn (1867–1956), a painter and sculptor who was born in Bruges of Welsh parents. Most of Brangwyn's life was spent in Britain, but he bequeathed this collection to Bruges, as well as his drawings, furniture and carpets. The dark and powerful canvases depicting industrial scenes are perhaps the most diverting.

Statue of Breydel and Pieter de Coninck

🖼 Concertgebouw
't Zand. **Map** A4. **Tel** (070) 22 3302.

Built as part of the celebrations for Bruges' European City of Culture, this terracotta concert hall features a 28-m (92-ft) tower that offers great views.

Groeninge Museum
Map B4. *See pp126–7.*

🏛 Onze Lieve Vrouwekerk
Mariastraat. **Map** A4. **Tel** (050) 34 5314. **Open** 9:30am–5pm Mon–Sat, 1:30–5pm Sun & holy days. **Closed** during services; mausoleum closed until 2016. 🖼

The Church of Our Lady took over 200 years to build, starting in 1220, and incorporates a variety of styles. The interior, with its white walls, stark columns and black-and-white tiled floor has a medieval simplicity, while the side chapels and pulpit are lavishly decorated.

One of the church's artistic highlights is Michelangelo's sculpture *Madonna and Child* (1504–5), at the end of the southern aisle. This marble statue was imported by a Flemish merchant, and was the only one of the artist's works to leave Italy during his lifetime. In the choir there are fine paintings by Pieter Pourbus including a *Last Supper* (1562), and the carved mausoleums of the Burgundian prince Charles the Bold and his daughter Mary.

The soaring spire of the Vrouwekerk

Gruuthuse Museum

The Gruuthuse Museum occupies a large medieval mansion close to the Dijver Canal. In the 15th century, it was inhabited by the merchant (or Lord of the Gruuthuse) who had the exclusive right to levy a tax on the "Gruut", an imported mixture of herbs added to barley during the beer-brewing process. The mansion's labyrinthine rooms, with their ancient chimneypieces and wooden beams, have survived intact and hold a priceless collection of fine and applied arts. There are tapestries, wood carvings, furniture and even a medical section devoted to cures of everyday ailments. The kitchen and original 1472 chapel transport visitors back to medieval times. The museum will be closed for restoration till mid-2016.

2nd Floor

1st Floor

Façade of the Gruuthuse
The museum's Gothic façade, with its elegant tower, stepped gables and fine stone windows, was built in the 15th century.

Ground Floor

★ **Charles V bust**
This incredibly life-like terracotta and wood bust of Habsburg king Charles V was carved in 1520 and is attributed to German sculptor Konrad Meit.

Entrance

The Seven Free Arts
Dating from around 1675, this exquisite tapestry depicts the "free arts", which includes music.

House on the Southern Bridge at Minnewater

VISITORS' CHECKLIST

Practical Information
Dijver 17, 8000 Bruges.
Map B4. **Tel** (05) 044 8743.
Open 9:30am–5pm Tue–Sun.
Closed 1 Jan, 25 Dec, Ascension
Day.

Transport
Markt.

Gallery Guide

*Laid out over three floors, the
collection is organized into types
of object from glassware,
porcelain and ceramics to
medical instruments in a series
of 22 numbered rooms. Visitors may view the rooms
in sequence from 1–22 and
get a good sense of the
original uses and layout of
the house in doing so.*

★ Chapel
Built in 1472, this oak-panelled
chapel on the museum's second
floor overlooks the high altar
of the church next door.

Key to Floorplan

- Glassware, porcelain and ceramics
- Kitchen
- Chapel
- Musical instruments
- Coins
- Tapestries
- Tools, weights and measures
- Entrance hall
- Textiles and lace
- Household implements
- Renaissance works
- Baroque works
- Reliquary and furniture
- Medical instruments
- Great Hall
- Weaponry

🏛 Sint-Janshospitaal
Mariastraat 38, 8000 Bruges.
Map A4. **Open** Tue–Sun.
Closed 1 Jan, 25 Nov.

This museum contains the works
of Hans Memling (1430–94), one
of the most talented painters
of his era. Among them, *The
Mystical Marriage of St. Catherine*
(1479), the central panel of a
triptych, is superb. The former
wards also house a collection of
paintings and furniture related
to the hospital's history.

⛪ St Salvators-Kathedraal
Steenstraat 1, 8000 Bruges. **Map** A4.
Tel (050) 33 61 88. **Open** Apr–Sep:
daily. **Closed** 1 Jan, 25 Dec.

Built as a parish church from
the 12th and 15th centuries,
this large, yellow-brick building
became Bruges' cathedral in
1834 when the French army
destroyed the existing one. The
interior is enormous and quite
plain except for a handsome set
of Brussels' tapestries hanging in
the choir, and a 1682 organ
adorned with angels.

Pale brick tower of St Salvators-Kathedraal
in Bruges

🏞 Minnewater
Map A5–B5.
Just south of the Begijnhof,
Minnewater is a peaceful
park with a canalized lake.
There were already swans here
in 1448 when Maximilian of
Austria ordered they be kept in
memory of his councillor, Pieter
Lanchals, who was beheaded
by the Bruges citizens.

Once this was a bustling
harbour which connected to
the canal network and the sea.
It is now a popular spot for
walkers and picnickers who may
view the pretty 15th-century
lock gate and house and the
1398 tower (Poedertoren). There
is an adjoining park which holds
music concerts in summer.

🏠 Begijnhof
Wijngaardplein 1, 8000 Bruges. **Map**
A4–A5. **Tel** (050) 33 00 11. **Open** daily.
Beguines were members of a lay
sisterhood active between the
13th and 16th centuries. They
lived and dressed as nuns but did
not take vows and were therefore
able to return to the secular
world at will. The begijnhof or
beguinage is the walled complex
in a town that housed the
beguines. In Bruges, this is an area
of quiet tree-lined canals faced
by white, gabled houses, with
a pleasant green at its centre.
Visitors and locals enjoy strolling
here and may visit the small,
simple church which was built in
1602. The nuns who live in the
houses are no longer beguines,
but Benedictine sisters who
moved here in the 1930s. One of
the houses is open to visitors and
displays simple rustic furniture
and artifacts that illustrate the
women's contemplative lives.

Groeninge Museum

Bruges' premier fine arts museum, the Groeninge, holds a fabulous collection of early Flemish and Dutch masters, featuring artists such as Jan van Eyck (d.1441) and Hieronymous Bosch (1450–94), famous for the strange freakish creatures of his moral allegories. Hugo van der Goes is well represented too, as is Gerard David (d.1523). These early works are displayed on the ground floor of the museum, as well as a collection of later Belgian painters, most notably Paul Delvaux (1897–1994) and René Magritte (1898–1967). Originally built between 1929 and 1930 on land belonging to the former Eeckhout Abbey, the museum is small and displays its collection in rotation, along with various temporary exhibitions.

★ Virgin and Child with Canon
(1436)
Jan van Eyck's richly detailed painting is noted for its realism. It shows van Eyck's patron, the canon, being presented to St Donatian by St George.

★ The Moreel Triptych
(1484)
This panel of the triptych, by German-born artist Hans Memling, was designed to adorn the altar in a Bruges church. It depicts the prominent Bruges family Moreel, and is said to be the first ever group portrait.

Last Judgement
Painted on three oak panels in the early 16th century, this detail from Hieronymous Bosch's famous triptych depicts scenes of cruelty and torture. The strong moral tone of the work suggests that man's sinful nature has created a hell on earth.

Portrait of Bruges Family
(1645)
Jacob van Oost the Elder's focus on the affluence of this family surveying their beloved city shows why he was Bruges' most popular artist of the Baroque period.

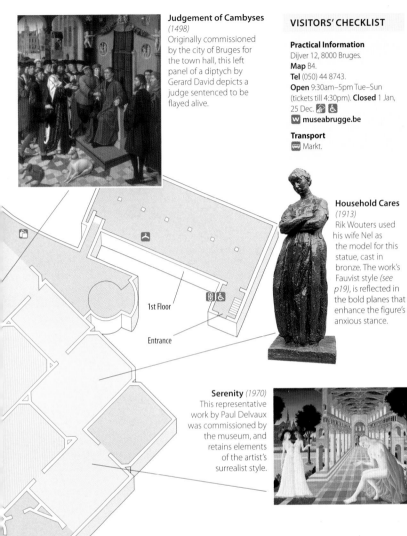

Judgement of Cambyses
(1498)
Originally commissioned by the city of Bruges for the town hall, this left panel of a diptych by Gerard David depicts a judge sentenced to be flayed alive.

VISITORS' CHECKLIST

Practical Information
Dijver 12, 8000 Bruges.
Map B4.
Tel (050) 44 8743.
Open 9:30am–5pm Tue–Sun (tickets till 4:30pm). **Closed** 1 Jan, 25 Dec. 🅿 ♿
Ⓦ **museabrugge.be**

Transport
🚌 Markt.

Household Cares
(1913)
Rik Wouters used his wife Nel as the model for this statue, cast in bronze. The work's Fauvist style *(see p19)*, is reflected in the bold planes that enhance the figure's anxious stance.

1st Floor

Entrance

Serenity *(1970)*
This representative work by Paul Delvaux was commissioned by the museum, and retains elements of the artist's surrealist style.

Gallery Guide
The Groeninge Museum is divided between two buildings. The main portion of the museum is on one level with a series of rooms displaying the early Flemish masters as well as works from the 17th to 20th centuries. Nearby, the Arentshuis (see p123), displays temporary exhibitions and houses a permanent collection of work by the artist Frank Brangwyn on its first floor.

Museum Façade
Originally built in 1930, the gallery was extended in 1994 to a design by architect Joseph Viérin. The old entrance is based on that of a Romanesque convent.

Key

☐ 15th and 16th centuries
☐ 17th to 19th centuries
☐ 20th century
☐ Cabinet displays
☐ Non-exhibition space

Exploring Northeast Bruges

In the height of the summer and on holiday weekends, tourists pour into Bruges, and parts of the city centre often get too crowded for comfort. Fortunately, the narrow cobbled streets and picturesque canals to the northeast of the Markt never suffer from this, and this fascinating area remains one of the most delightful parts of Bruges. Streets of charming terraced houses are dotted with grand, yet elegant 18th-century mansions. The best approach is via Jan van Eyckplein, in medieval times the city's busiest harbour, from where it is a short stroll along Spinolarei and Potterierei streets to the many museums and churches that are found in this historic district.

The historic buildings and lovely canals of northeast Bruges

Lace-making skills on show at the Kantcentrum lace centre

🏛 Kantcentrum

Balstraat 16. **Map** C2. **Tel** (050) 33 0072. **Open** Mon–Sat. 📷

The area from the white-washed cottages to the east of Potterierei Street is one of several old neighbourhoods where the city's lace workers plied their craft. Mostly, the women worked at home, receiving their raw materials from a supplier who also bought the finished product.

Lace-making skills are kept alive at the Kantcentrum, the Lace Centre on Balstraat, where local women (and a few men) fashion lace in a variety of styles, both modern and traditional. It is a busy place, and visitors can see the lace-making demonstrations held every afternoon during the summer. Some of the finished pieces are sold in the Kantcentrum shop at very reasonable prices.

🏛 Beluik der Gefusilleerden

Map C3.

Bruges was occupied by the German Army during both world wars. The bullet-marked "Wall of those who were shot

dead", as its name roughly translates, is located just south of the Kruispoort and commemorates a dozen men executed by German firing squad in 1916. Eleven of them were Belgian, shot for resisting German rule. The twelfth was Captain Fryatt, a British merchant navy officer. His arrest and execution here caused almost as much outrage around Europe as the death of Edith Cavell in Brussels a year earlier.

🏛 Jeruzalemkerk

Peperstraat. **Map** B3. **Open** Mon–Sat. 📷

The Jeruzalemkerk is Bruges' most unusual church. The present building dates from the 15th century, and was built on the site of a 13th-century chapel commissioned by a family of wealthy Italian merchants, the Adornes family, whose black marble tomb can be seen inside. Based on the design of the church of the Holy Sepulchre in Jerusalem, the structure possesses a striking tower with two tiers of wooden, polygon-shaped lanterns topped by a tin orb. Inside, the lower level contains a macabre altarpiece, carved with skulls and assorted

demons. Behind the altar is a smaller vaulted chapel; leading from this is a narrow tunnel guarded by an iron grate. Along the tunnel, a lifelike model of Christ in the Tomb can be seen at close quarters.

🏛 The Kruispoort and the Windmills

Map C2.

Medieval Bruges was heavily fortified. It was encircled by a city wall which was itself protected by a moat and strengthened by a series of massive gates. Most of the wall was knocked down in the 19th century, but the moat has survived and so has one

The Jeruzalemkerk, built in 1497

of the gates, the Kruispoort, a monumental structure dating from 1402 that guards the eastern approach to the city. The earthen bank stretching north of the Kruispoort marks the line of the old city wall, which was once dotted with some 20 windmills. Today, only four remain overlooking the canal. The first, the Bonne Chieremolen, was brought here from a Flanders village in 1911, but the second – St Janshuismolen – is original to the city, a restored structure erected in 1770. The northernmost mill of the four is De Nieuwe Papegai, an old oil mill that was relocated here in 1970.

The massive Kruispoort, one of the four remaining medieval gates

🏛 English Convent

Carmersstraat 85. **Map** C2. **Tel** (050) 33 2424. **Open** Mon & Tue; Mass 8:30am Sun. 📷 obligatory.

The English Convent was where dozens of English Catholics sought asylum following the execution of Charles I in 1649, and during Oliver Cromwell's subsequent rule as Lord Protector. The conventual buildings are not open to the public, but the nuns provide a well-informed tour of their beautiful church, which was built in the Baroque style in the 1620s. The interior has a delightful sense of space, its elegant proportions enhanced by its cupola, but the highlight is the altar, a grand affair made of around 20 types of marble.

🏛 Volkskundemuseum

Balstraat 43. **Map** B2–C2. **Tel** (050) 44 8764. **Open** 9:30am–5pm Tue–Sun, Easter & Whit Mon. 📷

The Volkskundemuseum is one of the best folk museums in

17th-century almshouses comprising the Volkskundemuseum

Flanders. It occupies an attractive terrace of low, brick almshouses located behind an old neighbour-hood café called the "Zwarte Kat" (Black Cat), which serves as the entrance. Each of the almshouses is dedicated to a different aspect of traditional Flemish life, with workshops displaying old tools. Several different crafts are represented here, such as a cobbler's and a blacksmith's, through to a series of typical historical domestic interiors.

🏛 Schuttersgilde St Sebastiaan

Carmersstraat 174. **Map** C2. **Tel** (050) 33 1626. **Open** May–Sep: 10am–noon Tue–Thu, 2–5pm Sat; Oct–Apr: 2–5pm Tue–Thu & Sat. 📷

The Archers' guild (the Schuttersgilde) was one of the most powerful of the militia guilds, and their 16th- and 17th-century red-brick guildhouse now houses a museum.

The commercial life of medieval Bruges was dominated by the guilds, each of

The St Sebastiaan guildhouse, now a museum

which represented the interests of a particular group of skilled workmen. The guilds guarded their privileges jealously and, among many rules and customs, marriage between children whose fathers were in different guilds was greatly frowned upon. The guild claimed the name St Sebastian after an early Christian martyr, whom the Roman Emperor Diocletian had executed by his archers. The bowmen followed orders – medieval painters often show Sebastian looking like a pincushion – but miraculously, Sebastian's wounds healed before he was finished off by club-wielding assassins. The guildhouse is notable for its collection of paintings of the guild's leading lights, gold and silver trinkets and guild emblems.

🏛 Museum Onze-Lieve-Vrouw-ter-Potterie

Potterierei 79. **Map** B1. **Tel** (050) 44 8711. **Open** 9:30am–12:30pm, 1:30–5pm Tue–Sun, Easter & Whit Mon. 📷

Located by the canal in one of the quietest parts of Bruges, the Museum Onze Lieve Vrouw ter Potterie (Our Lady of Pottery) occupies part of an old hospital that was founded in 1276 to care for elderly women. There is a 14th- and 15th-century cloister, and several of the sick rooms house a modest collection of paintings, the best of which are some 17th- and 18th-century portraits of leading aristocrats. The hospital church is in excellent condition, too; it is a warm, intimate place with fine stained-glass windows and a set of impressive Baroque altarpieces.

A 90-Minute Walk Around Bruges

Almost all the most famous sights of Bruges are in the centre and to the southwest of the centre. But the commercial and residential heart in Bruges' medieval golden age was to the north of the Markt. This is where a cosmopolitan collection of European merchants had their grand national "lodges", which oversaw the trade that passed into the city along a network of canals. Only small traces of this former glory remain, hidden among a collection of waterways, bridges, and residential streets of exceptional tranquillity and charm.

② The Provinciaal Hof housing the local government offices

Markt and Vlamingstraat

Like most of the old trading cities of Flanders, Bruges clusters around its old market square, the Markt *(see p123)*. The 19th-century statue in the centre celebrates Pieter de Coninck and Jan Breydel ①, the guildsmen who led a revolt against their French overlords in Bruges in 1302. It culminated in victory at the Battle of the Golden Spurs *(see p32)*, a key date in Flemish nationalism. Goods came into the square on a canal, and were unloaded under the roof of the Waterhalle. The canal was filled in during the 1780s and now the site of the Waterhalle has been taken by the Provinciaal Hof ②, which is now used for exhibitions and receptions. This Neo-Medieval building was designed by

① Statue of Pieter de Coninck and Jan Breydel

Louis Delacenserie (1838-1909), the architect responsible for much of the restoration of medieval Bruges. On the other side of the Markt, on the corner of St-Amandstraat, is the Huis Bouchoute ③; the compass on the façade, attached to a weathervane, was used by merchants to check the winds for the ships bringing goods to Bruges. Opposite it is the Craenenburg ④ (now a café), where Archduke Maximilian of Austria was imprisoned by the Bruges' authorities in 1488. A walk up Vlamingstraat leads past the Stadsschouwburg ⑤ (Municipal Theatre), a handsome Neo-Classical building from 1868. At No. 33 is the former Genuese Loge ⑥, the lodge of the Genoese traders, dating from 1399, which now houses the Friet Museum. No. 35 was the Huis Ter Beurze ⑦. The word "bourse" comes from the family Van de Beurse who ran an inn here in the 15th century, which became a meeting place for traders, much like Lloyds' coffee house in London gave its name to the insurance brokers who met there in the 17th century.

Spiegelrei

On the right-hand side of the Academiestraat stands the Poortersloge ⑧ (Burghers' Lodge), a clubhouse for leading citizens in medieval Bruges. Almost all the city's grand buildings of that era had a tower; this is a rare example where the tower (rebuilt in 1775) has survived. On the other side of the street is the Oud Tolhuis ⑨, the Old Customs House. It overlooked a weighbridge where customs charges were assessed; that area has been replaced by the square, Jan van Eyckplein, named after the city's great artist who is represented by a statue ⑩. The canal that once led to the city centre now stops

Key

• • • Walk Route

between Spiegelrei and Spinolarei. On the corner of Spiegelrei and Genthof is Roode Steen ⑪; this was the home of Georges Rodenbach, the author of the controversial novel *Bruges-la-Morte* (Bruges the Dead, 1892). Koningstraat, off Spinolarei, leads to the St Walburgakerk ⑫, Bruges' finest Baroque church, built for the Jesuits in 1612–42.

Jeruzalemkerk

Back on Spinolarei, cross the canal on Strooibrug. Straight ahead is Blekersstraat, with Café Vlissinghe ⑬ on the right. This is reputedly Bruges' oldest tavern, dating from 1515. Heading south down St-Annarei, the first left leads to the St Annakerk ⑭, a pretty parish church from

⑯ A room at Bruges' folk museum, the Volkskundemuseum

quarter. Cross the canal on the Vlamingbrug ⑳. At Naaldenstraat 19 is Hof Bladelin ㉑, a mansion built in about 1450 by Pieter Bladelin; after 1469, it was owned by the Medici Bank of Florence. Hotel Lucca ㉒, at Naaldenstraat 30, is on the site of the trading house of the merchants of the Italian city of Lucca. The alley off Naaldenstraat called Boterhuis ㉓ passes beneath the arch of the old Butter House and dairy market, and leads to St Jakobskerk ㉔. This fine Gothic church – with Baroque remodelling – contains art, ornate chapels, and tombs. The route along Moerstraat and Ontvangersstraat marks the bounds of the Prinsenhof, the former palace of the Dukes of Burgundy, which is now the first and only five star hotel in Bruges ㉕. Geldmuntstraat is named after the old mint that stood on the little square called Muntplein; it leads back to the Eiermarkt (Egg Market) ㉖ and the Markt.

1497. The Jeruzalemkerk (see p128) ⑮ on Peperstraat is very different, built in the 15th century and themed on pilgrimage sites in the Holy Land. On Balstraat is the Kantcentrum, the Lace Centre (see p128). A row of almshouses, also in Balstraat, is now the Museum voor Volkskunde (see p129) ⑯, a folk museum that paints a vivid picture of life in old Bruges. The only domed church in Bruges is in the English Convent (Engelsklooster) (see p129) ⑰, on Carmersstraat. Head back west along Carmersstraat, cross the canal on the Carmersbrug, and turn right to reach St Gilliskerk ⑱, an attractive church dating from the 13th–15th century. A series of cobbled streets leads to a picturesque section of canal at the Augustijnenbrug. The street on the opposite side called Spaanse Loskaai ⑲ recalls that this was once the Spanish

The Spinolarei canal, one of Bruges' principal waterways

Tips for Walkers

Starting point: The Markt
Length: 3.7 km (2.3 miles)
Getting there: The Markt is within walking distance of almost all hotels in Bruges; bus routes from all directions also go to this hub.
Stopping off points: There are a multitude of cafés and restaurants around the Markt, but very few beyond Vlamingstraat. A famous exception is the venerable old tavern called Cafe Vlissinghe in Blekersstraat (No. 13 on this walk).

TRAVELLERS' NEEDS

WHERE TO STAY

For most of the year, Brussels is primarily a business or political destination, and accommodation is often priced accordingly. The wide range of top hotels has one fine advantage for the visitor – weekend and summer deals make it possible to stay in some of Europe's most luxurious establishments even on a modest budget. The mid-range of hotels is also well represented in the city, with period houses turned into stylish family-run hotels and chain hotels. To keep accommodation costs to a minimum, choose from Brussels' abundance of youth hostels and bed-and-breakfast options. Also included are listings of accommodation in Antwerp, Bruges and Ghent for those who would like to stay overnight in these towns.

Hallway in the Hotel Métropole on Place de Brouckère, Brussels *(see p139)*

Where to Look

While Brussels does not have a specific hotel area, there are clusters of hotels in various parts of the city. Centrally, the most fertile ground is between Place Rogier and Place de Brouckère, which is within walking distance of both the Upper and Lower Towns and a short bus ride from most major sights. The streets to the west of the Grand Place are also well-supplied for those who want to be in the historic centre of town, but be aware that the noise from the roads can be a problem at night. To the north, Place Ste-Catherine or the streets behind Avenue de la Toison d'Or have plenty of options.

Bed-and-breakfast options are dispersed across the capital and can often be found in residential districts at very reasonable rates. When arriving in the city by train or plane, it is worth knowing that the Gare du Midi and the airport both have hotel colonies nearby, although the area around the station can be run down in some places. The airport has principally attracted chain hotels, which often offer good-value package deals with the national airlines, although sightseeing from here is more inconvenient.

Room Rates

Hotels at the top end of the market offer exceptional standards of comfort and convenience to their largely corporate clients, and their prices tend to reflect this. In general, room rates are higher than in the rest of Belgium, but on a par with other European capitals. For a night in a luxury hotel, expect to pay between €250 and €300 for a double room; the price for a room in the city averages in the €150 to €175 bracket. Following the pattern of cities worldwide, the price of a room generally reduces the further they are from the centre. However, there are numerous discounts available, so check before making a reservation *(see p136)*.

Single travellers can often find reasonable discounts on accommodation, although few places will offer rooms at half the price of a double. It is usual to be charged extra if you place additional guests in a double room, sometimes even if they are children, so make sure to call and check first. Youth hostels cater very well to the budget or student traveller and some also have family rooms.

Taxes and Charges

Room tax and sales tax should already be included in the cost of a room, so the price quoted will usually be what appears as the total. There may be an additional charge for car parking; some hotels offer free parking, while others might charge up to €25 a night. In hotels with no private

Unique frescoes decorate each room at the Hotel Bloom *(see p138)*

Warm interiors of Le Plaza, Brussels *(see p139)*

car park, it is worth checking discounts for public parking facilities if these are located nearby. While many hotels are happy to allow pets, others will add a small nightly charge to the bill.

Breakfast is usually included in the price of a room in Brussels; but confirm this when making a booking. The fare generally consists of Continental breakfasts, including coffee, warm croissants and brioche rolls, along with preserves and fruit juice. Bear in mind that if a high-end hotel is charging €20 for breakfast, there will be plenty of places nearby offering equal quality for much less money.

Phone calls from hotel rooms can be extremely expensive, with unit charges of €.60 for even a local call not uncommon. To make a long-distance call, buying a phonecard and using the efficient public payphone service is several times less expensive. Almost all Brussels hotels offer free Wi-Fi, although the speed of the connection may not be the best and usage time allowed to guests may be limited.

Hotel Gradings and Facilities

Approved hotels are issued with a shield by the Belgian Tourist Board which must be displayed in a prominent position near the entrance or lobby. Hotels carrying this sign conform to official standards set by Belgian law which guarantee certain standards of quality. Some hotels are also graded according to the Benelux system, ranging from one to five stars, with one as the minimum. It is worth keeping in mind, however, that membership to this scheme is voluntary and as a result, there may be high-quality hotels which are not included in this grading.

In a city with so many luxury hotels, fierce competition has led to ever more sophisticated gadgets and services being offered to attract businesspeople. Several private phone lines, screened calls, free Wi-Fi access, automatic check-out services, 24-hour news via Reuters, secretarial services, free mobile phones and even executive suites designed expressly for women are all on offer. Most of the top hotels also house extensive fitness facilities, including saunas and full gymnasiums, although there are few large swimming pools.

Brussels' reputation as a centre for fine dining is significantly enhanced by the hotel trade, with major hotels often offering several dining options, from expert gastronomy to excellent brasserie dining. For snacks and drinks, Brussels' hotels are known for their old-style, entertaining bars,

complete with live piano music, for those guests who prefer not to venture into the city at night. A handful have nightclub facilities where lively crowds meet in the evening for cocktails and dancing.

As one of Europe's major centres for the convention trade, Brussels is not short of meeting and function rooms. The big hotels offer dozens of spaces for anything from conferences to society weddings and even relatively modest hotels have good-sized rooms for business seminars and the like. Many hotels also offer serviced apartments, which provide greater freedom and more space.

Façade of the Crowne Plaza Hotel, one of the chain hotels *(see p139)*

View of the Grand Place from a room at Hotel Saint-Michel *(see p138)*

Travellers with Disabilities

Hotels in Brussels and the rest of Belgium take the needs of travellers with disabilities seriously. Many have one or more rooms designed with wheelchair-bound guests in mind. It is worth remembering, however, that many hotel buildings in Brussels are historic and, therefore, may not be fully suitable, but all hotels and their staff will go out of their way to accommodate guests with special needs. Most hotels will allow the visually handi-capped to bring a guide dog onto the premises, although it is best to call ahead and confirm.

How to Book

Rooms are available in Brussels at most times of the year, but book several days in advance to ensure you get the place of your choice. Visitors can usually book directly with the hotels, either on their websites or over the phone. However, the most efficient way to book a room is by using the services offered by Internet booking websites such as **booking.com** and **hotels.com**. These websites offer instant online bookings, often at rates far below those quoted by even the hotels themselves.

To book a room when already in Brussels, **Visit Brussels** offers a free, same-day reservation service on site. It also publishes a practical guide to Brussels hotels, updated annually, which is available on request.

Special Rates

Brussels is an exceptional destination, in that relatively few business travellers come for the weekend or in July and August, meaning that often great deals can be acquired at these times.

The cost of staying in one of the top hotels over the week-end or at off-peak times can plummet by as much as 65 per cent, for example, from €300 to €100 for a double room, so checking about any special deals before booking may save a large sum of money. A few hotels also offer discounts for guests who eat in their restaurants.

The best place to find special rates, however, is by using one of the major Internet hotel booking services, or the one offered by the Tourist Office on its website.

Youth Accommodation

Brussels has several excellent, centrally located youth hostels. Perhaps the best are Sleephere,

Stately exterior of the Hilton Brussels City *(see p139)*

DIRECTORY

How to Book	Youth Accommodation	Gay and Lesbian Accommodation	Self-Catering Apartments
Visit Brussels Rue Royale 2–4, Brussels 1000. **Map** 2 E4. **Tel** (02) 513 8940. Ⓦ visitbrussels.be	**Sleephere** Quai à la Chaux 8, Brussels 1000. **Tel** (02) 496 599 379. Ⓦ sleephere-la-source.com	**The Rainbow House** Rue du Marché au Charbon 42, Brussels 1000. **Map** 1 C3. **Tel** (02) 503 5990. Ⓦ rainbowhouse.be	**Airbnb** Ⓦ airbnb.com **Bed-and-Breakfasts**
Booking Through Websites Ⓦ booking.com Ⓦ hotels.com	**Sleep Well** Rue du Damier 23, Brussels 1000. **Map** 1 D1. **Tel** (02) 218 50 50. Ⓦ sleepwell.be	**Tels Quels** Rue du Marché au Charbon 81, Brussels 1000. **Map** 1 C3. **Tel** (02) 512 4587. Ⓦ telsquels.be	**Bed & Brussels** Rue Kindermans 9, Brussels 1050. **Tel** (02) 646 0737. Ⓦ bnb-brussels.be

close to Place Ste-Catherine, and Sleep Well, which has full access for travellers with disabilities. A bed in a four-person room should cost around €25, rising to around €45 for a single room. Breakfast is sometimes included or costs from €2.50 up, with lunch and dinner for a charge of around €10. For guests who are not members of Hostelling International, rates increase up to €5 extra per night; membership cards, priced €10–16, are available at most hostels.

The opulent lobby at the Meridien Hotel in Brussels' Lower Town *(see p140)*

Gay and Lesbian Accommodation

Same-sex couples should have few problems finding welcoming accommodation. Maison Noble *(see p139)*, Brussels' first luxury gay guesthouse, opened in 2009. The **Tels Quels** association, located on the Rue de Marché au Charbon, is the best source of information about gay-friendly options. It has a documentation centre covering most aspects of gay life in the city and publishes a monthly magazine. **The Rainbow House**, across the road, is a good place to find out about LGBT events taking place in and around the city centre.

Travelling with Children

Children are welcome at all hotels in Brussels, with many making concerted efforts to

cater for the needs of those travelling with children. Most allow one or two under-12s to stay in their parents' room without extra charge and some hotels will extend this to under-16s and even under-18s. Note, however, that not all do, and an increasing number of places add surcharges as high as €75 to hotel bills even when children share their parents' room. Always check with the hotel in advance while booking.

Self-Catering Apartments

There is no shortage of self-catering accommodation in Brussels, with many places available for a short stay as well as by the week or month. A few places are attached to hotels as suites, with the rest run by private companies. Prices start at around €600

per week, for a fairly basic but furnished one- or two-bedroom apartment, to €1,000 or more for more luxurious lodgings. Visit the Tourist Office for a detailed list of suggestions or try the Internet service Airbnb.

Bed-and-Breakfasts

Bed-and-breakfasts, also called chambre d'hôte, can be a very pleasant alternative to staying in a cheap hotel, and rooms can often be found even in the centre of town. A number of good Brussels bed-and-breakfasts can be found on the specialist website Airbnb and at Bed & Brussels.

Recommended Hotels

The many hotels featured in this guide have been selected across as wide a price range as possible for their excellent facilities, good location and usually great value. From historic, often centuries-old, buildings in the city centre to those slightly outside the major tourist areas in lovely garden settings, these hotels encompass all price levels.

For our pick of the very best, look out for hotels featuring the DK Choice symbol. These establishments have been highlighted in recognition of an exceptional feature – a stunning location, notable history, inviting atmosphere or outstanding value. Many of these are exceptionally popular, so reserve as early as possible.

Neatly laid-out tables at the stylish brasserie at Hotel Marivaux *(see p138)*

Where to Stay

Brussels

Lower Town

Aris Grand Place €
Historic   **Map** 2 D3
Marché aux Herbes 78–80, 1000
Tel *(02) 514 4300*
Ⓦ arishotel.be
Housed in a late 19th-century
building, the rooms here have
double-glazing to keep out the
city noise.

Astrid €
Modern   **Map** 1 C1
Place du Samedi 11, 1000
Tel *(02) 219 3119*
Ⓦ astridhotel.be
A comfortable and efficient hotel.
Rooms are large with modern
furnishings and facilities. Superb
complimentary breakfast.

Atlas €
Modern   **Map** 1 C2
*Rue du Vieux Marché aux Grains
30, 1000*
Tel *(02) 502 6006*
Ⓦ atlas-hotel.be
Three-star hotel just to the north
of Grand Place. Offers basic but
pleasant rooms and breakfast is
included in the price.

Congres €
Historic   **Map** 2 F2
Rue du Congres 42, 1000
Tel *(02) 217 1890*
Ⓦ hotelducongres.be
This peaceful three-star hotel
occupies four elegantly
renovated 19th-century town
houses. Polite and friendly staff.

Floris Arlequin Grand'Place €
Modern   **Map** 2 D2
*Rue de la Fourche 17–19,
Greepstraat, 1000*
Tel *(02) 514 1615*
Ⓦ florishotels.com
A modern, three-star hotel in
the heart of the historical centre.
Some of the rooms boast great
city views. Good breakfasts.

Grande Cloche €
Historic   **Map** 1 C4
Place Rouppe 10, 1000
Tel *(02) 512 6140*
Ⓦ hotelgrandecloche.com
Occupies a renovated 19th-
century town house. Ideal for
budget travellers.

Hotel La Madeleine €
Historic   **Map** 2 D3
Rue de la Montagne 20–22, 1000
Tel *(02) 513 2973*
Ⓦ hotel-la-madeleine.be
Charming hotel with room
options to meet all budgets.
Some have shared bathrooms.
Pet-friendly.

Hotel Saint-Michel €
Value   **Map** 2 D3
Grand Place 15, 1000
Tel *(02) 511 0956*
Ⓦ hotel-saint-michel.be
Rooms are basic but clean.
Friendly and helpful staff. Breakfast
can be served in the rooms.

Hotel Van Belle €
Modern   **Map** 1 A3
Chaussée de Mons 39, 1070
Tel *(02) 521 3516*
Ⓦ hotelvanbelle.be
Offers rooms that are comfortable
and well furnished. The communal
lounge area has a large open fire.

La Vieille Lanterne €
Value   **Map** 1 C3
Rue des Grands Carmes 29, 1000
Tel *(02) 512 7494*
Ⓦ lavieillelanterne.be
Good-value hostel with six
rooms. All are brightly decorated,
and benefit from great views
onto Manneken Pis.

Manhattan €
Modern   **Map** 2 D1
Blvd Adolphe Max 132–140, 1000
Tel *(02) 219 1619*
Ⓦ hotelmanhattan.be
Very well priced but pretty basic.
The neat, comfortable rooms have
an old-fashioned feel to them.

Marivaux €
Modern   **Map** 2 D1
Blvd Adolphe Max 98, 1000
Tel *(02) 227 0300*
Ⓦ hotelmarivaux.be
The rooms of this comfortable,
modern hotel are large and
pleasantly decorated. Stylish
bar and brasserie.

Queen Anne €
Value   **Map** 2 D1
Blvd Emile Jacqmain 110, 1000
Tel *(02) 217 1600*
Ⓦ queen-anne.be
Welcoming Queen Anne is small
and friendly, with nice rooms,
11 apartments and a generous
buffet breakfast.

9Hotel Central €€
Historic   **Map** 2 E3
Rue des Colonies 10, 1000
Tel *(02) 504 9910*
Ⓦ le9hotel.com
Historic, well-priced four-
star hotel near the Royal
Palace. Helpful, efficient
service. Complimentary
buffet breakfast.

Bedford €€
Family   **Map** 1 C3
Rue du Midi 135–137, 1000
Tel *(02) 507 0000*
Ⓦ hotelbedford.be
Four-star hotel with spacious
and comfortable rooms. Also
offers sumptuously decorated
executive rooms and suites
suitable for families.

Bloom €€
Design   **Map** 2 E2
Rue Royal 250, 1210
Tel *(02) 220 6611*
Ⓦ hotelbloom.com
Boutique hotel featuring
comfortable, contemporary
rooms, each decorated with
a unique fresco by a different
local artist.

Café Pacific €€
Design   **Map** 1 B2
Rue Antoine Dansaert 57, 1000
Tel *(02) 213 0080*
Ⓦ hotelcafepacific.com
Modern, boutique hotel in one
of the trendiest areas of Brussels.
Ideal for couples and families
alike. Breakfast included.

Simple, contemporary room at Hotel Bloom, Lower Town, Brussels

Carrefour de l'Europe
Business   **Map** 2 D3
Rue du Marché aux Herbes 110, 1000
Tel *(02) 504 9400*
w carrefourhotel.be
Elegant four-star hotel targeted at the business traveller. Eight conference rooms and 10 executive traveller rooms. Good lobby bar.

Cascade Midi
Modern   **Map** 1 B5
Av Fosny 5–7, 1060
Tel *(02) 533 1090*
w novotel.com
Modern hotel that offers a range of comfortable rooms. Guests can enjoy a buffet breakfast while looking out onto the rear garden.

Citadines St. Catherine
Family   **Map** 1 C1
Quai Au Bois A Bruler 51, 1000
Tel *(02) 221 1411*
w citadines.com
Studio apartments with a peaceful communal garden, on self-catering or half-board basis. A good choice for visitors coming for a week or more.

Crowne Plaza
Historic   **Map** 2 E1
Rue Gineste 3, 1210
Tel *(02) 203 6200*
w crowneplazabrussels.be
An Art Nouveau hotel dating back to 1908, combining turn-of-the-century style with modern facilities. Book in advance during the busy summer season.

George V
Historic   **Map** 1 B3
Rue T'Kint 23, 1000
Tel *(02) 513 5093*
w hotelgeorge5.be
Friendly hotel occupying an old English-inspired 19th-century town house. Large, opulent rooms with period furnishings and plenty of old-world charm.

Hilton Brussels City
Modern   **Map** 2 E2
Place Rogier 20, 1210
Tel *(02) 203 3125*
w hilton.com
Sophisticated city hotel offering large, comfortable rooms and multiple facilities for tourists and business travellers alike.

La Legende
Value   **Map** 1 C3
Rue du Lombard 35, 1000
Tel *(02) 512 8290*
w hotellalegende.com
La Legende is a modern two-star hotel. Reasonably priced and welcoming. Also offers four-bed family rooms.

Luxurious interiors at Hotel Metropole, Lower Town, Brussels

Le Plaza
Historic   **Map** 2 D1
Blvd Adolphe Max 118–126, 1000
Tel *(02) 278 0100*
w leplaza-brussels.be
An opulent five-star hotel, Le Plaza even has its own theatre. The building dates back to 1930 when it was built to model Paris' famous George V hotel.

Maison Noble
Historic   **Map** 1 C1
Rue Marcq 10, 1000
Tel *(02) 219 2339*
w maison-noble.eu
Stylish gay-friendly place located in a 19th-century town house with beautiful, painted wooden ceilings and sumptuous Art Deco stained-glass windows.

Marriott Brussels
Modern   **Map** 1 C2
Rue Auguste Orts 3–7, 1000
Tel *(02) 516 9090*
w marriott.com
This five-star hotel in the heart of Brussels offers all one has come to expect from a Marriott: from large rooms to plenty of little extras. Great breakfast included.

Matignon
Value   **Map** 1 C2
Rue de la Bourse 8–12, 1000
Tel *(02) 511 0888*
w hotelmatignon.be
Small yet rather gorgeous place offering simple but thoughtfully decorated rooms. The price includes a wonderful breakfast.

Métropole
Historic   **Map** 1 D2
Place de Brouckère 31, 1000
Tel *(02) 217 2300*
w metropolehotel.com
Built in 1895, this plush hotel boasts striking architecture and a mix of French Renaissance, Empire and Art Deco styles.

NH Grand Place Arenberg
Modern   **Map** 2 D2
Rue d'Assaut 15, 1000
Tel *(02) 501 1616*
w nh-hotels.com
A modern hotel within sight of Brussels' cathedral. The rooms have been wonderfully refurbished to their current spotless state.

Noga
Modern   **Map** 1 C1
Rue du Béguinage 38, 1000
Tel *(02) 218 6763*
w nogahotel.com
A friendly hotel near the church of St-Jean-Baptiste, Noga feels like a home away from home. Eclectic furnishings.

Novotel Tour Noire
Family   **Map** 1 C2
Rue de la Vierge Noire 32, 1000
Tel *(02) 620 0428*
w novotel.com
Well-priced base in the heart of the city, with plenty of family-friendly facilities – including a gym and pool.

Opera
Modern   **Map** 2 D2
Rue Grétry 53, 1000
Tel *(02) 219 4343*
w hotel-opera.be
Quiet and friendly spot, with simply decorated rooms. Well-priced for the location. Complimentary buffet breakfast.

Scandic Grand Place
Luxury   **Map** 2 D2
Rue d'Arenberg 18, 1000
Tel *(02) 548 1811*
w scandichotels.com
Luxury hotel with sumptuous rooms situated behind the façades of two listed town houses. Has a popular bar and restaurant, a sauna and a fitness room.

Welcome
Modern   **Map** 1 C1
Quai au Bois à Brûler 23, 1000
Tel *(02) 219 9546*
w hotelwelcome.com
This charming hotel lives up to its name. It offers a range of good rooms and serves a terrific complimentary buffet in its Art Deco breakfast room.

Amigo
Luxury   **Map** 1 C3
Rue de l'Amigo 1–3, 1000
Tel *(02) 547 4747*
w roccofortehotels.com
Five-star hotel providing an elegant setting in a great location. Rooms have king-size beds and marble bathrooms. Award-winning restaurant.

For more information on types of hotels *see page 137*

Le Chatelain   €€€
Luxury   Map 2 D5
Rue de Châtelain 17, 1000
Tel *(02) 646 0055*
w le-chatelain.com
This five-star hotel prides itself
on its traditional hospitality
and attention to detail.
Soundproof rooms and
luxurious bathrooms.

Le Meridien   €€€
Luxury   Map 2 D3
Carrefour de l'Europe 3, 1000
Tel *(02) 548 4211*
w lemeridienbrussels.com
One of Belgium's finest hotels,
offering all the amenities and
grand, opulent rooms designed
in a Victorian/English style.

Radisson Blu Royal   €€€
Design   Map 2 D2
Rue du Fosse-aux-Loups 47, 1000
Tel *(02) 219 2828*
w radissonblu.com
Fabulous five-star hotel behind
a glorious Art Deco façade,
designed by famed Belgian
designer, Michel Haspers.

DK Choice

Royal Windsor   €€€
Luxury   Map 2 D3
Rue Duquesnoy 5, 1000
Tel *(02) 505 5555*
w royalwindsorbrussels.com
This exquisitely luxurious
establishment by the Grand
Place is one of the best hotels
in the city. Marble bathrooms
and French antiques adorn the
rooms, some of which are very
spacious. The Grand Place
Suite is one of the finest
hotel rooms in Europe.

Upper Town

**Best Western Hotel
Royal Centre**   €
Modern   Map 2 F1
Rue Royale 160, 1000
Tel *(02) 219 0065*
w royalcentre.be
A well-priced four-star hotel
within walking distance of the
Royal Palace. Rates inclusive of
Continental breakfast.

Chambord   €
Modern   Map 2 E4
Rue De Namur 82, 1000
Tel *(02) 548 9910*
w hotel-chambord.be
The Penthouse Suite of the
Chamboard has a stunning
view from its terrace. Some of
the standard rooms have their
own balconies as well. Breakfast
is included.

Exquisite interiors at Royal Windsor Hotel,
Grand Place, Lower Town, Brussels

Chambres en Ville   €
Value   Map 2 F2
Rue de Londres 19, 1050
Tel *(02) 512 9290*
w chambresenville.be
Wonderfully chic guesthouse
designed by the artist-owner
Philippe Guilmin. Studio
apartments for longer stays.

Les Bluets   €
Value
Rue Berckmans 124, 1060
Tel *(02) 534 3983*
w bluets.be
Charming family-run, non-
smoking hotel in a 19th-century
bourgeois town house. Eight
rooms decorated with a mix of
antique furnishings.

Sabina   €
Value   Map 2 F2
Rue du Nord 78, 1000
Tel *(02) 218 2637*
w hotelsabina.eu
No-frills hotel tucked away in a
quiet corner in the city centre.
Although some rooms are
small, the hotel is, nevertheless,
excellent value for money.

Exe Sablon   €€
Design   Map 2 D4
Rue de la Paille 2, 1000
Tel *(02) 513 6040*
w exesablonhotel.com
This is a friendly boutique hotel
with a sauna and relaxation
centre. Boasts large rooms with
split-level suites.

La Dixseptieme   €€
Historic   Map 2 D3
Rue de la Madeleine 25, 1000
Tel *(02) 517 1717*
w ledixseptieme.be
The former home of a 17th-
century Spanish ambassador.
All rooms are named after
famous Belgian artists and the
lounge has its own art library.

New Hotel Charlemagne   €€
Business   Map 3 B2
Blvd Charlemagne 25–27, 1000
Tel *(02) 230 2135*
w new-hotel.com
Located in the heart of the
European district, the rooms
at this hotel are modern and
comfortably furnished.

Stanhope   €€€
Luxury   Map 2 F4
Rue du Commerce 9, 1000
Tel *(02) 506 9111*
w stanhope.be
Deluxe Belgian hospitality in
three converted town houses.
Elegant rooms, beautiful interior
garden and gourmet restaurant.

The Hotel Brussels   €€€
Luxury   Map 2 E5
Blvd de Waterloo 38, 1000
Tel *(02) 504 1111*
w thehotel-brussels.be
Five-star hotel offering luxury
facilities and efficient service in
a central location. The lobby is
decorated with a frieze of the
Grand Place.

Greater Brussels

Alliance Hotel Brussels Expo €
Business
Av Imperatrice Charlotte 6, 1020
Tel *(02) 478 7080*
w alliance-hotel.brussels.com
Near the Brussels Exhibition
Centre, with a metro station
close by. Rooms are basic but
comfortable. Complimentary
breakfast and parking.

Best Western County House   €
Business
Square des Heros 2–4, 1180
Tel *(02) 375 4420*
w bestwestern.be
Spacious rooms in a peaceful
park-side location. Enjoy
complimentary buffet breakfast.
Meeting and conference centre.

Capital   €
Modern
Chaussée de Vleurgat 191, 1050 Ixelles
Tel *(02) 646 6420*
w hotelcapital.be
Well-fitted rooms, with more
luxurious suites also available.
In summer, enjoy breakfast
on the terrace.

Les Tourelles   €
Value
Winston Churchill Av 135, 1180
Tel *(02) 344 9573*
w lestourelles.be
A fantastically atmospheric hotel,
the three-star Les Tourelles has
an old-fashioned feel with stone
fireplaces and antique furnishings.

Key to Price Guide *see page 138*

Kasteel Gravenhof €€
Historic
Alsembergsesteenweg 676, 1653 Dworp
Tel *(02) 380 4499*
🅦 gravenhof.be
A stately castle hotel built in 1649 in the middle of a magnificent stretch of parkland. The rooms have all the period fittings and luxurious furnishings.

Monty €€
Design **Map** 4 F3
Brand Whitlock Blvd 101, 1200
Tel *(02) 734 5636*
🅦 monty-hotel.be
A design hotel boasting luxurious rooms, a colourful lounge, a bar and large private gardens. Breakfast is included.

Sofitel Le Louise €€€
Luxury **Map** 2 D5
Av de la Toison d'Or 40, 1050 Ixelles
Tel *(02) 514 2200*
🅦 sofitel.com
Rooms at the Sofitel Le Louise are modern and comfortable. Good dining options and fitness centre. Well-placed for exploring antique shops and museums.

Antwerp

Boulevard Leopold €
Value
Belgielei 135, 2018
Tel *(03) 225 5218*
🅦 boulevard-leopold.be
Housed in a beautiful mansion in the atmospheric Jewish Quarter, this hotel offers grandeur at good prices. High-ceiling rooms with large windows.

Postiljon €
Value **Map** K1
Blauwmoezelstraat 6, 2000
Tel *(03) 231 7575*
🅦 hotelpostiljon.be
Antwerp's best bargain hotel. The rooms are smart and comfortable; ask for one with a view of the cathedral. No breakfast.

Antwerp Hilton €€
Historic **Map** K2
Groenplaats, 2000
Tel *(03) 204 1212*
🅦 hilton.com
An architectural landmark, located behind a listed Baroque façade. Rooms are large and great value.

Firean €€
Luxury
Karel Oomsstraat 6, 2018
Tel *(03) 237 0260*
🅦 hotelfirean.com
A welcoming four-star hotel in an early-20th century Art Deco mansion. With crystal chandeliers in the lounge, antique furnishings and a secluded garden. Breakfast not included.

DK Choice

Antwerp: m0851 €€
Design **Map** K2
Nationalestraat 19, 2000
Tel *(049) 621 3264*
🅦 m0851.be
Directly opposite the ModeMuseum, this minimalist B&B is the work of a Canadian textile company who sell their gorgeous products in the shop next door. The large rooms are packed with simple luxuries and the stylish, modernist bathrooms alone are well worth the room rate.

t' Sandt €€
Historic **Map** K2
Zand 13–19, 2000
Tel *(03) 232 9390*
🅦 hotel-sandt.be
Occupies a protected Neo-Rococo building from the mid-19th century. The rooms and apartments feature unique decor.

De Witte Lelie €€€
Luxury **Map** L1
Keizerstraat 16–18, 2000
Tel *(03) 226 1966*
🅦 dewittelelie.be
Five-star B&B made up of three

converted 17th-century canal houses. Rooms have great city views and a mix of antique furnishings and modern facilities.

Bruges

Goezeput €
Historic **Map** N4
Goezeputstraat 29, 8000
Tel *(050) 34 26 94*
🅦 hotelgoezeput.be
A converted monastery offering amazing-value rooms, some featuring original wooden floors and roof beams.

Prinsenhof €€
Historic **Map** N3
Ontvangersstraat 9, 8000
Tel *(050) 34 26 90*
🅦 prinsenhof.com
Set amid lovely grounds, this 15th-century building offers a range of rather contemporary rooms. Excellent breakfasts.

de Orangerie €€€
Luxury **Map** P3
Kartuizerinnenstraat 10, 8000
Tel *(050) 34 16 49*
🅦 hotelorangerie.be
Waterfront hotel set in a 15th-century former convent. Superb rooms, and common areas boasting antiques galore.

Pand €€€
Design **Map** P3
Pandreitje 16, 8000
Tel *(050) 34 06 66*
🅦 pandhotel.com
An 18th-century mansion in the heart of Bruges, offering historic charm with lots of modern, designer touches.

Ghent

De Waterzooi €€
Value **Map** S1
Sint-Veerleplein, 9000
Tel *(09) 330 77 21*
🅦 dewaterzooi.be
There are only two rooms at this B&B, so book well in advance. Both are gorgeous, especially the spilt-level Phara suite.

Sandton Grand Hotel Reylof €€€
Luxury **Map** R1
Hoogstraat 36, 9000
Tel *(09) 235 40 70*
🅦 sandton.eu
Grand in every way. One of the few hotels in the city to boast a swimming pool. Elegant rooms, many with balconies offering fine views.

Softly lit room at De Waterzooi, Ghent

For more information on types of hotels *see page 137*

WHERE TO EAT AND DRINK

It is almost impossible to eat badly in Brussels. Some say one can eat better here than in Paris, and even meals in the lower- to mid-price bracket are always carefully prepared and often innovative. Venues range from top gastronomic restaurants to unpretentious local taverns where diners can find generous servings of local specialities such as *moules-frites* (mussels and French fries). For those who might tire of Belgian fare, try the variety of excellent local seafood and the range of ethnic cuisine that reflects the city's lively cultural diversity.

The well-lit Brasserie Horta in Centre Belge de la Bande Dessinée *(see p150)*

Where to Eat

The Belgian love affair with dining out makes for an astonishing concentration of restaurants and eateries: a 10-minute stroll from almost anywhere in Brussels should bring visitors to a decent, and often almost undiscovered, tavern or brasserie. However, superb dining can be had without leaving the Ilôt Sacré, the area around the central Grand Place, where many very good and surprisingly well-priced restaurants abound. Beware of the many tourist traps around the Grand Place that make their living from gulling unwary visitors into spending far more than they intended to. The bill for a seemingly cheap meal may soar once expensive drinks have been added. The impressive displays of seafood, allowed during winter, adorning the pavements of Rue des Bouchers northwest of the Grand Place and Petite Rue des Bouchers can promote rather touristy restaurants, but those on pages 150–52 are recommended.

Types of Cuisine

The city centre has a wealth of quality fish restaurants, especially around the former fish market at Place Ste-Catherine, while the city's trendiest eateries can be found on Rue Dansaert and in the Place Saint-Géry district. For those planning to explore other parts of Brussels, or staying outside the city centre, there is plenty of good Belgian fare on offer in the southern communes of Ixelles and Saint-Gilles, and in Etterbeek, where the European Commission buildings are located. Ixelles also boasts the largest concentration of Vietnamese and Southeast Asian restaurants, especially in the student area around Chaussée de Boondael. The Matonge district is also home to several African restaurants, serving food from the Congo, Senegal and Rwanda.

North of the city centre, in the communes of Schaerbeek and Saint-Josse, Turkish and North African communities have sprung up, and excellent Moroccan and Tunisian cuisine is commonplace. There is also a growing trend for "designer couscous", with Belgian restaurateurs exploiting the popularity of North African food in spectacularly ornate venues, often featuring ethnic music in the evenings.

Spanish and Portuguese restaurants can be found in the Marolles district and in Saint-Gilles, reflecting the wave of immigration in the 1950s and 1960s when many southern Europeans chose to settle in Brussels. The city is also liberally sprinkled with Greek restaurants, although many try too hard to attract tourists and may be off-putting. A better bet is the modern Latin American eateries.

Vegetarians

Despite a marked upturn in recent years, Brussels is far from being a vegetarian-friendly city. Those who eat fish will find mainstream restaurants cater generously to their needs; Brussels is very strong on fish and seafood. There are only a handful of specialist vegetarian restaurants, but the traditional dish, *stoemp,* is a classic

The contemporary interior of Lola, a fashionable Brussels brasserie *(see p153)*

Opulent Belle Epoque dining room of the Belga Queen *(see p151)*

is a classic vegetarian dish. North African restaurants usually offer vegetarian couscous courses, and there are plenty of Italian options. Indian restaurants are few and far between, but most offer vegetable curries. Vegans may struggle to find a filling meal, particularly in European restaurants. Some health food shops, however, have cafés serving vegan dishes.

How Much to Pay

Most restaurants, taverns and cafés display a menu in the window and the majority take credit cards. Prices usually include VAT (21 per cent) and service (16 per cent), although it is worth checking the latter before tipping. In tourist and shopping districts, visitors should also check that menu prices inside match those shown as special deals in the window.

A meal at the city's most luxurious restaurant can cost up to €150 per head, but diners can eat superbly for around €50 per head (including wine) and a hearty snack in a tavern should cost no more than €20. The mark-up level on wine can be very high, especially in Mediterranean restaurants and in areas frequented by tourists, but most taverns do a reasonable *vin maison* and serve myriad varieties of cheap beer.

Service in all but the most expensive restaurants can be erratic by British and American standards. But beneath the sometimes surly exterior, you

will often find warmth and a cheerfully self-deprecating sense of humour that is unique to Belgium. There are no hard and fast rules, but some diners leave an additional tip of up to 10 per cent if they are especially satisfied with the quality of the meal and the service. Note that some restaurants cannot take service on a credit card slip, and this, plus the tip, will have to be paid in cash, as do other gratuities in the city.

Dining on a Budget

Many restaurants offer bargain, fixed-price or rapid lunchtime menus for under €15, plus a selection of reasonably priced dishes of the day. Even when dining at the city's most upmarket eateries, you can find similar lunchtime deals, meaning you can sample haute cuisine for less than €39. In the evening, look out for set menus with *vin compris* (wine included), which are often a way to save a

significant part of the dining bill. If wine is not included, opting to have a beer or a single glass of wine rather than a bottle can keep the drinks cost down.

At the other end of the scale, Brussels has most of the usual fast-food outlets, and sandwiches are sold at most butchers or *traiteurs* (delicatessens), usually with tuna, cheese or cold meat fillings. Some of the latter offer sit-down snacks too. Alternatively, visitors can take advantage of Belgium's national dish, *frites/frieten* (French fries, hand-cut and double-fried to ensure an even crispiness). There are *friteries/frituurs* all over town, serving enormous portions of French fries, traditionally in a paper cone, with mayonnaise and dozens of other sauces, plus *fricadelles* (sausages in batter), lamb kebabs, fish cakes or meatballs. Inevitably, these establishments vary in quality; one sure bet is Maison Antoine on Place Jourdan in Etterbeek, where they have been frying for over half a century.

Most cafés and taverns offer petite restauration (light meals) on top of or instead of a regular menu. These simple, traditional snacks include croque mon- sieur, shrimp croquettes, chicory baked with ham and cheese, salads, spaghetti bolognaise and américain (raw minced beef with seasoning). Do not be fooled by the word "light" – most of these dishes will keep you going from lunchtime well into the evening.

Elegant place settings at the restaurant La Truffe Noire *(see p155)*

Outdoor tables at Chez Leon on Rue des Bouchers *(see p151)*

Making a Reservation

When visiting one of the more celebrated restaurants, it is recommendable to book in advance. The listings indicate where booking is advisable. For those planning to go to the legendary Comme Chez Soi *(see p152)*, reserve weeks ahead rather than hoping for a last-minute cancellation.

Reading the Menu

Menus at most restaurants are written in French, at times in Dutch as well. Some, especially in tourist areas, may have explanations in English. Dishes of the day or suggestions are often scribbled on blackboards. Fortunately, most waiters speak some English and should be able to help. For details of some of the most popular Belgian specialities, see pages 146–7. The phrasebook on pages 197–200 also has translations of many menu items.

Budget Food

Brussels is home to a sizeable Turkish community, which means that kebab, gyros and pitta restaurants are ubiquitous, especially in the busy Saint-Josse neighbourhood and on the gaudy Rue du Marché aux Fromages, just off the Grand Place. The nearby L'Express, a Lebanese takeaway specializing in chicken and felafel pittas, generously crammed with fresh salad, is perhaps a better option.

Ethnic food can work out at a very reasonable price; large portions of couscous, pizza and African specialities are often to be found at good rates in student areas to the south and at stands throughout the city. There are also numerous Indian and Chinese restaurants, which offer decent takeaway food at affordable prices.

Breakfast and Snacks

Especially good breakfasts – as well as inventive light lunches and snacks – with an emphasis on vegetarian dishes are the staple of L'Ultime Atome, a bustling brasserie situated in the St Boniface quarter of the city. Breakfasting in a café or brasserie, such as the Belgian chain, Le Pain Quotidien (Het Dagelijks Brood in Dutch), is recommended if breakfast is not included in your hotel accommodation. For snackers with a sweet tooth, waffle stands or vans appear on almost every street corner, while cafés and taverns offer a tempting variety of waffles,

which can be topped with jam, cream or chocolate. Sweet crêpes/pannekoeken (pancakes), with lemon and sugar or chocolate, are just as popular – and filling – although you can cut down on the number of calories with a savoury wholewheat pancake at one of the city's many crêperies.

Opening Times

Time-consuming business lunches are still part of the culture in Belgium and most restaurants serve lunch from noon until 2 or 3pm. Dinner is generally served from 7pm onwards and last orders are taken as late as 10pm. Late-night restaurants, serving until midnight, can be found in the side streets of downtown Brussels and a handful provide meals after 1am. Breakfast bars usually open around 7am.

Ordering Food

On the whole, Belgians like to eat beef fairly rare. If you ask for a medium-rare steak, it is likely to be cooked more rare than medium. The quality of the beef usually justifies light cooking, but if you want your meat well done, insist on it, and ignore any raised eyebrows. Lamb is also served rare; ask for it to be well done when you order. Use the phrasebook at the back of this guide to help when ordering.

The elegant dining room of La Rose Blanche in the Upper Town *(see p151)*

The 16th-century cellar of 't Kelderke in the Grand Place *(see p152)*

Etiquette

Brussels is less relaxed than, say, Amsterdam and, although casual or smart-casual dress is acceptable in all restaurants, you will probably feel more comfortable dressing up for upmarket places.

Pets

The Belgians are great dog lovers and many bars and cafés have a relaxed attitude to clients bringing their pets. Do not be suprised to see a dog sitting beneath the next table at a restaurant.

Children

In general, Brussels is kid-friendly. Many establishments have children's menus, although they are not always a bargain. Highchairs should be available on request, and some restaurants have indoor play areas, including some of the big hotels, where children are usually welcome. On the outskirts of Brussels or near one of the parks, eateries can offer extensive outside playgrounds. Ethnic restaurants, in particular Vietnamese, Greek and the less formal Italian ones, tend to be especially accommodating. They do not always have children's menus, but are happy for adults to share their meal with youngsters. Children are usually allowed in cafés and bars, although they are forbidden to drink alcohol. Note that while some restaurants may be too formal for children to feel comfortable, not even the most celebrated Michelin-starred places will turn them away.

Smoking

Brussels is still very much a smokers' city, although smoking is prohibited inside restaurants, bars and cafés. Many bars and restaurants provide their customers with heated outdoor terraces where smoking is permitted. It is important, therefore, to make sure to enquire beforehand about smoking arrangements when reserving, or before you take a seat. Smokers should know that most restaurants and cafés do not sell cigarettes.

Travellers with Disabilities

While facilities for the disabled in Brussels are in general not as good as those in most other EU capitals, almost every restaurant in the city will go out of its way to make disabled diners feel comfortable. There are a limited number of restaurants with ramps and ground-floor bathrooms, so check the extent of the access before making a reservation.

Recommended Restaurants

The restaurants featured in this guide have been selected for their good food, value, location, atmosphere or a combination of these. As wide a range as possible of Brussels' dining scene has been included, from cafés, pubs and bistros to a large selection of the city's Michelin-starred restaurants.

Look out for the DK Choice symbol: these restaurants have been highlighted in recognition of an exceptional feature – exquisite food, an inviting atmosphere, an unusual setting or simply great value. The majority of these are exceptionally popular among local residents as well as visitors, so be sure to enquire regarding reservations or you may be faced with a lengthy wait for a table.

Art Nouveau interior of Comme Chez Soi *(see p152)*

The Flavours of Brussels

Most Belgians are passionate about food and standards are generally very high. The many first-class grocers, greengrocers, butchers, fishmongers, bakers and pâtissiers, including Belgium's noted chocolatiers, are held in high public esteem, alongside the nation's top chefs and restaurateurs. In Brussels, the culinary heart of the country, there are a wide range of fine eateries to suit all budgets, serving both sophisticated Walloon (Belgian-French) dishes alongside more basic, hearty Flemish fare. A history of invasion has also added a dash of other European culinary traditions, particularly those of Spain and Austria.

Belgian chocolates

Bunches of white asparagus, some of Belgium's finest produce

The North Sea

Brussels, being only 100 km (62 miles) from the North Sea, has a good supply of really fresh fish and seafood. In Place Sainte-Catherine, just to the west of the Grand Place, there used to be a bustling fish market and the area remains a centre for fish restaurants. The best sole, cod, turbot, skate, hake and monkfish, simply

grilled or fried in butter, or swathed in a well-judged sauce, are always on the menu, along with huge platters of *fruits de mer* (mixed seafood).

A uniquely Belgian fish dish that is well worth seeking out is *anguilles au vert* (*paling in't groen*), which consists of large chunks of eel, cooked with a mass of finely chopped, fresh herbs.

Pasture and Woodland

The flat, reclaimed land of northern Belgium and the hills of the south are home to herds of cattle. Quality beef is the stock-in-trade of any Belgian butcher, and *steak-frites* (steak and chips) is a classic dish on bistro menus. Belgians are so confident in their beef that they are happy to eat it raw: minced in *steak à l'américaine*

Cockles · Oysters · Lobster · Langoustine · Whelks

Selection of fine quality North-Sea seafood

Local Dishes and Specialities

Although Belgian chefs produce some of the world's most complex and sophisticated cooking, many of Belgium's great classic dishes are relatively simple, striking a healthy balance between nourishment and pleasure. Fine examples include steaming platefuls of *moules-frites* and warming stews such as *carbonnade flamandes* and *waterzooï* (which is made with either fish or chicken), all dishes that might well be labelled as "comfort" food. Endives However, the quality of the ingredients and the skill put into the making of such dishes in Belgium invariably turns such homely fare into a feast. Desserts include a host of sweet tarts and the ever-popular waffles. Endive, almost the national vegetable, gets in here too, as a flavouring for ice cream.

Moules-frites Mussels, steamed in their own juices with onion and white wine, are served with chips and mayonnaise.

Fish restaurant in the elegant Galéries St-Hubert shopping arcade

(or *steak tartare*) and on toast as the snack, *toast cannibale*. Dairy cattle are the source of fine cheeses, such as Herve, Chimay and Maredsous.

Pork products include a range of sausages, patés and the noted Ardennes ham. In autumn and winter, look out for game, such as wild boar, pheasant and venison, often served in a rich fruity sauce. Quail, guinea fowl, pigeon and rabbit are also popular.

The Vegetable Patch

Not long ago, most Belgian householders toiled to fill their gardens with tightly-packed rows of top-class vegetables – beans, leeks, lettuces, carrots, potatoes and onions. This tradition may be waning, but the same quest for quality lives on in commercial market-gardens. In the 1840s, Belgian gardeners created *chicon* (*witloof*) by forcing the roots of the chicorée lettuce. It is now one of Belgium's most widely used vegetables, although the most popular must be the potato, in the form of chips (French fries). *Frites* (*frietjes*),

Freshly made waffles on a street stall, a familiar sight in the city

served with a dollop of mayonnaise, are a favourite street-food.

The Pâtissier

No Belgian community is without a pâtisserie, selling superlative tarts, cakes and biscuits, and many pâtissiers double-up as chocolatiers. *Gaufres* (waffles) are another great sweet treat, sold at specialist shops and street stalls. Enjoyed freshly made, topped with knobs of butter and a sprinkling of sugar, they may be raised to perfection with spoonfuls of jam or fruit and fresh cream.

ON THE MENU

White asparagus An early summer speciality, it is usually served with melted butter or hard-boiled egg and parsley.

Jets d'houblon Spring menus feature this dish of young hop shoots in a creamy sauce.

Crevettes grises Tiny but big on flavour, these "grey" shrimps are a popular snack.

Stoemp Mashed potato, with flecks of vegetables or meat, make up this pub favourite.

Garnaalkroketten Deep-fried croquettes, filled with shrimp.

Speculoos These buttery, spicy biscuits are available in festive shapes for Christmas.

Carbonnade flamande Beef is cooked in Belgian beer, with a touch of sugar, to make this hearty casserole.

Waterzooî This classic stew from Ghent consists of fish or chicken and vegetables, poached in a creamy broth.

Flamiche aux Poireaux Leeks, fried in butter and whisked with cream and eggs, are baked in a crisp pastry shell.

Belgian Beer

Belgium makes more beers, in a greater mix of styles and flavours, than any other country in the world. The Belgian citizen drinks on average 100 litres (200 pints) a year, and even small bars will stock at least 20 varieties. The nation's breweries produce over 400 different beers.

The cheerful peasants in Brueghel the Elder's 16th-century medieval village scenes would have been drinking beer from their local brewery, many of which had been active since the 11th century, as every small town and community produced its own beer. By 1900, there remained 3,000 private breweries throughout Belgium. Today, more than 100 still operate, with experts agreeing that even large industrial concerns produce a fine quality beer.

Detail from *The Wedding Dance* by Pieter Brueghel the Elder

Chimay label with authentic Trappist mark

Label for Westmalle Trappist beer

Trappist Beers

The most revered of refreshments, Belgium's Trappist beers have been highly rated since the Middle Ages when monks began brewing them. The drink originated in Roman times when Belgium was a province of Gaul, Gallia Belgica. Beer was a private domestic product until the monasteries took over and introduced hops to the process. Today's production is still controlled solely by the five Trappist monasteries, although the brewers are mostly laymen. Trappist beers are characterized by their rich, yeasty flavour. They are very strong, ranging from 6.2 to 11 per cent in alcohol content by volume. The most celebrated of the 20 brands is Chimay, brewed at Belgium's largest monastic brewery in Hainaut. This delicate but potent bottled beer has three different strengths, and is best kept for many years before drinking. The strongest Trappist beer is Westvleteren, from Ypres.

Chimay served in its correct glass

Lambic Beers

Made for centuries in the Senne Valley around Brussels, the unique family of lambic beers are made using yeasts naturally present in the air to ferment the beer, rather than being added separately to the water and grain mix. Containers of unfermented wort (water, wheat and barley) are left under a half-open roof in the brewery and wild airborne yeasts, only present in the atmosphere of this region of Belgium, descend to ferment it. Unlike the sterility of many breweries and officially exempt from EU hygiene regulations, lambic cellars are deliberately left dusty and uncleaned in order for the necessary fungal activity to thrive. Matured in untreated wooden casks for up to five years, the lambic is deliciously sour to drink, with a moderate strength of 5 per cent alcohol.

Young and old lambic beers are blended together to produce the variant of gueuze. A tiny bead, distinctive champagne mousse and a toasty, slightly acid flavour, are its main characteristics. Bars and restaurants lay down their gueuze for up to two years before it is drunk.

Lambic cherry beer

Brewer sampling beer from the vat at a brewery outside Brussels

Speciality Belgian Beers

Duvel

Chimay

Brugse Tripel

De Verboden Vrucht

Kwak

Speciality beers are common in Belgium, where the huge variety of brands includes unusual tastes and flavours. Fruit beers are a Brussels speciality but are available throughout the country. The most popular, kriek, is traditionally made with bitter cherries grown in the Brussels suburb of Schaerbeek; picked annually, these are added to the lambic and allowed to macerate, or steep. The distinctive almond tang comes from the cherry stone. Raspberries are also used to make a framboise beer, or frambozen.

For a characterful amber ale, Kwak is good choice. Strong beers are also popular; apart from the Trappist beers, of which Chimay is a popular variety, the pilseners De Verboden Vrucht (meaning "forbidden fruit") and Duvel ("devil") are almost as strong as red wine. Brugse Tripel, from Bruges, is also popular. Even Belgium's best-sellers, Jupiler and Stella Artois, are good quality beers.

Fruit beer mat of Chapeau brewery

The façade of a beer emporium in Brussels

Blanche Beers

Hoegaarden

Belgium's refreshing wheat beers are known as "blanche", or white beers, because of the cloudy sediment that forms when they ferment. Sour, crisp and light, they are relatively low in alcohol at 5 per cent. Blanche is produced in the western region of Hoegaarden, after which the best-known blanche is named. Many people now serve them with a slice of lemon to add to the refreshing taste, especially on warm summer evenings.

How to Drink Belgian Beer

There are no snobbish distinctions made in Belgium between bottled and casked beer. Some of the most prestigious brews are served in bottles, and, as with casks, bottles are often laid down to mature. The choice of drinking glass, however, is a vital part of the beer-drinking ritual. Many beers must be drunk in a particular glass, which the barman will supply, ranging from goblets to long thin drinking tubes. Beers are often served with a complimentary snack; cream cheese on rye bread and radishes are a popular accompaniment.

The traditional drinkers' snack of *fromage blanc* on rye bread

Where to Eat and Drink

Brussels

Lower Town

A la Mort Subite €
Café **Map** 2 D2
Rue Montagne aux Herbes Potagères 7, 1000
Tel *(02) 513 1318*
The cavernous former haunt of Brussels' favourite son, Jacques Brel, and the origin of the Mort Subite brand, A La Mort Subite is an Art Deco wonder. Good sandwiches, salads and omelettes.

Arcadi €
Café **Map** 2 D2
Rue d'Arenberg 1B, 1000
Tel *(02) 511 3343*
Producing arguably the best quiches in a city that has some outstanding quiche-making outlets, Arcadi is perhaps best known for the salmon and broccoli variety. Has great cakes too.

Bar Bik €
Franco-Belgian **Map** 1 C1
Quai aux Pierre de Taille, 1000
Tel *(02) 219 75 00*
Good-value food in an area that has become a trendy hot spot. The menu has lots of seafood and also offers a good range of vegetarian dishes.

Bonsoir Clara €
Modern European **Map** 1 C2
Rue Antoine Dansaert 22, 1000
Tel *(02) 502 0990* **Closed** *Sat & Sun: lunch*
One of the prettiest restaurants in town, Clara is high on style and often bustling with the city's fashionable crowd. Find a range of European favorites, including many Mediterranean specials.

Brasserie Horta €
Belgian **Map** 2 E2
Rue des Sables 20, 1000
Tel *(02) 217 7271*
This brasserie doubles as the caféteria in the lobby of the Centre Belge de Bande Desinée. Excellent Belgian cuisine at an affordable price. The building is a spectacular example of Art Nouveau architecture.

Café Métropole €
Bar-Restaurant **Map** 2 D2
Place de Brouckère 31, 1000
Tel *(02) 214 2627*
Located at the Hotel Métropole, this slightly pricey café has a beautiful *belle-époque* interior and an enormous terrace. Open daily until 1am.

Comocomo €
Tapas **Map** 1 C2
Rue Antoine Dansaert 19, 1000
Tel *(02) 503 0330*
Comocomo combines a Basque tapas restaurant with a sushi bar-style conveyor belt. Pick out generously portioned *pintxos* as they slowly pass by.

De Noordzee - La Mer du Nord €
Seafood **Map** 1 C2
Rue St Catherine 45
Tel *(02) 513 1192*
Hugely popular fishbar selling delicious seafood, which you can eat with a glass of white wine at one of the stand-up tables on the square.

De Skieven Architek €
Café **Map** 1 C5
Place du Jeu de Balle 50, 1000
Tel *(02) 514 43 69*
The architect in question is Joseph Poelaert, who designed the nearby Palais de Justice.

Price Guide
Prices are based on a three-course meal for one, including half a bottle of house wine, tax and service.

€	up to €50
€€	€50 to 75
€€€	over €75

Enjoy tasty Belgian food and beer from a lengthy list in this café's relaxed interiors.

Delirium €
Bar **Map** 2 D3
Impasse de La Fidélité 4A, 1000
Tel *(02) 514 4434*
Beautifully decorated, subterranean tourist magnet with over 2,000 types of beers to be enjoyed with a selection of meats or cheeses.

Den Teepot €
Vegetarian **Map** 1 B2
Rue des Chartreux 66, 1000
Tel *(02) 511 9402* **Closed** *Sun*
One of the best vegetarian options in the city located above its sister health-food shop. Many of the dishes on its lunch-only menu feature beans and pulses.

Gecko €
Café **Map** 1 C2
Place St Gery 16, 1000
Tel *(02) 502 2999*
Gecko combines a relaxed atmosphere with charming service. Its reasonably priced menu offers hot sandwiches, quiche, lasagne and *waterzooi*.

Het Warm Water €
Café **Map** 1 C5
Rue des Renards 25, 1000
Tel *(02) 513 9159.* **Closed** *Mon–Wed*
A pleasant little Flemish café on the narrow Rue des Renards. A great spot to relax with some cake and a glass of *gueuze*.

Kafka €
Café **Map** 1 C2
Rue des Poissonniers 21
Tel *(02) 513 5489*
Mellow, unpretentious spot, with an amazing range of vodkas, *genevers* (Dutch gin) and other spirits alongside coffee, beer and substantial portions of finger-food.

Le Cirio €
Café **Map** 1 C2
Rue de la Bourse 18–20, 1000
Tel *(02) 512 1395*
In the shadow of La Bourse, the interior of Le Cirio is a marvel of Art Nouveau ostentatiousness. Simple dishes on offer include pasta and *waterzooi*.

Well-stocked bar at the opulently decorated Café Métropole

Le Pain Quotidien €
Café **Map** 1 C2
Rue Antoine Dansaert 16A, 1000
Tel *(02) 502 2361*
Famed for its large communal tables and the best croissants and *pain au chocolat* in Brussels. A great choice for its delicious and inventive lunchtime salads.

Le Roy d'Espagne €
Café **Map** 2 D3
Grand Place 1, 1000
Tel *(02) 513 0807*
A drink on the Grand Place is an essential part of any visit to Brussels. Le Roy d'Espagne is one of the best priced places with a huge two-tiered bar housed in the bakers' guild house. On the food menu are several appetizers, salads and Belgian dishes.

Neatly arranged tables in Belga Queen

DK Choice

Nüetnigenouth €
Belgian **Map** 1 C3
Rue du Lombard 25, 1000
Tel *(02) 513 7884*
A *nuëtnigenough*, in local dialect, means a person who can never have enough. This brasserie is successful in offering more than enough in terms of food choice, quality, prices and service. The focus is on Belgian classics, modernized and made using the freshest seasonal produce. Daily specials are written on the chalkboard, and there is a list of 40 exemplary beers.

Pin Pon €
Belgian **Map** 1 C5
Place du Jeu de Balle 62, 1000
Tel *(02) 540 8999* **Closed** *Mon–Tue*
Located in a former fire station overlooking the lively Jeu de Balle, this smart but easy-going restaurant offers modernized-classic Belgian cuisine.

Plattesteen €
Café **Map** 1 C3
Rue du Marché au Charbon 41, 1000
Tel *(02) 512 8203*
A chilled-out microcosm of the trendiest area of the city centre, with a decent menu offering Belgian classics, a good range of beers and a great atmosphere during the day and at night.

Belga Queen €€
Belgian **Map** 2 D2
Rue Fossé aux Loups 32, 1000
Tel *(02) 217 2187*
The chic Belga Queen is located in the former Hôtel de la Poste, a cavernous *belle-époque* bank. Special beer and tasting menu.

Big Mama €€
International **Map** 1 C2
Place de la Vieille Halle aux Blés 41, 1000
Tel *(02) 513 3659*
Warm and cosy eatery, where children are well catered for with their own menu. The four-course set menu, including an aperitif, changes often and is great value.

Chez Leon €€
Belgian **Map** 2 D2
Rue des Bouchers 18, 1000
Tel *(02) 511 1415*
Founded in 1893, this place is a stalwart of traditional Belgian culinary standards. There are several versions of the classic *moules et frites* to choose from. The children's menu is excellent and free for children under 12.

Chez Patrick €€
Belgian **Map** 2 D3
Rue des Chapeliers 6, 1000
Tel *(02) 511 9815*
Warm and inviting, Chéz Patrick is a great place for sampling traditional Belgian cuisine in a relaxed setting. The hearty lunchtime *plats du jour* are always excellent value.

Falstaff €€
Café **Map** 1 C3
Rue Henri Maus 19, 1000
Tel *(02) 511 8789*
With its Art Nouveau interior and Neo-Classical detailing, the Falstaff is something of a Brussels institution. Excellent food, ranging from omelettes to steaks.

In 't Spinnekopke €€
Belgian **Map** 1 B2
Place du Jardin aux Fleurs 1, 1000
Tel *(02) 511 8695* **Closed** *Sun*
Intimate, former 18th-century coaching inn, "In the Spider's Head" has a strong range of unusual local brews and food items that are cooked in these brews.

La Belle Maraichere €€
Belgian **Map** 1 C2
Place Ste-Catherine 11, 1000
Tel *(02) 512 97 59* **Closed** *Wed & Thu*
A fine restaurant which proves that good food does not have to break the bank. Two set menus offer terrific choice and value. Dine in a warm, bistro-like atmosphere.

La Cantina €€
South American **Map** 1 C3
Rue du Jardin des Olives 13–15, 1000
Tel *(02) 513 4276* **Closed** *Sun*
Customers to La Cantina come for the *feijoada*, the rather heavy Brazilian national dish of rice, red beans, pork, smoked bacon and spicy sausages.

La Kasbah €€
Moroccan **Map** 1 C2
Rue Antoine Dansaert 20, 1000
Tel *(02) 502 4026*
Sample North African food in a dark interior decked out with ethnic knick-knacks. The attentive service and decent Moroccan wines ensure that it is always busy, but it remains intimate.

La Manufacture €€
French **Map** 1 B2
Rue Notre-Dame du Sommeil 12, 1000
Tel *(02) 502 2525*
Formerly a printer's workshop and leather factory, this is now a very 21st-century dining establishment complete with polished wood and iron pillars.

La Rose Blanche €€
Belgian **Map** 2 D3
Grand Place 11, 1000
Tel *(02) 513 6479*
Founded in 1905, this authentic brasserie on the Grand Place serves delicious traditional Belgian dishes, with many of the specialities cooked in beer – try the duck cooked in *kriek*.

For more information on types of restaurants *see page 145*

Contemporary interiors of Strofilia

Le Cap
€€
Belgian   **Map** 1 C3
Place de la Vieille Halle aux Blés 28, 1000
Tel *(02) 512 9342*
A popular local meeting place; look out for the daily specials alongside a good selection of Old and New World wines, all at decent prices.

Le Greenwich
€€
Café   **Map** 1 C2
Rue des Chartreux 7, 1000
Tel *(02) 540 8878*
An Art Nouveau gem, Le Greenwich was once a favourite of René Magritte, and has retained its charm. A good choice for a quiet beer.

L'HPO
€€
French   **Map** 1 C2
Place Ste-Catherine 1, 1000
Tel *(02) 511 6221*   **Closed** *Sun & Mon*
Small, family-run tavern that features contemporary decor. Serves fresh seasonal food, including oysters. Good-value set menus.

Le Paon Royal
€€
Belgian   **Map** 1 C2
Rue du Vieux Marché-aux-grains 6, 1000
Tel *(02) 513 0868*
Enjoy scrumptious traditional Belgian cuisine in a 17th-century house. Loyal customers roll in especially for the veal and the superb beer list.

Mappa Mundo
€€
Café   **Map** 1 C2
Rue du Pont de la Carpe 2–6, 1000
Tel *(02) 514 3555*
This Latin-flavoured hang-out is arguably the best café, with the best terrace, in St Géry. It has its bars spread over three floors and the seating booths are actually old wooden train seats.

O Bifanas
€€
Portuguese   **Map** 2 D2
Rue des Dominicains 30, 1000
Tel *(02) 502 2548*
The good-value O Bifanas serves a cheerful representation of the cuisine of the city's large Portuguese community. Fish is the order of the day; above all, the *bacalhau* (salt cod).

Strofilia
€€
Greek   **Map** 1 C1
Rue du Marché aux Porcs 11–13, 1000
Tel *(02) 512 3293*
Amid candlelight and brick walls, try the Strofilia salad, which includes spinach, capers, scampi and calamari. Mains include aubergine minced-meat roulade and suckling pig.

't Kelderke
€€
Belgian   **Map** 2 D3
Grand Place 15, 1000
Tel *(02) 513 7344*   **Closed** *Sun*
In a vaulted 17th-century cellar on the Grand Place, *moules frites* are served in their traditional, huge black pails at a fast and furious pace.

Alexandre
€€€
French   **Map** 1 C4
Rue du Midi 164, 1000
Tel *(02) 502 40 55*
Savour superbly inventive seasonal French cuisine in a refined atmosphere. Though expensive, the three-course set menu is excellent value. There are only a few tables, so reserve well in advance.

Aux Armes de Bruxelles
€€€
Seafood   **Map** 2 D2
Rue des Bouchers 13, 1000
Tel *(02) 511 5550*
Aux Armes de Bruxelles was a favourite haunt of Brussels' most famous chanteur, Jacques Brel. The lobster and mussels are the top recommendations.

Comme Chez Soi
€€€
Fine Dining   **Map** 1 C4
Place Rouppe 23, 1000
Tel *(02) 512 2921*   **Closed** *Sun & Mon*
Possibly the city's best restaurant, Comme Chez Soi is run by Chef Lionel Rigolet and boasts two Michelin stars. It features a mahogany bar, a bookcase and over-stuffed leather couches in the lounge area. Absolutely delicious food, but the menu changes often, though seafood usually features. The dessert trilogy is unmissable. Book well in advance.

Jaloa
€€€
Modern European   **Map** 1 C2
Place Ste-Catherine 5–7, 1000
Tel *(02) 512 1831*
Located in an 18th-century house once inhabited by Vincent van Gogh. Serves European cuisine, with both à la carte and set menu.

L'Idiot du Village
€€€
Modern European   **Map** 1 C4
Rue Notre-Seigneur 19, 1000
Tel *(02) 502 5582*   **Closed** *Sat & Sun*
"The Village Idiot"- a favoured establishment of the Belgian royalty – offers such intriguing concoctions as the escalope of hot *foie gras*, pepper and vanilla.

L'Ogenblik
€€€
French   **Map** 2 D2
Galeries des Princes 1, 1000
Tel *(02) 511 6151*   **Closed** *Sun*
This Parisian-style bistro with a relaxed ambience is a gastronomic wonder. Dishes such as salmon and crayfish cake, or carpaccio of scallops stand out. Lovely desserts.

Sea Grill
€€€
Seafood   **Map** 2 D2
Rue Fosse aux Loups 47, 1000
Tel *(02) 212 0800*   **Closed** *Sat & Sun*
Located at the Radisson Blu Hotel, a superb two Michelin-starred fish restaurant with good-value set menus, particularly at lunchtime. Great wine list too.

Bouillabaisse (fish stew) served in a bowl at an eatery in Brussels

Vincent
€€€
Seafood **Map** 2 D2
Rue des Dominicains 8–10, 1000
Tel *(02) 511 2607* **Closed** *Jan 1–15 & Aug 1–15*
Seafood restaurant featuring dark-wood panelling and sea-themed murals. Turbot served in a mousseline sauce - a must try.

Vismet
€€€
Seafood **Map** 1 C2
Place Sainte-Catherine 23, 1000
Tel *(02) 218 8545* **Closed** *Sun & Mon*
Vismet boasts a big open kitchen in which fine seafood, and much more, is prepared. Popular with both locals and travellers, so reserve well in advance.

Upper Town

Bier Circus
€
Belgian **Map** 2 D3
Rue de l'Enseignement 57, 1000
Tel *(02) 218 0034*
While it serves wholesome Belgian dishes, the real draw is the beer menu, one of the most extensive in the country.

Comics Café
€
Belgian **Map** 2 D4
Place du Grand Sablon 8, 1000
Tel *(02) 513 1323*
A bande *dessinée*-themed restaurant on the Sablon serving Belgo-American cuisine, where burgers and bagels rub shoulders on the menu with carbonnade and *chicon au gratin*.

L'Entree des Artistes
€
Franco-Belgian **Map** 2 D4
Place du Grand Sablon 42, 1000
Tel *(02) 502 3161*
Good selection of classic dishes, including a fine house steak tartare and *chicons au gratin*. Great option for late night snacks, as they stay open till midnight.

Les Larmes du Tigre
€
Thai **Map** 1 C5
Rue de Wynants 21, 1000
Tel *(02) 512 1877* **Closed** *Mon & Sat*
One of the city's best Asian restaurants. The peaceful, elegant ambience is in marked contrast to the rather explosive variety of flavours found in the dishes.

Restobieres
€
Belgian **Map** 1 C5
Rue des Renards 9
Tel *(02) 511 5583*
When even the vinaigrette for the Abbey cheese salad is made from beer, you know you're in for a true Belgian culinary experience. Well worth a visit for its warm

atmosphere and remarkable range of dishes cooked in Belgium's favourite tipple.

Tutto Bene
€
Italian **Map** 2 D4
Rue Joseph Stevens 28, 1000
Tel *(02) 512 4095* **Closed** *Tue & Wed*
In a rustic interior, accompanied with contemporary music and jazz, a friendly Italian family serves a regularly changing menu of simple Italian staples.

Au Vieux Saint-Marten
€€
Modern European **Map** 2 D4
Place du Grand Sablon 38, 1000
Tel *(02) 512 6476*
A great modernist eatery on the Sablon serving delicious Euro fare. Also serves as a gallery for contemporary painters, a number of whose works hang on the walls.

Havana
€€
Cuban **Map** 1 C5
Rue de l'Epée 4, 1000
Tel *(02) 502 1224* **Closed** *Sun–Wed*
For dinner and dancing with a Latin flavour, take the outside lift that descends from Avenue Louise to Marolles and head to Havana, one of the city's more colourful establishments.

JB
€€
Franco-Belgian **Map** 2 D5
Rue du Grand Cerf 24, 1000
Tel *(02) 512 04 84*
Given the food, the value for money is outsanding. Small, intimate space, with an open kitchen provides a nice touch.

L'Atelier Europeen
€€
Franco-Belgian **Map** 3 C2
Rue Franklin 28, 1000
Tel *(02) 734 9140*
This legendary eatery boasts large dining rooms and the highlights of its Belgian-inflected French cuisine include the veal

Colourful decor at Kwint in the Upper Town

escalope with Roquefort butter. Open on weekends only by prior group reservation.

Le Cap Sablon
€€
Belgian **Map** 3 D4
Rue Lebeau 75, 1000
Tel *(02) 512 0170*
A cosy bistro just off the Grand Sablon, serving imaginative Franco-Belgian cuisine at a reasonable price.

Lola
€€
Fusion **Map** 2 D4
Place du Grand Sablon 33, 1000
Tel *(02) 514 2460*
A contemporary setting where diners can expect to find only the best seasonal ingredients on a changing menu of healthy, light fusion dishes.

Orphyse Chaussette
€€
Belgian **Map** 2 D4
Rue Charles Hanssens, 5, 1000
Tel *(02) 502 7581* **Closed** *Sun & Mon*
The chef at Orphyse Chaussette uses only seasonal, regional produce, although the menu always carries the Chaussette's most popular dish – the red tuna tartare. Good wine list.

Wine Bar Sablon
€€
French **Map** 1 C5
Rue Haute 198, 1000
Tel *0496 820105*
Great food in a more relaxed, less formal atmosphere than many places in Brussels. Offers a bistro menu which changes regularly.

Kwint
€€€
Belgian **Map** 2 D3
Mont des Arts 1, 1000
Tel *(02) 505 9595* **Closed** *Sun*
Designed by leading Belgian conceptual artist Arne Quinze, the dazzling Kwint serves food with delicious flavours added to traditional Belgian cuisine.

Classy decor at L'Entree des Artistes, a Franco-Belgian eatery

For more information on types of restaurants *see page 145*

Diners at L'Ultime Atome in Greater Brussels

La Tortue du Sablon €€€
Seafood **Map** 2 D4
Rue de Rollebeek 31, 1000
Tel *(02) 513 1062*
The menu at the Tortue is solidly based around lobster, but there are plenty of other seafood treats too. Go for one of the alfresco tables in the summer.

L'Ecailler du Palais Royal €€€
Seafood **Map** 2 D4
Rue Bodenbroek 18, 1000
Tel *(02) 512 8751* **Closed** *Sun, Aug*
L'Ecailler du Palais Royal is housed in a 17th-century mansion. The menu is dominated by fish and seafood dishes. It is particularly strong on the range and quality of its oysters.

Les Petits Oignons €€€
Franco-Belgian **Map** 2 D4
Rue de la Régence 25, 1000
Tel *(02) 511 7615* **Closed** *Sun*
The family-friendly Les Petits Oignons offers up French and Belgian brasserie-style cuisine. The fried goose liver with caramelized onions is a must-try.

L'Esprit de Sel Brasserie €€€
Belgian **Map** 3 B4
Place Jourdan 52–54, 1000
Tel *(02) 230 6040*
The beef on offer here, stewed in Belgian beer, is perfectly complemented by the soft wood and velvet decor. Pair the meal with one of the many beers or wines on the menu.

L'Estrille du Vieux Bruxelles €€€
Belgian **Map** 2 D4
Rue de Rollebeek 7, 1000
Tel *(02) 512 5857* **Closed** *Wed*
The old establishment of L'Estrille du Vieux Bruxelles has something of a venerable literary pedigree: La Tribune Poétique once held their meetings here. The eatery specializes in traditional, beer-soaked Belgian cuisine.

Greater Brussels

Café Belga €
Café
Place Flagey 18, 1050 Ixelles
Tel *(02) 640 3508*
Café Belga is located in an Art Deco building complex and has a bohemian feel. Serves a decent range of light meals alongside great coffee.

Café des Spores €
Belgian
Chaussée d'Alsemberg 103, 1060 Saint-Gilles
Tel *(02) 534 13 03* **Closed** *Sun*
With the entire cuisine based around different kinds of mushrooms, including unique desserts, Café des Spores is an excellent and quirky dining option. Also has an exciting wine list.

La Buvette €
Wine Bar
Chaussée d'Alsemberg 108, 1060 Saint-Gilles
Tel *(02) 534 1303*
Opposite Café des Spores lies its twin wine bar, La Buvette. The focus here is on the quality wine list, but the rustic dishes on offer are more than generous.

La Fin de Siecle €
Belgian
Rue des Chartreux 9, 1000
Tel *(02) 512 5123* **Closed** *Sun*
Located in a side street near the Bourse, this cosy Belgian restaurant in a 19th-century building offers generous portions of traditional dishes. Friendly service and lovely atmosphere.

Le Rubis €
Cambodian **Map** 4 E4
Av de Tervueren 22, 1040 Etterbeek
Tel *(02) 733 05 49* **Closed** *Sun*
Quite simply, a real find. On tables set among an eye-catching collection of Khmer art, adventurous diners get to try lightly spiced, aromatic Cambodian dishes.

L'Ultime Atome €
Belgian
Rue St Boniface 14, 1050 Ixelles
Tel *(02) 513 48 84*
This cavernous, bustling and noisy, brasserie has a good range of vegetarian options, and serves fantastic crêpes for breakfast.

Mille-et-une Nuits €
North African
Rue de Moscou 7, 1060 Saint-Gilles
Tel *(02) 537 4127* **Closed** *Mon & Lunchtimes*
This undiscovered gem – decorated to give the impression of the inside of a Bedouin tent – lies hidden away in bohemian St Gilles. Delicious North African food at reasonable prices. The service is cordial.

Musical Instruments Museum Restaurant €
Belgian **Map** 2 E4
Rue Montagne de la Cour 2, 1000
Tel *02) 502 9508* **Closed** *Mon*
Located on the top floor of the museum, this restaurant affords superb views of the city. The menu offers Belgian cuisine and a Sunday brunch that is famed throughout the city.

Tout Près Tout Prêt €
Sandwiches
Chaussée de Boondael 413, 1050
Tel *(02) 640 8080* **Closed** *Sun*
Between the twin universities Université Libre de Bruxelles and Vrije Universiteit Brussel, this cheap, no-frills sandwich bar offers quick, inventive snacks to a largely student crowd.

Bon-Bon €€
Fine Dining
Av de Tervueren 453, 1150
Tel *(02) 346 66 15* **Closed** *Sat & Sun*
With two Michelin stars, Bon-Bon serves food at prices a bit lower than some of the other resturants with that honour in Brussels. The wines on offer are as good as the scrumptious food.

Brasserie Georges €€
French
Av Churchill 259, 1180
Tel *(02) 347 2100*
Gorgeous Parisian-style seafood brasserie with numerous waiters in floor-length aprons and a conspicuous shellfish stall at the front doors.

Brasserie La Paix €€
Belgian
Rue Ropsy Chaudron 49, 1070
Tel *(02) 523 09 58* **Closed** *Sat & Sun*
A family-run eatery that has been serving up Belgian classics for more than three decades. Terrific

food with something for all tastes and budgets – despite the Michelin star.

Bruneaux €€
Modern European
Av Broustin 73, 1083
Tel *(02) 421 70 70* **Closed** *Tue & Wed*
With a choice of set menus (three or five courses), there is something for everyone at this creative, Michelin-starred restaurant.

La Terrasse €€
Belgian/International **Map** 4 E4
Av des Celtes 1, 1040
Tel *(02) 732 2851*
A lovely old brasserie, where European Union journalists, MEPs and Commission *fonctionnaires* sit cheek by jowl while munching on huge plates of *steak americain* and sipping delicious beers.

Le Fils de Jules €€
Basque
Rue du Page 35, 1050 Ixelles
Tel *(02) 534 0057* **Closed** *for Lunch Mon-Sat*
Art-Deco Basque bistro popular for its tartare of tuna, spicy squid and the rest of the menu's resolutely Basque repertoire.

Le Loup Voyant €€
International
Av de la Couronne 562, 1050 Ixelles
Tel *(02) 640 02 08*
This restaurant in the student area offers a wide variety of Belgian favourites as well as a good selection of Italian pasta dishes.

Le Passage €€
Belgian
Avenue Jean en Pierre Carsoel 17, 1180 Uccle
Tel *(02) 374 6694* **Closed** *Sat for Lunch & Sun*
Serves simple yet exquisite Michelin-starred food in a bright setting. Great set menus, both extravagant (in the evening) and accessible (at lunchtime).

Le Variétés €€
Belgian
Place Ste-Croix 4, 1050 Ixelles
Tel *(02) 647 0436*
Located in a magnificent Art Deco building, Le Variétés has splendidly re-created a 1930s brasserie. The beef tartare is particularly good.

Les Fils à Papa €€
French
Chaussée de Waterloo 1484, 1180 Uccle
Tel *(02) 374 4144* **Closed** *Sat & Sun: lunch*
It is worth the 15-minute drive from the city centre to Uccle to

dine at this charming old house with a delightful terrace serving top French food..

Relais St-Job €€
Belgian
Place Saint-Job 1, 1180
Tel *(02) 375 5724*
Far from the bustle of the city, sit on the roof of the Relais in good weather, and enjoy chilled rosé and dishes such as knuckle of ham and creamy mustard sauce.

Senza Nome €€
Italian
Rue Royale-Sainte-Marie 22, 1030 Schaerbeek
Tel *(02) 223 1617* **Closed** *Sat & Sun*
Traditional Italian food with a contemporary twist and good wines. The *aglio e olio* with squid ink pasta is a wonderful treat.

Bouchery €€€
Modern European
Chaussée d'Alsemberg 812a, 1180
Tel *(02) 332 3774* **Closed** *Sun & Lunchtimes*
Elegant, understated decor and outstanding French gastronomic cuisine make for an exquisite dining experiences.

Café Maris €€€
Seafood
Chaussée de Waterloo 1260, 1180
Tel *(02) 374 8834*
This splendid Parisian-style brasserie, complete with an Art Deco interior and a warm atmosphere, has a strong following. Fish and seafood dishes are the order of the day.

En Face de Parachute €€€
French
Chaussée de Waterloo 578, 1050 Ixelles
Tel *(02) 346 4741* **Closed** *Sun & Mon*
This Corsican-Marseillaise fusion establishment has a chalkboard menu that changes daily

and includes vegetarian options. Cosy ambience and relaxed service.

Kamo €€€
Japanese
Av des Saisons 123, 1050 Ixelles
Tel *(02) 648 7848* **Closed** *Sat & Sun*
Probably Belgium's best Japanese restaurant with a Michelin star. Sit at the bar and watch the chefs in action in the open kitchen. A small space, so reservations are highly recommended.

La Quincaillerie €€€
Belgian
Rue du Page 45, 1050 Ixelles
Tel *(02) 533 9833* **Closed** *Sun lunch*
Visually stunning restaurant, housed in a former hardware store from the 1900s; serves excellent steaks and the seafood counter is one of the best in Brussels. Good international wines.

La Truffe Noire €€€
Fine Dining
Blvd de la Cambre 12, 1050 Ixelles
Tel *(02) 640 4422* **Closed** *Sat lunch & Sun*
Extravagant, with one Michelin star and prices to match. The menu includes such items as a Périgord truffle cooked in a Porto *jus*, or warm duck *foie gras* with honey-roasted carrots.

Le Chalet de la Forêt €€€
Fine Dining
Drève de Lorraine 43, 1180
Tel *(02) 374 5416*
With two Michelin stars, Le Chalet de la Forêt serves first-class food with the best seasonal and local ingredients. The superb fish is a hallmark, alongside the brilliant wine list.

Outdoor tables on the charming terrace of Bouchery

For more information on types of restaurants *see page 145*

Stylish interiors of WY, an upmarket gastronomic restaurant

Rouge Tomate €€€
Modern European
Av Louise 190, 1050
Tel *(02) 647 70 44*   **Closed** *Sat lunch & Sun*
Though it may not be the place for a hearty stew, Rouge Tomate always satisfies with its exceptionally delicious food. The quality of produce and the seasonal menu is a matter of pride.

Salon 58 €€€
Fine Dining
Av de l'Atomium 6, 1020
Tel *(02) 479 8400*   **Closed** *Sun*
A stylish dining experience in the beautifully converted spaces of the listed and protected "vision-of-the-future" building built for the 1958 Brussels Universal Exhibition.

Touareg €€€
Morrocan
Chaussée de Charleroi 80, 1060 Saint-Gilles
Tel *(02) 534 5400*   **Closed** *Sun*
Touareg offers a traditional Moroccan mix of Berber, Arab and Andalusian cuisines, made using only the most authentic ingredients and following traditional recipes.

Va Doux Vent €€€
Fine Dining
Rue des Carmelites 93, 1180
Tel *(02) 346 65 05*   **Closed** *Sat lunch, Sun & Mon*
Sophisticated, Michelin-starred food in an outstanding dining room. For those who find the prices prohibitive, the good-value lunchtime set menu may be an accessible option.

WY €€€
Modern European
Bodenbroekstraat 22–24, 1000
Tel *(02) 400 42 50*
Savour contemporary, inventive Michelin-starred food in a chic, spacious setting. On offer are superb steaks and seafood,

as well as a wide range of champagnes and wines from its excellent bar.

Antwerp

Amadeus €
Belgian
Sint-Paulusplaats 20, 2000
Tel *0493 093329*
Former glass factory that is now a haven for fans of spare ribs. The Art Nouveau interior, with glasswork and wooden carvings, along with the food, helps create a traditional brasserie atmosphere.

Brasserie Appelmans €
French   **Map** K2
Papenstraatje 1
Tel *(03) 226 2022*
Excellent brasserie fare – big salads, pastas, juicy burgers and steaks – at affordable prices. Comes complete with its own absinthe bar.

Ciro's €
Belgian
Amerikalei 6, 2000
Tel *(03) 238 1147*   **Closed** *Mon*
The best steaks in Antwerp are served at Ciro's, which was last redecorated in 1962. The place is best defined as "rough and ready", but that's how the regulars like it.

De Foyer €
Belgian   **Map** L2
Komedieplaats 18, 2000
Tel *(03) 233 5517*
Opulent space in the foyer of a 19th-century theatre. Red velvet drapes and marble columns add to the sumptuous feel. The prices, however, are reasonable.

De Groote Witte Arend €
Belgian
Reyndersstraat 18, 2000
Tel *(03) 233 5033*
Located in a fine building dating from the 15th century. There is

nothing fancy about the food here, but diners are guaranteed good, hearty Flemish fare.

Fong Mei €
Chinese
Van Arteveldestraat 65–67, 2060
Tel *(03) 225 0654*
Offers very good, outstanding value Chinese food in a city where dining is seldom cheap. Does an excellent dim sum set menu. Also has several vegetarian dim sums to choose from.

Het Kathedraal €
Café   **Map** K2
Torfbrug 10, 2000
Tel *(03) 289 3466*
Het Kathedraal is a mandatory pit stop when wandering through the centre of town. This café's decor is kitschy yet great fun. Offers a good value three-course set lunch.

Mie Katoen €
Fondue   **Map** K1
Koolkaai 9, 2000
Tel *(03) 231 1309*
Popular little fondue house located on a farm in central Antwerp. Choose one of the traditional fondues or try something different – the Japanese fondue served with tempura, for instance.

De Kleine Zavel €€
Seafood   **Map** K2
Stoofstraat 2, 2000
Tel *(03) 231 9691*   **Closed** *Mon*
An affordable inventive menu paired with delicious wines has made this place popular with both travellers and locals. Specialities include a dish with seven preparations of tuna.

Hangar 41 €€
Café   **Map** J3
Sint-Michielskaai 41, 2000
Tel *(03) 257 0918*
Hangar 41 is a hugely popular venue that has become a hangout for Antwerp's more fashionable crowd. Its features include a cool, industrial interior and a terrace space. Serves stiff cocktails and sound Belgian cuisine.

Hippodroom €€
Franco-Belgian   **Map** J3
Leopold De Waelplaats 10, 2000
Tel *(03) 248 5252*   **Closed** *Sun*
The early 20th-century building that houses Hippodroom is also home to an enviable collection of art and photography. The cuisine here is as modern as its contemporary fittings.

InVINcible €€
Seafood **Map** K2
Haarstraat 9, 2000
Tel *(03) 231 3207* **Closed** *Sat & Sun*
Many of the items on the menu here are based on that morning's catch from the North Sea, and the open kitchen allows diners to watch the chefs at work.

Lam & Yin €€
Chinese **Map** K2
Reyndersstraat 17, 2000
Tel *(03) 232 8838* **Closed** *Wed–Sun evenings*
An upmarket Michelin-starred Chinese restaurant which is very popular with locals, so make sure to reserve a table in advance. The duck dishes particularly good.

Le Zoute Zoen €€
French **Map** K1
Zirkstraat 17, 2000
Tel *(03) 226 9220* **Closed** *Sat lunch & Mon*
A gorgeous restaurant offering a fine-dining experience for a little less than what diners may be asked to shell out elsewhere. For the best value for money, go for the set menu.

L'Epicerie du Cirque €€
Franco-Belgian **Map** K3
Volkstraat 23, 2000
Tel *(03) 238 0571* **Closed** *Sun & Mon*
Sample excellent old-school Franco-Belgian food in modern bistro-like surroundings. The space is not very big, but is charming and warm. Reservations advised.

't Karveel €€
Café
Vlaamse Kaai 11, 2000
Tel *(03) 237 3623* **Closed** *Mon*
This themed bar is styled on a 16th-century ship and includes portholes, ropes, barrels, rigging and cannons

in its decor. The beer can be ordered at the rudder. Bar food is available.

The Glorious €€
American **Map** J3
De Burburestraat 4a, 2000
Tel *(03) 237 0613* **Closed** *Sun & Mon*
A Belgian take on an upscale New York bistro, located south of the city centre, close to the Koninklijk Museum voor Schone Kunsten.

Dome €€€
French
Grotehondstraat 2, 2018
Tel *(03) 239 9003* **Closed** *Sun & Mon*
Inventive, contemporary, Michelin-starred French food in a quite wonderful Art Nouveau building. The wine list is one of the city's best. A grand dining experience in every way.

Het Gebaar €€€
Modern European **Map** L2
Leopoldstraat 24, 2000
Tel *(03) 232 3710*
A Michelin-starred, well-priced, good-value (although hardly cheap) contemporary restaurant that is one of Roger van Damme's creations. Its location in the Botanical Gardens might be one of the city's most picturesque.

Het Pomphuis €€€
Fusion
Droogdok, Siberiastraat 7, 2030
Tel *(03) 770 8625*
A Pacific Rim bistro that is in keeping with the city's appetite for industrial resto-bar conversions. This large, very dramatic space has retained much of the original hydraulic machinery. An extensive wine list accompanies the superlative fusion cuisine.

DK Choice

Kommilfoo €€€
Franco-Belgian
Vlaamsekaai 17, 2000
Tel *(03) 237 3000* **Closed** *Sun & Mon*
Even in a city as famed for eating out as Antwerp, the Michelin-starred Kommilfoo still stands out. The four-course set menu is, at €65, an absolute bargain, and while the decor is very plain, this is a deliberate choice so that the diner's attention stays on the food. The à la carte menu changes almost daily, and the wine list is as impressive as the food.

Pazzo €€€
Wine Bar
Oudeleeuwenrui 12, 2000
Tel *(03) 232 8682* **Closed** *Sat & Sun*
This wine bar in an old warehouse offers wines by the glass, each intended to match the various tapenades, stir-fries, tempuras and risottos on offer.

Rooden Hoed €€€
Seafood
Oude Koornmarkt 25, 2000
Tel *(03) 289 0909* **Closed** *Mon*
The oldest restaurant in Antwerp – it opened around 1750 – the Rooden Hoed is also one of the city's most renowned eateries. Their speciality is seafood, especially mussels.

't Fornuis €€€
Fine Dining **Map** K2
Reyndersstraat 24, 2000
Tel *(03) 233 6270* **Closed** *Sat & Sun*
Expect Michelin-starred excellence from Chef Johan Segers who often visits the tables to present his food to diners. Every dish at this formal restaurant is a gourmet extravaganza.

The elegant dining area of Le Zoute Zoen in Antwerp with crystal chandeliers and dark wood furniture

For more information on types of restaurants *see page 145*

't Zilte €€€
Belgian
Hanzestedenplaats 5, 2000
Tel *(03) 283 4040* **Closed** *Sat, Sun & Mon lunch*
Located on the top floor of the Museum aan de Stroom (MAS), this amazing two Michelin-starred restaurant offers modern Belgian food and great wines along with a terrific view.

Bruges

Bhavani €
Indian **Map** A4
Simon Stevinplein 5, 8000
Tel *(050) 33 9025* **Closed** *Wed*
Excellent, welcoming eatery that serves a wide range of Indian dishes, of which the Kashmiri *rogan josh* (a signature aromatic lamb dish) is one of its best.

Café Vlissinghe €
Café **Map** B2
Blekerstraat 2, 8000
Tel *(050) 34 3737* **Closed** *Mon & Tue*
The genuinely medieval Vlissinghe dates back to 1515 and is the city's oldest hostelery. The interior is an historical marvel and there is also a beautiful beer garden.

De Republiek €
Café **Map** A3
St Jacobsstraat 36, 8000
Tel *(050) 34 0229*
A medium-sized café, popular with students and artists who drink in the courtyard at night. It is also part of a cinema and theatre complex.

Den Huzaar €
International
Vlamingstraat 36, 8000
Tel *(050) 33 3797* **Closed** *Wed & Thu*
Hearty old-school Flemish cooking, but with a touch of class and a dash of inventiveness, making this centrally-located bistro a favourite among locals and visitors..

Lotus €
Vegetarian **Map** B3
Wapenmakersstraat 5, 8000
Tel *(050) 33 1078* **Closed** *Sat & Sun*
There are usually just two options on the menu at this vegetarian café. These are served in three sizes but lunch – the only meal served – is hearty no matter what size chosen.

Brasserie Erasmus €€
Belgian **Map** B3
Wollestraat 35, 8000
Tel *(050) 33 5781*
Found in the centrally located hotel of the same name, every

single dish on the menu here is made with beer. Try the rabbit in beer sauce or the fish *waterzooi*.

Café Craenenburg €€
Café **Map** A3
Markt 16, 8000
Tel *(050) 33 3402*
Situated in the north-west of Grote Markt, this bar is a little away from the more tourist-heavy bars. The limited menu includes pasta dishes, salads and sandwiches.

Cafédraal €€
Belgian **Map** A4
Zilverstraat 38, 8000
Tel *(050) 34 0845* **Closed** *Sun*
One of the most attractive restaurants in Bruges. Its medieval setting is a delight and provides a highly atmospheric backdrop to the inventive dishes based around meat and shellfish.

De Gouden Meermin €€
Café **Map** A3
Markt 31, 8000
Tel *(050) 33 1805*
Perhaps the best café on the Grote Markt, which is home to many tourist traps. Although the menu is mainly Italian, the mussels and frites are excellent.

De Stove €€
Belgian **Map** A3
Kleine Sint-Amandsstraat 4, 8000
Tel *(050) 33 7835* **Closed** *Mon & Fri lunch , Wed & Thu dinner*
The *foie gras* at this restaurant is exceptional, but do also try the fresh North Sea fish, supplied daily – particularly the breaded cod in butter sauce. Intimate spot, with just a few tables.

De Karmeliet €€€
Belgian **Map** C3
Langestraat 19, 8000
Tel *(050) 33 8259* **Closed** *Sun & Mon*
In 1996, Chef Geert Van Hecke became the first Flemish chef to

be awarded three Michelin stars. Many dishes at De Karmeliet are made with Belgian *genever;* try the popular roasted French scallops and marinated sea urchin.

De Visscherie €€€
Seafood **Map** B3
Vismarkt 8, 8000
Tel *(050) 33 0212* **Closed** *Tue*
Overlooking the centuries-old Vismarkt (fish market). Any of the turbot variations served here are a must-try. Popular among locals, so book ahead.

Den Dijver €€€
Belgian **Map** B4
Dijver 5, 8000
Tel *(050) 33 6069*
This stylish restaurant makes creative use of regional Belgian beers in many of its dishes. Three-, four- or five-course set menus are available in addition to a sophisticated à la carte selection. All dishes are prepared using locally sourced produce.

DK Choice

Den Gouden Harynck €€€
Seafood **Map** B4
Groeninge 25, 8000
Tel *(050) 33 7637* **Closed** *Sun & Mon*
Chef Philippe Serruys and his wife run this restaurant located in a 17th-century building in the museum district. The restaurant is very attuned to the seasonal, and the menu doesn't always stays the same, but the sea bass with coarse sea salt and rosemary is a must-try.

Duc de Bourgogne €€€
Seafood **Map** B3
Huidenvettersplein 12, 8000
Tel *(050) 33 2038*
Overlooking a canal in the historical city centre, the Duc is always busy, so do make a

Wood-beamed interior of Café Vlissinghe, Bruges

reservation. The delicious bouillabaisse made with local sea fish is the house speciality.

Ghent

Chez Liontine €
Belgian **Map** E1
Groentenmarkt 10–11, 9000
Tel *(09) 225 0680* **Closed** *Mon–Wed*
A friendly little restaurant in which diners can savour fresh Flemish specialities, some of which are made with beer. The rustic setting, with four separate dining rooms, enhances the unique atmosphere.

DK Choice

De Frietketel €
Fries **Map** D2
Papegaaistraat 89, 9000
Tel *(09) 329 4022* **Closed** *Sat & Sun lunch*
Widely regarded as serving the very best fries in all of Belgium, this chip shop is a Ghent legend, and the queues outside at busy times speak for themselves. There are burgers too, including a great vegetarian variety. If the place is full, just grab some fries and the excellent gravy, and eat them on the go. A must for anyone visiting Ghent.

Groot Vleeshuis €
Belgian **Map** E1
Groentenmarkt 7, 9000
Tel *(09) 233 2324* **Closed** *Mon*
This medieval butcher's hall makes a spectacular setting for a meaty lunchtime sandwich or even meatier tourist "formule". The *gentse waterzooi* (chicken stew) is particularly great.

Kapittelhuis €
International **Map** F2
Lange Kruisstraat 4, 9000
Tel *(09) 336 8519* **Closed** *Sun*
This restaurant offers a wide choice of dishes, ranging from steaks to pasta. The adjoining tea room serves great waffles and pancakes. Good choice for families.

Brasserie Pakhuis €€
Belgian **Map** E2
Schuurkenstraat 4, 9000
Tel *(09) 223 5555* **Closed** *Sun*
An ultra-hip renovated 19th-century warehouse. Sit on oak and marble tables amongst exposed giant cast-iron pillars. The menu features seafood platters and Flemish favourites.

Minimalistic decor at Vrijmoed, an expensive Belgian restaurant in Ghent

Keizershof €€
Belgian
Vrijdagmarkt 47, 9000
Tel *(09) 223 4446* **Closed** *Sun & Mon*
Located in a narrow 17th-century building on the market square; serves well-priced Belgian staples and salads. Paintings by local artists decorate the walls.

Coeur d'Artichaut €€€
Fusion **Map** E2
Onderbergen 6, 9000
Tel *(09) 225 3318* **Closed** *Sun & Mon*
Prepares a monthly changing menu that features classic European dishes made with a twist, in addition to inventive Asian selections. Great location in an impressive mansion.

Georges IV €€€
Seafood **Map** E2
Donkersteeg 23–27, 9000
Tel *(09) 225 1918* **Closed** *Mon & Tue*
A Ghent institution, this family business is one of the city's pricier restaurants but offers superior, wonderful food. The oysters, crab and mussels of Lélande are the main attractions.

Horseele €€€
French
Ottergemsesteenweg-Zuid 808, 9000
Tel *(09) 330 23 20* **Closed** *Sat for Lunch, Sun & Mon*
A Michelin-starred eatery in a highly unusual location (Ghent's football stadium) offering fantastic food with multiple amazingly inventive set menus to choose from. Closed on days when there is a match.

Jan van den Bon €€€
Fusion **Map** E5
Koning Leopold II-laan 43, 9000
Tel *(09) 221 9085* **Closed** *Sat for Lunch, Sun & Mon*
Outstanding Michelin-starred food featuring all sorts of flavours from around the world. Offers both tasting and à la carte menus. Outstanding quality guaranteed.

Nestor €€€
Belgian **Map** E1
Kraanlei 17, 9000
Tel *(09) 225 1880* **Closed** *Sun*
One of the city's best mid-range bistros, with a friendly atmosphere and a dark, modern decor. Specialities on the menu include charcoal-grilled meat and fish dishes.

Tapasbar La Malcontenta €€€
Spanish **Map** E1
Haringsteeg 7–9, 9000
Tel *(09) 224 1801* **Closed** *Mon*
Spanish eatery that serves specialities from the Canary Isles and Latin America. The seafood pancake is recommended, but their best item is the paella.

Valentijn €€€
French **Map** E1
Rodekoningstraat 1, 9000
Tel *(09) 225 0429* **Closed** *Sun evening, Thu, Mon-Sat for Lunch.*
A favourite with the city's locals, who come especially for the great-value four-course menu. The restaurant prides itself on using only the freshest ingredients.

Volta €€€
Seafood **Map** E1
Nieuwe Wandeling 2b, 9000
Tel *(09) 324 0500* **Closed** *Sun*
This über cool converted turbine hall just outside the centre is home to one of Ghent's finest new restaurants, with a superb menu of highly imaginative fish and seafood dishes..

Vrijmoed €€€
Belgian **Map** F2
Vlaanderenstraat 22, 9000
Tel *(09) 279 9977* **Closed** *Sun & Mon*
Terrific-value set menus are the main draws at this contemporary Michelin-starred eatery, popular with Ghent's youth. The offerings include a decent range of vegetarian dishes, which is quite unusual in this town.

For more information on types of restaurants *see page 145*

SHOPPING

Brussels may traditionally be known for its high-quality chocolate shops, but this great shopping city has much more to offer. It is fast gaining on fashion capital Antwerp for its own collection of cutting-edge designers, and the city also happens to be the world capital of comic books, with almost as many shops selling comics as there are vending chocolate. Throw in department stores selling luxury goods and street markets for bargain-hunters and you have a city that caters for all shopping styles and budgets. Of the other cities, Antwerp is renowned for its diamond and fashion outlets, Ghent offers vibrant music and clothes shops, while you can find beer and classical music in Bruges.

Rue Neuve crowded with shoppers

Where to Shop

Brussels' Grand Place is surrounded by lace vendors, chocolate shops and souvenir outlets, but just one street south is Rue des Éperonniers, with shops selling vintage clothing, posters and specialist teas. North-west of the Grand Place is Avenue Antoine Dansaert, centre of the Bruxellois fashion scene.

To the south-west of the Grand Place is the Rue du Midi, where you can find shops selling second-hand records, clothing, comic books, stamps and coins. Between the Lower and Upper Towns lies the antiques district of Rue Haute and Rue Blaes, leading into the Place du Grand Sablon, where exquisite chocolate shops can be found alongside high-end florists and antique shops.

South of the Palais du Justice lies Avenue Louise and Boulevard de Waterloo, where you can find top boutiques such as Gucci and Louis Vuitton. Perpendicular to Avenue Louise is Rue du Bailli, with its art boutiques, game shops and tea importers. To the west of the Avenue

lies the Matonge, the city's most multi-cultural area, where street markets are held on some weekends, and where you can find skatewear, rare vinyl and vintage denim in the St Boniface area. It is a pleasant district to wander around on a Sunday afternoon.

For all the major high-street chains, head to pedestrianized Rue Neuve, a short walk from the Grand Place.

Renowned Dandoy biscuit shop on Rue au Beurre

Opening Hours

Most shops open from around 10am to 6pm, but at a few of the arcades, and in the Rue Neuve area, there is late-night shopping on Fridays until 8pm. Apart from the "night shops" (or corner stores), almost all shops are closed on Sundays (except for the shops in the Quartier Marolles) and many on Mondays. The night shop chain White Nights is the best option for Sunday and late-night convenience shopping.

Sales in Belgium are regulated, with summer sales running from 1 to 31 July, and winter sales taking place from the first weekday after New Year's Day through to the end of January.

How to Pay

There is a noticeable lack of ATMs in and around the Grand Place, and a number of the smaller shops, newsagents, supermarkets, cafés, and even some restaurants do not accept debit or credit cards. It is wise, therefore, to ensure that you always take out sufficient cash if you are planning to spend the day in the city centre.

Visitors from outside the EU are entitled to a refund on VAT of purchases of more than €125 in one store. As the sales tax on items can be as much as 21 per cent, this can be a considerable saving. Look out for the "Tax-Free Shopping" logo on a shop door and request a tax-free cheque, which you can redeem at customs on your way out of the EU.

Galéries Saint-Hubert historic 19th-century shopping arcade

Department Stores and Arcades

Brussels has a selection of shopping malls, though they differ little from those found in other cities. However, **City 2** at the northern end of Rue Neuve, is host to the exhaustive French book and CD emporium, **Fnac**, and the Belgian department store **Inno**. Further south on the same street lies **Hema**, a Dutch low-cost store, selling everything from clothes to kitchen utensils. Closer to the Grand Place is the **Centre Anspach**, which includes a casino, concert hall, restaurant, a hotel and upmarket shopping. Possibly the most impressive collection of shops is the delightful **Galéries Saint-Hubert**, an opulent 19th-century covered arcade – Europe's first – housing a selection of upscale outlets.

A Dries van Noten design

Markets and Antiques

Brussels is blessed with a range of markets. Most weekends you can find a "brocante" – a glorified car boot sale combined with street party – somewhere in the city. These are listed in most of the city's free events magazines, as are the various farmers' markets found across the city where you can try some remarkable local breads and cheeses. Cheapest and most extensive of the traditional markets is the **Marché**

du Midi (Sundays 6am to 1pm) near the Gare du Midi that reflects the tastes of the area's North African community.

The eclectic **Marolles Marché aux Puces** (flea market) in Place du Jeu de Balles (daily 6am to 2pm, but best at weekends) dates back to 1873 and is the starting point for any antiques hunter. It can take time to sort through the various boxes of items but there are definitely bargains to be found. For pre-sorted antiques, head instead for the more expensive market in the Place du Grand Sablon (weekends only).

Fashion

Though Antwerp has long been regarded as Belgium's international fashion centre, these days it is the capital city itself that is creating a stir. Downtown's Rue Antoine Dansaert is at the heart of Brussels' thriving fashion industry, and the principal outlet remains **Stijl**. Since 1984, it has sold the work of fashion graduates from the Antwerp Art Academy such as Dries van Noten, and still offers the best wares produced by domestic talent. Further down the street, peruse the beautiful knitwear of **Annemie Verbeke**, and **Martin Margiela**'s shop in Rue de Flandre, which offers the apparel of one of Belgium's most talked about designers. On Avenue Louise, check out Brussels' trendiest hat designer, **Elvis Pompilio**.

Chocolates

There are 81 chocolatiers listed in the Brussels phone book – not including franchise outlets – almost all of high quality. The three biggest chains in Belgium are **Godiva, Neuhaus** and **Leonidas**. **Galler** and **Corné Port-Royal** are also excellent and have numerous outlets throughout the city.

While the area around the Grand Place has many chocolate shops – including the impressive **Dandoy** on Rue au Beurre – it is worth visiting the Sablon to find the **Wittamer** shop *(see p81)*, which are probably the best – and most expensive – in Brussels, and **Pierre Marcolini** (who also happens to be a champion pastry-maker) on the corner of the Sablon. **La Maison des Maîtres Chocolatiers** is also worth a stop.

Beer

Having fallen in love with Belgium's beers, you may want to take a few bottles home with you. Most local supermarkets, such as **Delhaize**, GB and Match, have quite comprehensive selections of many of the country's finest beers. However, for rarer finds – as well as appropriate glasses for each beer, gift boxes and other beer paraphernalia – visit **Beer Mania** in Ixelles where you can try the beer before you buy it. Also recommended are **De Bier Tempel** and **Delices et Caprices**, both near the Grand Place.

Specialist beer glasses can be found at the Marolles flea market on Saturday mornings.

Browsers at the Marolles flea market

Brüsel, one of Brussels' many comic bookshops

Comics

Brussels is the world capital for comic books, and the best of its many shops is **Brüsel**, which has a vast collection of comics in French, Dutch and English; it also has a gallery of framed original art for sale on the second floor. In Rue des Renards is **Utopia**, which leans towards American super-hero strips and science fiction but also has a selection of Japanese anime titles. **La Boutique Tintin** is a short walk from the Grand Place and offers a variety of Tintin-imprinted knick-knacks.

A more economical bet is the well-stocked comic shop on the ground floor of the **Centre Belge de la Bande Dessinée** (see pp52–3). Separate from the musuem itself, it is free to enter, and despite being a main tourist destination, is one of the better stocked comic shops in the city.

Bookshops

The Brussels outlet of the English bookstore, **Waterstone's**, and the friendly, independent store **Sterling Books** both have a wide selection of English-language books. Nestled among the high-fashion boutiques of Rue Antoine Dansaert is **Passa Porta**, which calls itself a tri-lingual bookstore and "Inter-national House of Literature". **Bibliopolis**, a popular and cheap French second-hand bookstore, has a number of outlets in the city.

Antwerp

Apart from the city's diamond district – located west of the railway station – modern jewellery outlets can be found in Schutterhofstraat. Then try **Nadine Wijnants**' shops for clever but inexpensive contemporary pieces from one of the country's most exciting young jewellery designers. The **Atelier Solarshop** sells clothes by designer Jan-Jan van Essche, along with jewellery and shoes, and is the last word in Antwerp cool.

Cutting-edge fashion can be found just a few streets away from Antwerp's main high-street shopping district, the Meir. **Ann Demeulemeester**, Dries van Noten's **Het Modepaleis** and Walter van Beirendonck and Dirk van Saene at **DVS** are all must-sees for fashionistas.

Het Modepaleis in Antwerp, housing Dries van Noten's collections

Ghent

Ghent is a university town, so it has a high number of hip record stores, streetwear outlets and second-hand shops to service the youthful population. The pedestrianized main shopping area, the Veldstraat, also has all the typical chain stores. For upscale second-hand retro furniture, visit **N'Importe Quoi**; for more organized bargain-hunting, go to **De Kaft**, where you will find used CDs, vinyl and other second-hand goods. **Music Mania** covers three floors and specializes in drum 'n' bass, reggae and jazz. **Het Oorcussen** is another outlet for Antwerp's famed fashion designers, as is the men's boutique **Hot Couture**.

Ghent's quirkiest shop may be **Vve Tierenteijn-Verlent**, a mustard shop dating back to 1858. The recipe for the mustard sold here was first concocted by a Madame Tierenteijn-Verlent in 1790, and it remains a firm favourite over 200 years later.

Bruges' Bottle Shop has a range of beers

Bruges

While Bruges is considered less of a shopping destination than Belgium's other major cities, the main shopping thoroughfare of Steenstraat is a little quieter and less stressful than Brussels' Rue Neuve or Antwerp's Meir. What's more, the Belgian fashion scene has spilled over into this quaint city. There's the boutique of Brussels' designer **Olivier Strelli**, and L'Heroine, which sells works by a number of Antwerp's famed young designers and their contemporaries.

The Bottle Shop has a more comprehensive range of Belgian beer than its Brussels-based competitors, with an array of some 850 beers and genevers.

Medieval Bruges is the perfect setting for **Rombaux**, which has been selling classical records and sheet music for three generations.

DIRECTORY

Department Stores and Arcades

Centre Anspach
Boulevard Anspach 30–36.
Map 2 D2.

City 2
Rue Neuve 123.
Map 2 D2.
Tel (02) 211 4060.
W city2.be

Fnac
City 2, Rue Neuve 123.
Map 2 D1.
Tel (02) 700 9191.
W fnac.be

Galéries Saint-Hubert
Galérie de la Reine.
Map 2 D2.

Hema
Rue Neuve 13.
Map 2 D2.
Tel (02) 227 5210.
W hema.be

Inno
Rue Neuve 111–123.
Map 2 D2.
Tel (02) 211 2111.

Markets and Antiques

Marché du Midi
Gare du Midi. **Map** 1 A5.

Marolles Marché aux Puces
Place du Jeu de Balle.
Map 1 C5.

Fashion

Annemie Verbeke
Rue Antoine Dansaert 64.
Map 1 C2.
Tel (02) 511 2171.
W annemieverbeke.be

Elvis Pompilio
Avenue Louise 437.
Tel (02) 512 8588.
W elvispompilio.com

Martin Margiela
Rue de Flandre 114. **Map** 1 B1. **Tel** (02) 223 7520.
W maisonmartin
margiela.com

Stijl
Rue Antoine Dansaert 74.
Map 1 C2.
Tel (02) 512 0313.

Chocolates

Corné Port-Royal
Rue de la Madeleine 9.
Map 2 D3. **Tel** (02) 512 4314.
W corneportroyal.com

Dandoy
Rue au Beurre 31. **Map** 2 D3. **Tel** (02) 511 0326.
W maisondandoy.com

Galler
Rue au Beurre 44. **Map** 2 D3. **Tel** (02) 502 0266.
W galler.com

Godiva
Grand Sablon 47–48. **Map** 2 D4. **Tel** (02) 502 9906.
W godivachocolates.eu

La Maison des Maîtres Chocolatiers
Grand Place 4, Grote Markt. **Map** 2 D3.
Tel (02) 888 6620.

Leonidas
Rue au Beurre 34.
Map 2 D3. **Tel** (02) 512 8737. W leonidas.com

Neuhaus
Galerie de la Reine 25–27.
Map 1 C3. **Tel** (02) 512 6359. W neuhaus.be

Pierre Marcolini
Rue des Minimes 1.
Map 1 5C.
Tel (02) 514 1206.
W marcolini.be

Wittamer
Place du Grand Sablon 6, 12 & 13.
Map 2 D4.
Tel (02) 512 3742.
W wittamer.com

Beer

Beer Mania
Chausée de Wavre 174–176.
Map 2 F5.
Tel (02) 512 1788.
W beermania.be

De Bier Tempel
Rue Marché aux Herbes 56.
Map 2 D3.
Tel (02) 502 1906.

Delices et Caprices
Rue des Bouchers 68.
Map 2 D3.
Tel (02) 512 1451.

Comics

Brüsel
Boulevard Anspach 100.
Map 1 C3.
Tel (02) 511 0809.

Centre Belge de la Bande Dessinée
Rue des Sables 20.
Map 2 F5.
Tel (02) 219 1980.

La Boutique Tintin
Rue de la Colline 13.
Map 2 D3.
Tel (02) 514 5152.

Little Nemo
Boulevard Maurice Lemonnier 25.
Map 1 C3.
Tel (02) 514 6804.

Utopia
Rue de Midi 39.
Map 1 C5.
Tel (02) 514 0826.

Bookshops

Bibliopolis
Rue du Midi 93.
Map 1 C3.
Tel (02) 502 4676.
W bibliopolis.be

Passa Porta
Rue Antoine Dansaert 46.
Map 1 C2.
Tel (02) 502 9460.
W passaporta.be

Sterling Books
Fossé aux Loups 23–25.
Map 2 D2.
Tel (02) 223 6223.
W sterlingbooks.be

Waterstone's
Boulevard Adolphe Max 71–75. **Map** 2 D1.
Tel (02) 219 2708.

Antwerp

Ann Demeulemeester
Leopold de Waelplaats.
Tel (03) 216 0133.

Atelier Solarshop
Dambruggestraat 48.
W ateliersolarshop.be

DVS
Schuttershofstraat 9 (1st Floor).
Tel 0488 492814.

Het Modepaleis
Nationalestraat 16.
Tel (03) 470 2510.

Nadine Wijnants
Kloosterstraat 26.
Tel (03) 226 4569.
W nadinewijnants.be

Ghent

De Kaft
Kortrijksepoortstraat 5.
Map E4.
Tel (09) 329 6438.

Het Oorcussen
Vrijdagmarkt 7.
Map F1.
Tel (09) 233 0765.

Hot Couture
Onderbergen 29.
Tel (09) 233 7407.

Music Mania
St. Pietersnieuwstrwat 19.
Tel (09) 278 2338.
W musicmaniarecords.com

N'Importe Quoi
Burgstraat 11.
Map D/E1.
Tel (09) 223 0617.

Vve Tierenteijn-Verlent
Groentenmarkt 3.
Map E1.
Tel (09) 225 8336.

Bruges

Olivier Strelli
Eiermarkt 3. **Map** A3.
Tel (050) 343837.
W strelli.be

The Bottle Shop
Wollestraat 13.
Map B3.
Tel (050) 349980.

Rombaux
Mallebergplaats 13.
Tel (050) 332575.
W rombaux.be

For Ghent and Bruges map references refer to the inside back cover

ENTERTAINMENT

Lying at at the crossroads of London, Paris, Amsterdam and Cologne, Brussels benefits from the best international touring groups passing through the city. In its own right, Brussels is one of the top destinations in Europe for modern dance and jazz, is host to a world-renowned classical musical competition, and has a knowledgeable, cinephilic population.

The visitor really is spoilt for entertainment choice. Knowingly hip Antwerp, the country's clubbing and fashion capital, offers a similar range of options, while Ghent's large student population gives the city a lively urban scene. Bruges, although quieter, is equipped with a clutch of cosy pubs and jazz bars to while away the evening.

The 19th-century interior of La Monnaie Opera House

Listings and Tickets

Up-to-date and tuned in to the city's goings-on is *Agenda*, a trilingual listings magazine that can usually be found freely distributed in boxes outside supermarkets and in cafés. *The Bulletin* magazine, highly popular with expatriates for five decades, now has a purely online presence in Brussels, but it still provides a good range of news, reviews and events listings, along with other useful information and links. Visit the website at www. xpats.com.

The French-language newspapers *La Libre Belgique* and *Le Soir* both publish their entertainment supplements every Wednesday. For cinema times online, check www. cinenews.be or www.cinebel. be. Visit www.jazzinbelgium. com for a trilingual schedule of

Magazines on sale in Brussels

jazz gigs throughout the country. If you are interested in reggae, ska and dancehall, visit www.irielion.com. The best online arts agenda is found at www.netevents.be (although the information is only available in French and Dutch).

On foot, head to the Tourist Information Office, which, as well as offering free maps and other information, will also help you book tickets.

Opera and Classical

Students from around the world come to study at the Royal Conservatory of Music, which is the site of the initial rounds of the Concours Musical International Reine Elisabeth de Belgique, one of the most challenging musical contests in the world,

which instantly places its winners at the very height of their profession.

The **Théâtre Royal de la Monnaie** *(see p50)* is one of Europe's finest opera houses, and its season runs from September to June. Tickets can be cheap, but beware, many productions sell out months in advance. The **Palais des Beaux-Arts**, the country's most notable cultural venue, is home to the **Belgian National Orchestra** and site of the final rounds of the Concours Musical. Its Art Nouveau hall, Salle Henri LeBoeuf, has recently been renovated, vastly improving the building's acoustics. Its season also runs from September to June.

Dance

For its size, Belgium is particularly strong in the field of modern dance, with its leading choreographers – above all Anne Teresa de Keersmaeker, Michèle Anne de Mey and Wim Vandekeybus (www. ultimavez.com) – having enormous influence internationally. De Keersmaeker is a former resident at the Brussels opera and director of the world-renowned Rosas company (www.rosas.be).

Venues naturally vary, but the **Théâtre Les Tanneurs**, tucked away in the cobbled streets of the Marolles district, puts dance at the centre of its programme. Ticket prices are reasonable.

Jazz

Brussels is one of the key cities in the world for jazz, and the leading soloists and groups are sure to include the town in their tour schedules.

Every May, jazz fans from around the world congregate for the **Brussels Jazz Marathon**, which hosts hundreds of gigs in all forms, many of them for free.

The quintessential Brussels jazz venue is the venerable **L'Archiduc**, an Art Deco gem in the centre of town where Miles Davis once popped in to jam. There are regular concerts at weekends and occasionally in the week. For jazz ranging from Big Band to contemporary, head to **Jazz Station**, in a former railway station in St Josse. For international acts, head to the classy **Music Village**, which stretches across two 17th-century buildings close to the Grand Place, and features local and international names. Regular jazz gigs are held in the Art Deco splendour of the **Flagey** building in Ixelles. **Sounds** is another popular venue with a prolific agenda of concerts every day except Sunday.

L'Archiduc, hosting regular jazz concerts in Art Deco surroundings

Rock, Folk, World and Reggae

Brussels is one of the best cities in Europe to catch up-and-coming acts, and ticket prices don't usually go much above €20 for a concert.

The **Forêst-National**, lying southeast of the city centre, is Belgium's top arena for big-name acts. Closer to the centre, Brussels' other venues tend to be more intimate places, with

their own favoured musical genres. **Café Central** favours R&B, blues, bossa nova and ambient. **Cirque Royale** leans towards indie rock, and has a reputation for booking rock and new-wave bands long before they are household names.

The downtown **Ancienne Belgique** has a similar line-up to Cirque Royale, if for more established acts. Flemish student venue **Kultuur Kaffee** at the Vrij Universitiet Brussel (the Dutch-language university) always has a strong line-up of bands and serves the cheapest beer in town. **Recyclart** showcases avant-garde techno, hardcore, punk and a bit of world music in a refitted abandoned train station. Look out for the old wood-and-brass ticket windows which have been turned into the bar. **Magasin 4** is dedicated to the promotion of French punk and ska. Visit the **Halles de Schaerbeek**, a 19th-century former market, for a range of different groups, **Vaartkapoen**

Logo for rock venue Ancienne Belgique

(also known as **VK Club**) for reggae, the **Beursschouwburg** – the Flemish Cultural Community centre – for Flemish acts, and **La Tentation** for flamenco, salsa and Flemish folk.

Although the city has few noted bands of its own, nearby Liège has quite a strong indie rock scene, centring around the Jaune-Orange label, whose acts often play in Brussels.

Theatre

There is a substantial English-language theatre scene in Brussels. The city's five English-language troupes – the **American Theater Company**, the **Brussels Light Opera Company**, the **Brussels Shakespeare Society**, the **Irish Theatre Company** and the **English Comedy Club** – are an established part of the Brussels theatre society. Performances are far from amateur and all plays are advertised in the city's listings magazines.

The most important Belgian theatre is the **Théâtre National**, which stages high-quality productions of mainly French classics as well as welcoming visiting companies, such as the Royal Shakespeare Company. Young Belgian playwrights have the opportunity to be showcased at the private **Théâtre Public**, while French 20th-century and burlesque pieces are staged in the glorious and beautifully restored surrounds of the **Théâtre Royal du Parc**.

Le Botanique cultural centre, venue for Les Nuits Botanique festival

Cinema

For the latest blockbuster films – always in their original language and never dubbed – head to the massive **Kinepolis Laeken**, boasting 28 screens (including IMAX) and free parking. Two central UGC cineplexes will also satisfy most mainstream tastes.

For more intriguing programmes and ambience, try the **Nova** for truly independent films, the **Actors Studio** for foreign and art films, and **Arenberg-Galeries**, which has its own eclectically chosen, summer-long festival, "Ecran Total". For mainstream films in Art Deco movie palace surrounds, go to **Movy Club**. Tickets cost from €6–7.50.

Brussels has a packed agenda of film festivals for all genres including fantasy (**Brussels International Fantastic Film Festival**, April), animation (**Anima**, February) and gay (**Belgian Gay and Lesbian Film Festival**, January).

Poster for BIFFF film festival, held annually in April

Clubs and Nightlife

Brussels' bright young things start off their weekend in St Géry, a square of trendy cafés and clubs just off the fashion district of Rue Antoine Dansaert. Formerly a run-down quarter surrounding the old grain exchange, the area is now home to latin-flavoured **Mappa Mundo**, popular **Le Roi des Belges** and the elegant **Gecko Bar**. The most renowned club in Brussels, **The Fuse**, has

Latin-inspired Brussels hot spot Mappa Mundo

earned a reputation for top-name techno and dance DJs. Once a month it becomes La Demence, a gay night that draws crowds from Germany, France and the Netherlands (www.lademence.com).

Ric's Boat, an actual boat turned nightclub, has a popular Single Friends night the first Friday of the month. **Les Jeux d'Hiver**, in the middle of the Bois de la Cambre woods, attracts an affluent crowd. Big, bold and occupying a church in Ixelles, **Spirito Brussels** is a night club with a difference. In the Marolles, Cuban disco **Havana** stays open until 7am at weekends.

Check www.noctis.com for up-to-date nightlife listings.

Music Festivals

A definite high point on the classical music calender is **Ars Musica**, a festival where composers often premiere their works. The festival takes place over several weeks, usually in March.

Les Nuits Botanique is a festival of over a hundred concerts, with indie rock, *chanson Française* and rap figuring prominently; it takes over the Botanique for the whole of May. In June, hundreds of free concerts are on offer during the **Fete de la Musique** festival. In the last weekend of the same month, the biggest pop and rock festival in the country comes to the village of Werchter (15 km/9 miles from Leuven) when the giant **Rock Werchter** festival takes place.

Antwerp

Antwerp is home to Belgian ballet. The **Royal Ballet of Flanders**, founded in 1969, performs both classical and contemporary works. Tickets start at €15.

The city also claims two opera houses and some fine theatres and jazz venues. Try Art Dethe atmospheric **De Muze** for first-rate jazz and jam sessions.

Clubbers from across the country flock to **Café d'Anvers**. The former church, located in Antwerp's red light district, was turned into a house club in 1991. **Petrol Club**, meanwhile, blends electro, hip-hop and rock.

Ghent

For Ghent jazz, the mandatory visit is to Art Nouveau **Damberd Jazz Café**, which has live jazz on Tuesdays. Ghent's popular **Hotsy Totsy** jazz bar also offers occasional stand-up comedy.

The country's most warm-spirited festival, **De Gentse Feesten**, is a centuries-old celebration that lasts for ten days in July. Buskers, street performers, rock and jazz bands compete for the attention of a lively crowd.

Bruges

Bruges is a real pub-goer's town more than anything, yet jazz lovers have plenty to choose from, notably the family-friendly art centre **De Werf** in Werfstraat and **Het Zwart Huis**. This friendly bistro puts on live jazz, folk and blues twice monthly on Sunday nights.

DIRECTORY

Opera & Classical

Belgian National Orchestra
Galeries Ravenstein 28.
Map 2 E3.
Tel (02) 552 0460.

Palais des Beaux-Arts
Rue Ravenstein 23.
Map 2 E3. **Tel** (02) 507 8200. W **bozar.be**

Théâtre de la Monnaie
Place de la Monnaie. **Map** 2 D2. **Tel** (02) 229 1211. W **lamonnaie.be**

Dance

Théâtre Les Tanneurs
Rue des Tanneurs 75.
Tel (02) 512 1784.
W **lestanneurs.be**

Jazz

Brussels Jazz Marathon
W **brusselsjazz marathon.be**

Flagey
Place Ste Croix. **Tel** (02) 641 1020. W **flagey.be**

Jazz Station
Chaussée de Louvain, 193a–195. **Tel** (02) 733 1378. W **jazzstation.be**

L'Archiduc
Rue Antoine-Dansaert 6.
Map 1 C2. **Tel** (02) 512 0652. W **archiduc.net**

Sounds
Rue de la Tulipe 28. **Map** 2 F5. **Tel** (02) 512 9250. W **soundsjazzclub.be**

The Music Village
Rue des Pierres 50. **Map** 1 C3. **Tel** (02) 513 1345. W **themusicvillage.com**

Rock, Folk, World & Reggae

Ancienne Belgique
Boulevard Anspach 110.
Tel (02) 548 2424.
W **abconcerts.be**

Beursschouwburg
A Ortstraat 20–28.
Tel (02) 550 0350.
W **beursschouwburg.be**

Café Central
Rue de Borgval 14.
W **lecafecentral.com**

Cirque Royale
Rue de l'Enseignement 81.
Tel (02) 218 2015.
W **cirque-royal.org**

Forêst-National
Avenue Victor Rousseau 208. **Tel** (02) 340 2123.
W **forestnational.be**

Halles de Schaerbeek
Rue Royale Sainte-Mairie 22a. **Tel** (02) 218 2107.
W **halles.be**

Kultuur Kaffee
Boulevard de la Plaine 2.
Tel (02) 629 2325.
W **kultuurkaffee.be**

La Tentation
Rue de Laeken 28.
Tel (02) 223 2275.
W **centrogalego.be**

Magasin 4
Avenue du Port 51B.
Tel (02) 223 3474.
W **magasin4.be**

Recyclart
Rue des Ursulines 25.
Map 1 C4. **Tel** (02) 502 5734. W **recyclart.be**

VK Club
Schoolstraat 76.
W **vkconcerts.be**

Theatre

American Theater Company
Rue Waelhem 69a.
W **atcbrussels.com**

Brussels Light Opera Company
Tel 0499 943721.
W **bloc-brussels.be**

Brussels Shakespeare Society
W **theatreinbrussels. com**

English Comedy Club
Rue Waelhem 73. W **ecc. theatreinbrussels.com**

Irish Theatre Co
W **irishtheatrebrussels. com**

Théâtre National
Boulevard Emile Jacqmain 111–115.
Tel (02) 203 4155.
W **theatrenational.be**

Théâtre Le Public
Rue Braemt 64–70.
Tel 0800 94444.
W **theatrelepublic.be**

Théâtre Royal du Parc
Rue de la Loi 3.
Tel (02) 505 3040.
W **theatreduparc.be**

Cinema

Actors Studio
Petite Rue des Bouchers 16.
Tel (02) 512 1696.
W **cinenews.be**

Anima
Tel (02) 534 4125.

Arenberg-Galeries
Galerie de la Reine 26.
Tel (02) 512 8063.
W **arenberg.be**

Belgian Gay and Lesbian Film Festival
W **fglb.org**

Brussels Intl Festival of Fantastic Film
W **bifff.net**

Kinepolis Laeken
Bruparck, Boulevard du Centenaire 20.
W **kinepolis.be**

Movy Club
Rue des Moines 21.
Tel (02) 537 6954.

Nova
Rue d'Arenberg 3.
Tel (02) 511 2477.
W **nova-cinema.org**

Clubs & Nightlife

Spirito Brussels
Rue Stassart 18. **Tel** 0483 580697. **Map** 2 E5.
W **spiritobrussels.com**

Gecko Bar
Place Saint-Géry 16.
Map 1 C2.

Havana
Rue de l'Epée 4.
Tel (02) 502 1224.
W **havana-brussels.com**

Le Roi des Belges
Rue Jules Van Praet 35.
Tel (02) 503 4300.

Les Jeux d'Hiver
Chemin du Croquet 1.
Tel (02) 649 7002.
W **jeuxdhiver.be.**

Mappa Mundo
Rue du Pont de la Carpe 2.
Tel (02) 514 3555.

Ric's Boat
Quai des Péniches 44.
Tel (02) 203 6728.

The Fuse
Rue Blaes 208.
Tel (02) 511 9789.
W **fuse.be**

Music Festivals

Ars Musica
W **arsmusica.be**

Fete de la Musique
W **conseildelamusique. be**

Les Nuits Botanique
W **botanique.be**

Rock Werchter
W **rockwerchter.be**

Antwerp

Café d'Anvers
Verversrui 15.
Tel (03) 226 3870.
W **cafe-d-anvers.com**

De Muze
Melkmarkt 15.
Tel (03) 226 0126.

Petrol Club
D'Herbouvillekaai 25.
Tel (03) 226 4963.
W **petrolclub.be**

Royal Ballet of Flanders
Kattendijkdok-Westkaai 16.
Tel (03) 234 3438.
W **balletvlaanderen.be**

Ghent

Damberd Jazz Café
Korenmarkt 19.
Map E2.
Tel (09) 329 5337.
W **damberd.be**

De Gentse Feesten
Tel (09) 269 4600.
W **gentsefeesten.be**

Hotsy Totsy
Hoogstraat 1.
Map D1–2.
Tel (09) 224 2012.
W **hotsytotsy.be**

Bruges

De Werf
Werfstraat 108.
Tel (050) 330529.
W **dewerf.be**

Het Zwart Huis
Kuipersstraat 23.
Tel (050) 691140.
W **bistrozwarthuis.be**

For Ghent and Bruges map references refer to the inside back cover

SURVIVAL
GUIDE

PRACTICAL INFORMATION

Although comfortable with its status as a major political and business centre, Brussels has sometimes struggled with its role as a tourist destination. It can be hard to find all but the most obvious sights: the same goes for inexpensive hotels. The tourist office, however, goes out of its way to help travellers enjoy the city and provides help with everything from finding hidden sights to medical and financial information. Brussels is a very cosmopolitan city, and its residents, many of whom are foreigners themselves, are usually charming and friendly, with most speaking English. Both the Upper and Lower Town can be negotiated on foot, and although Brussels' reputation as a rainy city is overplayed, bring a raincoat in summer and warm clothing for winter.

Customs and Immigration

Belgium is one of the signatories to the 1985 Schengen agreement, which means that travellers moving from one Schengen country to another are not subject to border controls. However, carry your passport as there are occasional spot checks, and always carry ID with you in Belgium.

Britain does not belong to Schengen, so travellers coming from the UK must present a valid passport when entering Belgium. This also applies to US, Australian and Canadian citizens.

British travellers no longer benefit from duty-free goods, but visitors from non-EU countries are entitled to a VAT refund if they spend more than €125 in a single transaction.

Tourist Information

The city is rarely crowded, so you should not have to wait at major attractions and museums unless a special event is taking place. If you are planning to do extensive sightseeing, the one-day tram and bus pass (see p177) is a must. Better still, pick up a Brussels Card from the Tourist and Information Office in Grand Place. The 72-hour Brussels Card costs €43 (also available for 24 and 48 hours) and includes free access to 25 of the city's museums, discounts for some attractions, restaurants and shops, and a guide to the city. The tourist office also publishes a variety of maps, guides and tours.

Language

Brussels is officially bilingual, which means that everything from street signs to bus destination boards must be in French and Dutch. Visitors will find that the locals are also remarkably adept at other languages too, and English in particular is spoken to an impressive level across much of the city.

Things become slightly more complicated outside Brussels, in part due to historical issues over language between the French and Flemish communities. Long-standing resentment at the dominance of French in Belgium means that initiating a conversation or ordering in a restaurant in French while you are in Flanders doesn't go down that well. A simple *"goed dag"* will do the trick, after which the conversation will almost certainly revert to your own language.

In Wallonia, on the other hand, there will be almost no Dutch and little English spoken outside the main tourist areas.

A useful start would be to look through the Phrase Book on p197.

Opening Hours

Most shops and businesses are open Monday to Saturday from 10am to 6pm. Supermarkets are usually open from 9am to 8pm. For late-night essentials and alcohol, "night shops" stay open until 1 or 2am. Banks are usually open weekdays from 9am to 1pm and 2 to 4pm.

Many sights are closed on Monday. Public museums are usually open Tuesday to Sunday from 10am to 5pm.

Admission Charges

Most of Brussels' major attractions charge an entrance fee, currently around €8–10, though there are often reductions available for students, senior citizens and the unemployed, while children under 12 usually get in free. Some museums, such as the Musées Royaux des Beaux-Arts

The sculpture court in the Musées Royaux des Beaux-Arts in summer

◀ Bicycles for hire at the Grand Place, Brussels

Visitors taking a break from sightseeing at a pavement café

de Belgique and the Musée des Instruments de Musique, have free entry for all visitors after 1pm on the first Wednesday of each month. There are still a few sights with no admission charge, including the Cathédrale des Sts Michel et Gudule and the Musée Royal de l'Armée et d'Histoire Militaire.

Tipping

A service charge is included in all hotel and restaurant prices. A small tip for the chambermaid and porter should be given personally to them, or left in your vacated room. Most diners round up the bill or add about 10 per cent if the service has been particularly good. Service is also included in taxi fares, although a 10 per cent tip is customary.

Travellers with Special Needs

The Belgian capital is not the easiest city for the disabled traveller to negotiate, but the authorities have recognized that there is significant room for improvement. Most of the more expensive hotels have some rooms designed specifically for people with disabilities; there are designated parking spaces for disabled drivers and newer trams provide wheelchair access, through only 10 metro stations have lifts. The **Brussels For All** website has information for travellers with reduced

mobility on everything from transport to restaurants and exhibitions. The Tourist Office also provides information and advice about facilities within the city.

Travelling with Children

Brussels is one of the most child-friendly cities in Europe. There are some excellent museums aimed specifically at younger children, such as the Musée du Jouet, packed with vintage toys, and the Musée des Enfants in Ixelles. Attractions like the Natural Science Museum, Bruparck and the Walibi theme park, just outside the city, will appeal to older kids. There are almost always discounts available for children: at the Musées Royaux des Beaux-Arts, under-18s are free if accompanied by an adult, and there are price reductions at Walibi for kids aged six to 11. Children under six have free entry to most museums, and they can travel for free on buses, trams and trains.

Public Toilets

Many public toilets in Brussels, including those in bars, restaurants and even cinemas and railway stations, have attendants, who should be given 40–50 cents. If they are unmanned, an honour system applies and you'll be expected to leave the money in a dish at the entrance.

Responsible Tourism

Awareness of the environment and local culture is subtly, yet powerfully felt in Brussels. Recycling has become second nature: public litter bins are colour-coded for different types of rubbish and super-markets across the capital charge for using plastic bags.

Every commune has excellent weekly food markets offering the best in fresh, local produce. Two of these markets, at Place de la Monnaie and the Ateliers des Tanneurs in the Marolles, offer organic (or "bio") vegetables, cheese, bread, fruit, meat and charcuterie. Even the tradi-tional Cantillon Brewery in Anderlecht uses cereal that is 100% organic for its beer.

Under the auspices of **Karikol**, a union of food-producers and restaurateurs founded in 2007, the week-long Goûter Bruxelles festival in late September celebrates the Slow Food movement. Events held at locations throughout the city are dedicated to savouring long, convivial meals and the ideals of "eco-gastronomy".

DIRECTORY

Tourist Information

Tourist and Information Office of Brussels
Grand Place 1, 1000 Brussels.
Map 2 D3.
Tel (02) 513 8940.
W visitbrussels.be

UK Tourism Flanders
W visitflanders.co.uk

US Belgian Tourist Office
W visitbelgium.com

Travellers with Special Needs

Brussels For All
W bruxellespourtous.be

Responsible Tourism

Karikol Slow Food Society
W karikol.be

Personal Security and Health

Brussels is one of Europe's safest capitals, with street crime against visitors a relatively rare occurrence. The poorer areas west and north of the city centre, including Anderlecht, Molenbeek and parts of Schaerbeek and St-Josse, have quite a bad reputation, but these areas are perfectly safe during the daytime for everyone except those who flaunt their wealth. After dark, it is sensible not to walk around on your own in these areas. Public transport is usually safe at all hours.

Police

There are two levels of integrated police in Brussels. Major crimes and motorway offences are handled by the national gendarmerie. However, visitors are most likely to come across the communal police, who are responsible for law and order in each of the capital's 19 administrative districts. All Brussels police officers must speak French and Flemish, and many will be proficient in English too.

Police officer on patrol

The main police station for central Brussels is on Rue du Marché au Charbon, close to the Grand Place. If stopped by the police, visitors will be asked for identification, so carry your passport on you at all times. Be aware that talking on a mobile phone while driving and possession of cannabis is illegal here; not using road crossings correctly is also illegal and may be subject to on-the-spot fines.

What to be Aware of

Most of Brussels' main tourist attractions are located in safe areas. When driving, make sure car doors are locked and any valuables are kept out of sight. If you are sightseeing, limit the amount of cash you carry. Handbags should be worn with the strap across the shoulder and the clasp facing towards the body. Wallets should be kept in a front, not back, pocket. Hotel rooms often come with a safe; if not, there should be one at reception to keep valuables locked up.

At night, avoid the city's parks, especially at Botanique and Parc Josaphat in Schaerbeek, both of which are favoured haunts of drug-dealers.

In an Emergency

For emergencies requiring police assistance, call 101; for medical or fire services, phone 100. Hospitals with emergency departments include **Institut Edith Cavell** and **Hôpital Universitaire Saint Luc**. The **Community Help Service**'s (CHS) 24-hour English-language help line is for expatriates, but it may be able to assist tourists.

Lost Property

Your chance of retrieving property that was lost in the street is minimal. For insurance purposes, contact the police station for the commune in which the article disappeared. (If you are not sure where that is, contact the central police station on Rue du Marché au Charbon.) The public transport authority **STIB/MIVB** operates a lost-and-found service for the metro, trams and buses. Report items lost in a taxi to the police station nearest your point of departure, and quote registration details and the taxi licence number.

Travel and Health Insurance

Travellers from Britain and Ireland are entitled to free healthcare under reciprocal agreements within the EU. To obtain this, you must carry an EHIC (European health insurance card). Europeans should make it clear that they have state insurance, or they may end up with a large bill. State healthcare subsidies do not cover all problems and it is worth taking out full travel insurance. This can also cover lost property.

Medical Matters

Whether or not you have insurance, doctors in Belgium will usually expect you to settle the bill on the spot – and in cash. Arrange to make a payment by bank transfer (most doctors will accept this if you insist).

Pharmacies are usually open Monday to Friday from 8:30am to 6:30pm and Saturday from 8:30am to noon, with each commune operating a rota system to cover holiday and other periods.

DIRECTORY

Police

Central Police Station
Rue du Marché au Charbon 30, 1000 Brussels.
Map 1 C3.
Tel (02) 279 7711.

In an Emergency

Ambulance and Fire Services
Tel 100.

Community Help Service
Tel (02) 648 4014.

Hôpital Universitaire Saint Luc
Ave Hippocrate 10, 1200 Brussels.
Tel (02) 764 1111.

Institut Edith Cavell
Rue Edith Cavell 32, 1180 Brussels.
Tel (02) 340 4001.

Police
Tel 101.

Lost Property

Central Police Station
Tel (02) 274 1690.

STIB/MIVB
Inside the Porte de Namur metro station. **Map** E5.
Tel (070) 23 2000.
W stib.be

Banking and Communications

Along with an array of banks and exchange bureaux in Brussels, there are hundreds of 24-hour cashpoints located around the city, and international credit and debit cards are widely accepted. The postal system is efficient and although Internet cafés are not common in Brussels, phone shops and Wi-Fi access in hotels, cafés and bars make up for this. As the capital of Europe, Brussels is a multilingual media hub; all aspects of publishing and broadcasting are available whatever your language.

Banks and Bureaux de Change

Most banks in Brussels are open weekdays from 9am to 1pm and 2 to 4pm; some open late on Friday until 4:30 or 5pm, and a few on Saturday mornings.

Banks often offer very competitive exchange rates, and most will happily serve non-clients. Many transactions (especially money transfers) are liable to banking fees, so ask in advance what these rates might be. Most banks will be able to cash traveller's cheques with the signatory's passport or other form of photographic identification. Visitors are also usually able to exchange foreign currency, again with valid ID. You will find that many bank attendants speak good English.

There is a 24-hour automated exchange machine at Grand Place 7, while in the streets around the square, there are several bureaux de change that are open until 7pm or later. Some of these charge no commission for exchanging cash, though it's always worth comparing prices between different bureaux. There are currency exchange booths at all of the city's major stations.

Red Belgian postbox

Credit Cards

American Express, Diners Club, MasterCard and Visa are widely accepted in Brussels, although it is wise to check in advance if booking a hotel or restaurant. Most hotels will accept a credit card booking, and the cardholder may be asked for a credit card imprint at check-in. Check first in shops and supermarkets whether they take credit cards, as some will only accept cards issued by Belgian banks, most notably the popular Mister Cash card.

ATMs

Almost all bank branches have 24-hour cashpoint facilities. Most ATMs will accept a wide range of credit or debit cards including those belonging to the Cirrus, Plus, Maestro and Star systems, as well as those from MasterCard and Visa.

Post and Communications

Brussels' central post office, 1 Boulevard Anspach, is open from 9am to 7pm Monday to Friday and from 10am to 4:30pm on Saturday.

Public payphones are run by Belgacom and accept both coins and telephone cards. The operator can be contacted by dialling 1380 or for directory enquiries in English dial 1404.

The ability to use your mobile phone in Belgium depends on your network and you should ask your provider whether this service is available to you before travelling.

There are almost no large Internet cafés, though in and around Boulevard Anspach in particular are phone shops and corner stores that have a few computers with Internet access. Instead, the city is especially big on Wi-Fi. Even the Grand Place is a designated free Wi-Fi hotspot.

Newspapers, TV and Radio

Most British and American daily newspapers produce international editions, which are on sale along with English-language magazines at specialist bookshops and newsstands across the city.

Belgium has one of the world's most advanced cable TV networks, with access to more than 40 channels, including both BBC 1 and 2, CNN and Arte.

Classical music radio stations include Musique 3 (91.2 FM) and Radio Klara (89.5 FM). Internet radio stations, such as StarRadio (www.star-radio.net), offer pop music, as well as news and chat in English.

A magazine stand

TRAVEL INFORMATION

Brussels is well suited to both casual and business travellers, with excellent connections by air, rail and road. The increasing political significance of Brussels in its role as the heart of Europe has led to greater competition between airlines, with many operators offering discounted fares.

The Eurostar and Thalys high-speed trains link the city with London, Paris, Amsterdam and Germany, and compare favourably with flying in terms of time. British travellers can use the Channel Tunnel or a range of cross-Channel ferry services if they want to bring their car with them.

An aeroplane from Belgian carrier Brussels Airlines' fleet

Arriving by Air

Situated 14 km (9 miles) northeast of the city centre, **Brussels National Airport** is in the Flemish commune of Zaventem (the name by which it is known to most citizens, including taxi drivers). A centre for Belgian carrier **Brussels Airlines**, the airport is also served by major carriers such as **British Airways**, **KLM**, **Air Canada**, **Delta** and **Lufthansa** and low-cost operators like **Ryanair**. A typical journey from London takes around 45 minutes. A scheduled return flight can be as much as £270, though prices can be significantly reduced if you are flexible regarding dates and keep an eye on airline websites for offers.

Reaching Brussels from the US can be more expensive than reaching other European cities. Flights average US$1000 for a charter return from New York. Prices from Canada are comparable.

Brussels **South-Charleroi** Airport has become a second hub since Ryanair began operating scheduled flights from various European destinations (including Glasgow Prestwick and Edinburgh in the UK). The airport is located 55 km (34 miles) from the centre of Brussels and can be reached by train or coach.

Getting into Town

The cheapest way of getting from Zaventem to the city centre is the express train from the airport to Gare du Nord, Gare Centrale or Gare du Midi. Tickets (about €3) are on sale in the airport complex or can be purchased online. Three trains run each hour between 5am and midnight; the journey to Gare Centrale takes 20 minutes. There is also an airport bus, Line 12, which runs hourly between 6am and 11pm. It stops at only the main train stations and Schuman metro stop, terminating at Place Luxembourg, near the European Parliament.

There is a taxi rank outside the arrivals hall. A one-way fare from the airport to the centre of Brussels will cost €40–45 and should take around 20 minutes (though this may be longer at rush hour). If you plan to return by taxi, ask the driver about deals, as some companies offer discounts on return fares.

An SNCB/NMBS *(see p178)* train runs from Charleroi to Gare du Midi. The journey takes about 45 minutes to/from the station. Ryanair also operates a shuttle bus between Brussels South-Charleroi Airport and Gare du Midi, with a journey time of approximately 1 hour.

Arriving by Rail

Brussels is at the heart of Europe's high-speed train networks, connected to London by the **Eurostar** service and to Paris, Amsterdam and Cologne by the **Thalys** network. These trains have a top speed of 300 kph (186 mph) and have slashed journey times between northern Europe's major cities significantly.

Eurostar passengers should book their tickets early to take advantage of reduced fares; they should also arrive at the terminal a minimum of 20–40 minutes before departure to go through the check-in and customs procedures before boarding. It is possible that you may be refused access to the train if you arrive after this time, although you can often be transferred to the next service at no extra charge.

Eurostar train at the Gare du Midi, Brussels

Trains run hourly between London's St Pancras International station and Brussels via the Channel Tunnel; the journey takes just under 2 hours and arrives at the Gare du Midi, which is served by metro trains, buses and trams. Taxis to the centre cost around €12.

Many visitors to Brussels arrive from mainland Europe. The high-speed train company Thalys also operates from the Gare du Midi and offers a comfortable journey, with Paris accessible in 1 hour and 25 minutes, Amsterdam in around 2 hours and Cologne in under 3 hours.

Arriving by Sea

Belgium can easily be reached from the UK by ferries which arrive several times a day. Cross-Channel ferries run frequently from Dover to Calais and Dunkirk, and from Hull to Zeebrugge. Services are offered by several companies, including **DFDS Seaways** and **P&O Ferries**. Foot passengers do not usually need to book, but those with vehicles should always reserve a space and arrive promptly.

DFDS Seaways does not take foot passengers.

Arriving by Car

Le Shuttle, operated by **Eurotunnel**, takes vehicles from the Channel Tunnel entrance near Folkestone direct to Calais, a journey of about 35 minutes. From there, Brussels is just a 2-hour drive via the A16 motorway, which becomes the E40 when you cross the Franco-Belgian border. Follow signs first to Brugge (Bruges), and then on to Brussels. Those planning to use the Eurotunnel should book tickets in advance and try to arrive early. Three trains per hour operate between 6:30am and midnight, with one train running hourly from midnight to 6:30am. There are a number of special offers that are intermittently available.

Arriving by Coach

Eurolines, a group of coach companies forming Europe's largest coach network, operates daily bus services

Eurolines coach running between London and Brussels

from Victoria Coach Station in London to Brussels' Gare du Nord, via the Channel Tunnel. Prices are extremely competitive compared to other forms of travel to Brussels, though this is offset by a journey time of around 7 hours. Note that coaches are sometimes checked at the border with France, so be sure to keep passports handy. From Gare du Nord, the centre can be reached either by mainline SNCB trains, prémetro trams or city buses. Small discounts are available for travellers aged under 26 and over 60. **Megabus** runs a daily service to Brussels from London's Victoria Coach station. Coaches arrive at Gare Centrale, close to the Grand Place and with excellent metro and bus links to other areas of the city.

DIRECTORY

Arriving by Air

Air Canada
Tel (0871) 220 1111 (UK).
w aircanada.com

British Airways
Tel (0844) 493 0787 (UK).
w britishairways.com

Brussels Airlines
Tel (0902) 51600.
w brusselsairlines.com

Brussels National Airport Information
w brusselsairport.be
Flight Information
Tel 0900 70000.
Disabled Travellers and Special Needs
Tel (02) 753 2212.
Airport Police
Tel (02) 709. 6666.
Customs
Tel (02) 572 4640.

Delta
Tel (800) 241 4141 (US).
Tel (0871) 221 1222 (UK).
w delta.com

KLM
Tel (0871) 231 0000 (UK).
Tel (1 866) 434 0320 (US).
Tel (61 1) 30 039 2192 (AUS).
w klm.com

Lufthansa
Tel (0871) 945 9747 (UK).
w lufthansa.com

Ryanair
Tel (0871) 246 0000.
w ryanair.com

South-Charleroi Airport
Tel (0)90 202 490.
w charleroi-airport.com

Arriving by Rail

Belgian & International Railway Info
w belgianrail.be

Eurostar
Tel 08432 186 186.
w eurostar.com

Thalys
Tel (07) 066 7788.
w thayls.com

Arriving by Sea

DFDS Seaways
Tel (0871) 574 7235.
w dfdsseaways.co.uk

P&O Ferries
Tel (0871) 664 2121.
w poferries.com

Arriving by Car

Eurotunnel
Tel 08443 35 35 35.
w eurotunnel.com

Arriving by Coach

Eurolines
Tel (0871) 781 8178.
w eurolines.com

Megabus
w megabus.com

Getting Around Brussels

Although its public transport system is clean, modern and efficient, Brussels is a city best explored on foot. Most of the key attractions for first-time visitors are within a short walk of the Grand Place, and the Art Nouveau architecture in Ixelles and Saint-Gilles is also best enjoyed on a leisurely stroll. For those anxious to see the main sights in limited time, the tram and metro network covers most of the city at speed, while buses are useful for reaching more out-of-the-way areas. Although expensive, taxis are recommended for late-night journeys. Cycling can be hazardous for the inexperienced.

Bus at a stop in Brussels city centre

Green Travel

Brussels is the perfect place to reduce your carbon footprint. The centre is small enough to make walking around its ancient cobbled streets one of the highlights of any visit, while the use of bicycles is encouraged through the imaginative **Villo** rental scheme and kilometres of bicycle lanes. Each September, a popular "car-free" day is held, when traffic is banned and pedestrians and cyclists take over the streets.

Brussels also has an excellent public transport system, with a highly integrated, affordable metro, tram and bus network. The city is committed to an Eco-drive scheme, reducing energy consumption by lowering speeds on all modes of public transport and accessing electricity from renewable sources for trams and metro trains, and the development of hybrid and fuel cell engines on its buses.

There's little need for a car even when you go beyond Brussels. The other main cities aren't that far away and are served by an excellent national train network.

Several special tariffs are available, including discounts for young adults aged under 26 and seniors, and weekend tickets, which reduce the price by up to 40 per cent.

Planning your Journey

If you are seeing Brussels by car, avoid its major roads during rush hours, which are weekdays from 8 to 9:30am and 5 to 7pm as well as Wednesday lunchtimes during the school year, when there is a half day. Tram and bus services run frequently at peak times and are usually not too crowded. However, the small size of Brussels means that walking is often a viable option.

Walking in Brussels

The short distance between sights and the interest in every corner make central Brussels easy to negotiate on foot. Outside the city centre, walking is the only way to appreciate the concentration of Art Nouveau buildings on and around Square Ambiorix, around the district of Ixelles and near St-Gilles Town Hall.

Drivers in Brussels have a bad reputation, and it is important to be alert to traffic while crossing roads. Motorists are obliged to stop at pedestrian crossings but you will find that this rule is often ignored. At traffic lights, drivers turning right or left may pay no attention to the walker's priority. It is essential to be careful even in residential areas.

Blue or white street signs are placed on the walls of buildings at one corner of a street, and can be somewhat hard to locate. Street names are always in French first, then Flemish, with the name in capital letters and the street type in small letters to the top left and bottom right corners (for example, Rue STEVIN straat).

Cycling

Car traffic can be fierce, but happily the number of cycle lanes is ever on the increase, as is the ease with which visitors can rent a bike. One of the most convenient ways is the Villo scheme. You can take a Villo unisex bike by the day or week, paying online or at one of the 180 cycle stations across the city. Use your credit card for the €150 deposit. The bike can be parked or returned to any of the stations. Base rates are €1.60 per day and €7.50 per week. Rates go up with usage.

Children enjoying the sights of Brussels by bike

A city tram travelling down Rue Royale towards the city centre

Travelling by Bus, Tram and Metro

The authority governing Brussels' public transport is the bilingual **STIB/MVIB**, which runs buses, trams and metro services in the capital. Tickets are valid on all three services, which run between 5:30am and 12:30am on weekdays with shorter hours on Sundays and public holidays.

A single ticket, which allows unlimited changes within 1 hour (excluding the Nato-Brussels Airport Line 12), costs €2.10. You can also buy a five-journey Jump ticket for €8, or a 10-ride Jump ticket for €14. Single tickets can be bought on buses and trams but cost €2.50. Tickets should be stamped in the machines next to the exits; you must restamp your ticket if the journey involves a change. A map of the whole network is available at most metro stations. STIB is gradually replacing transport tickets with a single pass, called MOBIB, which can store different travel options at the same time, such as a season ticket, a ten-day journey or a day pass, on an electronic chip.

At street level, metro stations are marked by a large white 'M' on a blue background. Tickets must be bought and stamped before you reach the platform. They can be obtained from metro ticket offices and automated machines inside stations, as well as many newsagents. Metro stations in the city centre have electronic displays showing where each train is in the system and all the stops on the route.

The older yellow trams are slowly being phased out. Unlike newer models, these have no information on what the upcoming stop is, so you need to have a copy of the tram network or ask the driver to call out the relevant stop.

As well as the main network, a few bus services in the capital are run by the Walloon transport group (TEC) and the Flemish operator De Lijn. These services have lettered rather than numbered codes, but most tickets are valid on all the services.

Driving in Brussels

Belgium drives on the right, and the *priorité à droite* rule – which means that the driver coming from the right at junctions has absolute priority to pull out unless otherwise indicated – is enforced with sometimes startling regularity. Always watch for vehicles coming from the right, no matter how small the road; some drivers have been known to take their priority even though it means a crash, secure in the knowledge that they are legally correct. Always give way to trams, who will ring their bells should a car be blocking their path. Street parking, usually by meter, is becoming increasingly difficult in the centre of the city.

One-day travel pass

Essential safety precautions should be adhered to at all times. Safety belts are obligatory in all seats, and children under 12 years old are not allowed to sit in the front. Drink-driving is illegal (the limit in Belgium is currently 0.5g/l), as is talking on a mobile while driving (though not on "hands free" phones so far). The Belgian police are notorious for suddenly targeting an offence, so you might find one day they ignore you completely and the next give you a €50 on-the-spot fine.

Most international car rental agencies have branches in Brussels, many at the National Airport in Zaventem or at the Gare du Midi, where the Eurostar, Thalys and other main train services arrive.

The success of the Belgian Mister Cash bank card means that many petrol stations, when unattended on Sundays and out of hours, only accept this card, so fill up during the week if possible.

Taking a Taxi

Brussels' taxis are fairly expensive, but most journeys are short and cabs are the city's only 24-hour transport service. All taxis have a rooftop sign which is illuminated when the vehicle is vacant. Cabs are generally picked up at a taxi rank or ordered by phone rather than flagged down on the street. Tips are included in the fare, but an extra tip is usually expected. Give the taxi's registration number, its make and colour when making a complaint.

Traffic on a busy main street in central Brussels

Getting Around Belgium

As you might expect from a country that is small, modern and predominantly flat, Belgium is an extremely easy place in which to travel. The toll-free motorways compare favourably with any in France, train travel is swift and there are good bus services in those areas not covered by the railway network. Intercity trains leave from all three of the city's main stations and take 40 minutes to Antwerp (for the section on getting around Antwerp see p96), 40 minutes to Ghent (see p116) and one hour to Bruges (see p122). Public transport is clean and efficient and the range of touring tickets allows a great deal of freedom and the ability to see the whole country inexpensively. In the level Flemish countryside to the north, hiking and cycling are pleasant ways to get around.

Car travelling through Durbuy in the scenic Ardennes

Travelling by Car

After the rather enervating traffic in Brussels, driving in the rest of Belgium comes as something of a relief. The motorways are fast, reasonably well maintained and toll-free, while major roads are also excellent. Drivers in cities outside the capital tend to be more relaxed, although the trend in Flanders for car-free city centres can make navigation through them demanding. The only difficulty most drivers come across is an occasional absence of clear signs for motorway exits and junctions, which can necessitate taking extra care when approaching junctions (in Flanders, many drivers are confused by signs for "Uitrit". It means exit).

Speed limits are 50 kph (30 mph) in built-up areas, 120 kph (75 mph) on motorways and dual carriageways and 90 kph (55 mph) on all other roads. These limits are reduced to as low as 20 kph in some residential areas and near schools. If you break down, three motoring organizations should be able to provide assistance: **Touring Club de Belgique**, **Royal Automobile Club de Belgique** and **Vlaamse Automobilistenbond** in Flanders. It is worth getting breakdown coverage before you leave, and you must have a valid driving licence (from the EU, US, Australia or Canada) or an International Driving Licence on your person. It is also essential to have comprehensive insurance and/or a Green card. Visitors are expected to carry a first-aid kit, a reflective orange or yellow jacket and a warning triangle at all times.

All the major car rental agencies operate in Belgium, although renting one can be an expensive business. To hire a vehicle, you must be 21 or over, with a year's driving experience, and be in possession of a credit card. A week's rental with unlimited mileage will cost €370 or more but might be reduced as the big firms offer regular special deals. Local rental agencies may also be cheaper, but be sure to check the terms and conditions.

Bicycle hire is available in most Flemish towns with a modest deposit of €15.

Travelling by Rail

Run by **Belgian National Railways** (Société Nationale Chemins de Fer Belges/ Belgische Spoorwegen), Belgium's train network provides a fast and economical means of getting to and from major towns and cities. As most journeys are fairly short, only light refreshments, including good Belgian beers, are available on board.

Fares for standard second-class tickets are calculated by distance,

French/Dutch Place Names

One of the most confusing aspects of travel in Belgium is the variation between French and Dutch spellings of town names. On road signs in Brussels, both names are given, while in Flanders only the Dutch and in Wallonia only the French are shown. The following list gives main towns:

French	Dutch	French	Dutch
Anvers	Antwerpen	Malines	Mechelen
Ath	Aat	Mons	Bergen
Bruges	Brugge	Namur	Namen
Bruxelles	Brussel	Ostende	Oostende
Courtrai	Kortrijk	Saint-Trond	Sint-Truiden
Gand	Gent	Tongres	Tongeren
Liège	Luik	Tournai	Doornik
Louvain	Leuven	Ypres	Ieper

Train travelling through Belgium on a spring evening

so return tickets generally offer no savings and are usually valid only until midnight. Children aged under six travel free, with a maximum of four children allowed per adult, and those aged between six and 11 receive a 50 per cent discount. A range of special tariffs are available for people under 26 and senior citizens.

Belgian railway logo

A variety of rail passes are available for extensive travel. The Railpass costs €76 and allows ten trips within Belgium over one year, while the Benelux Pass costs €158 for 4 days or €212 for 6 days, and offers unlimited travel on any five days within one month of purchase. The Benelux Pass can be used on trains in Belgium, the Netherlands and Luxembourg.

Travelling by Bus

While slower and less comfortable for travelling between major cities, buses come into their own in the more remote or rural areas of the rest of Belgium, as well as in city suburbs. In Flanders, buses are run by the **De Lijn** group; in Wallonia, the network is operated by **TEC**. Fares are calculated according to distance, and are bought from the driver. Bus stops and terminals are generally close to railway stations. Buses have priority on public roads, so journeys are often swift.

Specialist Tours

Brussels is a city rich in culture and there are many tours on offer to visitors. The Tourist and Information Centre (*see p177*) in the city centre runs over 40 walking, bus and car day tours that cover all of the capital with topics as diverse as "Humanist Brussels" and "Industrial Belgium". The focus is largely on the city's exceptional range of art and architecture, but many themes are covered. In each major regional city, detailed multi-lingual private tours are available in the historic town centre; you should contact the city's main tourist office for full information.

Belgium's position as one of Europe's most fought over territories is reflected in the range of battlefield tours available. Check at local tourist offices in Waterloo, Ypres and Bastogne for information on guided visits to battlefields from the Napoleonic era to World War II.

Away from cities, Belgium also offers hiking and cycling excursions, ranging from one-day adventures to five-day hikes. The Ardennes is a popular destination for hikers, who can appreciate the area's flora and fauna as well as its history. Contact the **Wallonia-Brussels** tourist office for more details.

DIRECTORY

Travelling by Car

Tel Avis (02) 720 0944.
Tel Budget (02) 720 0944.
Tel Europcar (02) 721 0592.
Tel Hertz (02) (02) 720 6044.

Police Road Information
w polfed-fedpol.be

Royal Automobile Club de Belgique
Rue d'Arlon 53, 1040 Brussels.
Map 3 A3. **Tel** (02) 287 0911.

Touring Club de Belgique
Rue de la Loi 44, 1040 Brussels.
Map 3 A2. **Tel** (070) 344777.

Vlaamse Automobilistenbond
Pastoor Coplaan 100,
Zwijndrecht. **Tel** (070) 22 40 30.

Travelling by Rail and Bus

De Lijn
Tel 070 220 200.

SNCB/BS (Belgian National Railways)
Tel (02) 528 2828.

TEC
Tel (010) 235353.

Specialist Tours

Arau
Boulevard Adolphe Max 55.
Map 1 A2. **Tel** (02) 219 3345.

La Fonderie
Rue Ransfort 27. **Tel** (02) 410 9950. Industrial heritage, chocolate and beer walks.

Wallonia-Brussels Tourist Office
w opt.be

A long-distance bus in a city suburb in Belgium

BRUSSELS STREET FINDER

The page grid superimposed on the area by area grid below shows which parts of Brussels are covered in this *Street Finder*. The central Upper and Lower Town areas are marked in the colours that are also the thumbtab colours throughout the book. The map references for all sights, hotels, restaurants, shopping and entertainment venues described in this guide refer to the maps in this section only. A street index follows on pp186–8. The key, set out below, indicates the scales of the maps and shows what other features are marked on them, including transport terminals, emergency services and information centres. All the major sights are clearly marked so they are easy to locate. The map on the inside back cover shows public transport routes.

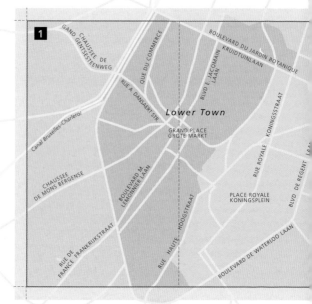

Key

⬛ Major sight
⬜ Other sight
⬜ Other building
Ⓜ Metro station
🚉 Train station
🚊 Tram stop
🚌 Bus station
ℹ️ Tourist information
➕ Hospital
🔵 Police station
✝️ Church
═══ Railway line
▬ Pedestrian street

Scale of Maps   1:11,500

0 metres	250
0 yards	250

Façade of La Maison des Ducs de Brabant, Grand Place *(see pp44–5)*

The Triumphal arch in the
Parc du Cinquantenaire,
built in 1905 *(see pp76–7)*

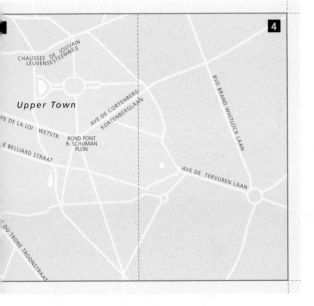

4

CHAUSSEE DE LOUVAIN
LEUVENSESTEENWEG

Upper Town

AVE DE CORTENBERG
KORTENBERGLAAN

BVD BRAND WHITLOCK LAAN

E DE LA LOI   WETSTR.

ROND PONT
R. SCHUMAN
PLEIN

E BELLIARD STRAAT

AVE DE TERVUREN LAAN

DU TRONE TROONSTRAAT

| 0 metres | 500 |
| 0 yards | 500 |

Cathédrale Sts Michel et
Gudule *(see pp72–3)*

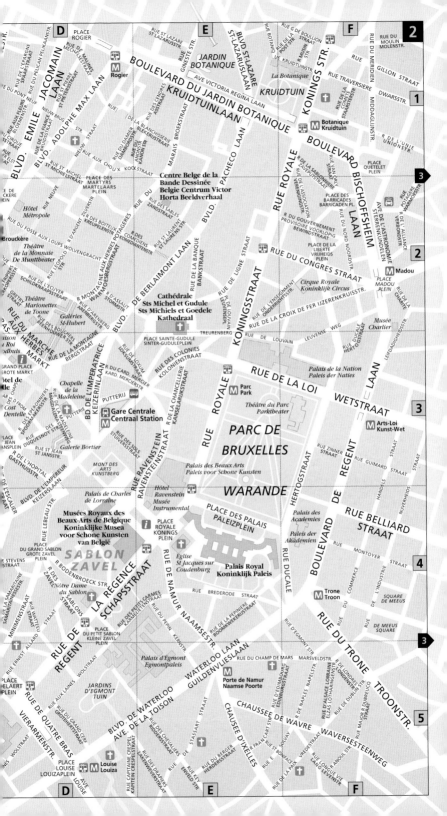

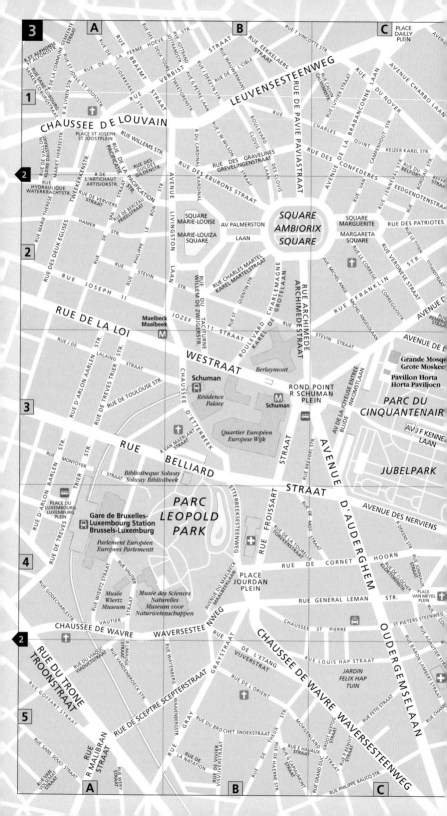

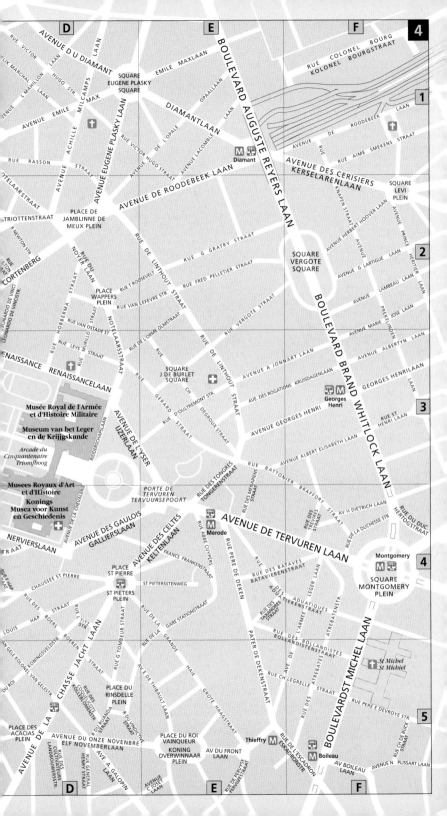

Street Finder Index

General Index

Acknowledgments

Dorling Kindersley would like to thank the following people whose assistance contributed to the preparation of this book:

Main Contributors
Zoë Hewetson is based in London but works in Brussels as a simultaneous translator for the European Commission. She is also a keen walker and has recently published a guide to walking in Turkey.

Philip Lee lives and works in Nottingham. A veteran travel writer, he has contributed to numerous *Rough Guide* and *Dorling Kindersley Travel Guide* publications, including the *Rough Guide to Belgium*. He frequently writes on travel for British newspapers and magazines.

Zoë Ross is a London-based writer and editor. She has worked on several Dorling Kindersley travel guides, and is now a freelance author.

Sarah Wolff has lived and worked in Brussels for several years. An editor and journalist, she is currently working for *The Bulletin*, Brussels' English-language newsweekly magazine.

Timothy Wright lived in Brussels for most of the 1990s. A successful journalist, he contributed to several English-language magazines published in Brussels and elsewhere in the Benelux countries.

Julia Zyrianova is a freelance journalist and translator. She lived in Brussels and Paris for several years and is now based in London.

Additional Contributors
Antony Mason, Emma Jones, Leigh Phillips.

For Dorling Kindersley
Gillian Allan, Douglas Amrine, Claire Baranowski, Marta Bescos Sanchez, Louise Bostock Lang, Dan Colwell, Paula da Costa, Vivien Crump, Simon Davis, Rhiannon Furbear, Donald Greig, Amy Harrison, Marie Ingledew, Jude Ledger, Carly Madden, Catherine Palmi, Lee Redmond, Marisa Renzullo, Ellen Root, Meredith Smith, Susana Smith, Lesley Joan Williamson.

Proofreader
Sam Merrell.

Indexer
Hilary Bird.

Revisions and Relaunch Team
Ashwin Adimari, Stuti Tiwari Bhatia, Madhura Birdi, Dipika Dasgupta, Mohammad Hassan, Shobhna Iyer, Darren Longley, Craig Turp, Tanveer Abbas Zaidi.

Additional Photography
Anthony Cassidy, Steve Gorton, Ian O'Leary, Roger Mapp, Neil Mersh, David Murray, William Reavell, Tim Ridely, Stuti Tiwari, Jules Selmes, Anthony Souter, Clive Streeter, Matthew Ward, Lesley Joan Williamson.

Special Assistance
Many thanks for the invaluable help of the following individuals: Joanna at Belgo; Derek Blyth; Christiana Ceulemans at Institut Royal Du Patrimonie Artistique; Charles Dierick at Centre Belge de la Bande Dessinée; Anne at Gaspard de Wit; Elsge Ganssen and Georges Delcart at Rubenshuis; Doctor Janssens at the Domaine de Laeken; Leen de Jong at Koninklijk Museum Voor Schone Kunsten; Antwerpen; Noel at Leonidas; Chantal Pauwert at Stad Brugge Stedelijke Musea; Marie-Hélène van Schonbroek at Cathédrale Sts Michel et Gudule; Elaine de Wilde and Sophie van Vliet at Musées Royaux des Beaux-Arts.

Photography Permissions
Dorling Kindersley would like to thank all the cathedrals, churches, museums, hotels, restaurants, shops, galleries and sights too numerous to thank individually for their assistance and kind permission to photograph at their establishments.

Placement Key - a–above; b–below/bottom; c–centre; f–far; l–left; r–right; t–top.

Works of art have been produced with the permission of the following copyright holders: ©Casterman 22 br, Ted Benoit Berceuse Electrique 52clb; ©DACS 2011 20bl, 53tl/cra/crb/b, 84ca/bl/br; ©Dupuis 1999 22tr, 23ca; Sofa Kandissy ©Alessandro Medini 117cr; Lucky Luke Licensing ©MORRIS 22br; @Moulinsart SA 4, 22cr/cl/bc, 52tr/cra/crb, 53cla/clb; ©Peyo 1999 - Licensed through I.M.P.S. (Brussels) 23bc; 53cla;

The publishers would like to thank the following individuals, companies, and picture libraries for their kind permission to reproduce their photographs:

Accueil Et Tradition: 144br; **AKG, London**: 33br, 36tr, 38bl, 39bl, 39br, 148tr; Galleria Nazdi Cupodimonte 24-5c; Erich Lessing 30, / Kunsthistoriches Museum 33tl; Musée du Louvre 31b; Musée Royaux d'Arts et d'Histoire, Brussels 37cr; Museum Deutsche Geschichte, Berlin 33c; Pushkin Museum 32c; Victoria and Albert Museum, London 34cl; **Ancienne Belgique**: 165c; **Alamy Images**: Pat Behnke 147tl, 101bl; Gary Cook 130cla; Ian Dagnall 118cl, 118br; Richard Wayman 173cr; INSADCO Photography/Martin Bobrovsky 146cla; Andre Jenny 80cla; Art Kowalsky 8bl; Angus McComiskey 9br; mediacolor's 80br; Paul Thompson Images/Chris Ballentine 130bc; picturesofeurope.co.uk 147c; Ray Roberts 107br; Joern Sackermann 81br; Rudi Theunis 138bl; Justin Kase ztwoz 168-9; **L'Archiduc**: Antoine Huart 165tr; **Art Archive**: Imperial War Museum, London 111br.

Duncan Baird Publishers: Alan Williams 149br. **CH. Bastin & J. Evrard**: 20tr/cb/bc, 21tr/br, 78br; 88br; 99tr, 109tl, 120bc; **Belga Queen**: 151tr; **Bouchery**: 155br; **The Bridgeman Art Library**: Christie's Images, London Peter Paul Rubens (1557–1640) *Self Portrait* 19tl; Musée Crozatier, Le Puy-en-Velay, France designed by Berain (c.1725–1730) *Dawn*, Brussels lace 25br; Private Collection/ Marie-Victoire Jaquotot (1778–1855) *Portrait of the Duke of Wellington* 37b./ Max Silbert (b.1871) *The Lacemakers of Ghent* 1913 25tr; Private Collection French School (19th century) *Louis XIV (1638–1715) of France in the costume of the Sun King in the ballet 'La Nuit' c.1665* 34br; Private Collection/ Bonhams, London/Robert Alexander Hillingford (1825–1904) *The Turning Point at Waterloo* (oil on canvas) 36bl; St. Bavo Cathedral, Ghent Hubert Eyck (c.1370–1426) & Jan van

Eyck (1390–1441), *Adoration of the Mystic Lamb*, Oil on panel 116bl; Stad Brugge Stedelijke Musea: Groeningemuseum 126cla/clb/br, 127tl; Paul Delveaux *Serenity*, 1970 ©Foundation P. Delveaux – St idesbald, Belgium 127crb; Gruithuis 124clb/bc, 125cl; Gruuthusemuseum 32tl; **Brüsel:** 162tl;

Brussels Airlines: 174cla; **Brussels International Fantastic Film Festival:** 166clb.

Cafe Couleur: 27ca; **Cephas:** TOP/A. Riviere-Lecoeur 148bl; **Chez Leon:** 144tl; **Chimay:** 148cr; **Alan Copson:** 17br, 39c; **Corbis:** David Bartruff 23cb; Jon Hicks 107tr; Wolfgang Kaehler 174br; Ludovic Maisant 143tl; Patrick Ward 27br.

Das Photo: 164cla, 172c, 178cla; **Dreamstime.com:** Anmalkov 11tl; Johan Vanden Borre 40-1; Kobby Dagan 132-3; Veronika Druk 2-3; Rob Van Esch 10tc; Fotojeroen 106cb; Kotomiti_okuma 90-1; Magition 10br; Mikhail Markovskiy 92; Tupungato 42, 56; **Dries Van Noten:** 8cra, 161c, 162bc.

L'Entree des Artistes: 153bc; **Eurolines:** 175tr.

Getty Images: 82; AFP/Getty Images / Dominique Faget 176br; AFP/Herwig Vergult 164cb; **Groeninge Museum Brussels:** Sarah Bauwens 127br.

Robert Harding Picture Library: Charles Bowman 95tr; Julian Pottage 177br; Roger Somvi 19bc, 26cr; **Hemispheres Images:** Monde/Suetone Emilio 160bc; **Hollandse Hoogte:** 118clb, 119bl; **Hotel Bloom:** 134br; **Hotel Marivaux:** 137bl; **Hulton Getty Collection:** 35t, 36cl, 38clb; Keytone 39tl.

Institut Royal Du Patrimoine Artistique/Koninklijk Instituut Voor Het Kunstpatrimonium: 24tr, Societé Des Expositions Du Palais Des Beaux-Arts De Bruxelles 55tr.

Glenda Kapsalis/Www.photographersdirect.com: 131bl; **Koninklijk Museum Voor Schone Kunsten, Antwerp:** Delvaux *Pink's Bow* ©Foundation P. Delveaux – St Idesbald, Belgium/DACS, London 2006 102br; J. Jordaens *As the old sang, the young ones play pipes* 103br; R. Magritte *Madame Recamier* ©ADAGP, Paris and DACS, London 2006 102bl; P.P. Rubens *Adoration of the Magi* 103cr; J. Van Eyck *Saint Barbara* 103tc; R. Wouters *Woman Ironing* 102clb; **Kwint:** 153tr.
Leonardo Mediabank: 106tr, 137tr;
Lonely Planet Images: Martin Moos 106bl; Rockoxhuis,

Frans Snijders, Fishmarket Antwerp, detail 101ca.
Mappa Mundo: 166tr; **Café Metropole:** 150bl; **Hotel Metropole:** 139tc; **ModeMuseum, Antwerp:** 100cl; **MUSEA BRUGGE:** Museum of Folklore 131tr; **Musée De L'art Wallon De La Ville De Liège:** Legs M. Aristide Cralle (1884) 37tl; **Musées Royaux Des Beaux-Arts De Belgique, Bruxelles-Koninklijke Musea Voor Schone Kunsten Van België, Brussel:** 68bl, photo Cussac 6–7, 18cl, 36–7, 64cl, 65crb/bl, 68tr, 69tr, 69b, /©ADAGP, Paris and DACS, London 2011 66bl; photo Speltdoorn 18br, 19c, 24cl, 65cr, 67br, 67cra,/©ADAGP, PARIS AND DACS, London 2006 66cl.

Document Pot: Alain Mathieu 179tl. **Photoshot:** Michael Owston 173bl; **Hotel Le Plaza, Brussels:** 135t; Robbie Polley: 120bl, 124cla, 125bc, 126tr, 176cla, 179bl; **Private Collection:** 36.

Rex Features: 26br, 28ca, Action Press 38t.

©**Standaard Strips:** 23bl; **Sensum.be:** 142br; Neil Setchfield: 94t, 161br; **Strofilia:** 152tl; **Sundancer:** © Moulinsart 22cl.

Archives Du Theatre Royal De La Monnaie: 37tr; **Tony Stone Images:** Richard Elliott 29cr; ©**Toerisme Ooost-Vlaanderen:** 109crb; **Tourism Antwerp:** 97cr; 98clb; 119cl; **La Truffe Noire:** 143br; **Service Relations Exterieures City Of Tournai:** 24bl.

L'Ultime Atome: 154tl

Roger Viollet: 34t; Musee San Martino, Naples 35b; **Café Vlissingel:** 158br; **Vrijmoed:** 159tr.

De Waterzooi: 141bl; **Royal Windsor Hotel:** 140tc; **World Pictures:** 28br; **WY:** 156tl.

Le Zoute Zoen: 157br.

Front Endpapers: **Dreamstime.com:** Tupungato Rcla, Lbl.

Map Cover: **Superstock:** Age Fotostock

Jacket:
Front and spine- **Superstock:** Age Fotostock

All other images ©Dorling Kindersley.
For further information see: www.dkimages.com

Special Editions of DK Travel Guides

DK Travel Guides can be purchased in bulk quantities at discounted prices for use in promotions or as premiums. We are also able to offer special editions and personalized jackets, corporate imprints, and excerpts from all of our books, tailored specifically to meet your own needs.

To find out more, please contact:
in the United States **SpecialSales@dk.com**
in the UK **travelspecialsales@uk.dk.com**
in Canada DK Special Sales at **general@tourmaline.ca**
in Australia **business.development@pearson.com.au**

Phrase Book

Tips for Pronouncing French

French-speaking Belgians, or Walloons, have a throaty, deep accent noticeably different from French spoken in France. Despite this, there are few changes in the vocabulary used in spoken and written language. Consonants at the end of words are mostly silent and not pronounced. Ch is pronounced sh; th is t; w is v; and r is rolled gutturally. Ç is pronounced s.

In Emergency

Help!	**Au secours!**	oh sek**oor**
Stop!	**Arrêtez!**	aret-**ay**
Call a doctor!	**Appelez un medecin!**	apuh-**lay**un meds**añ**
Call the police!	**Appelez la police!**	apuh-**lay** lah pol-**ees**
Call the fire brigade!	**Appelez les pompiers!**	apuh-lay leh poñ-**peeyay**
Where is the nearest telephone?	**Où est le téléphone le plus proche?**	oo ay luh tehleh**fon** luh ploo prosh
Where is the nearest hospital?	**Où est l'hôpital le plus proche?**	oo ay l**opeetal** luh ploo prosh

Communication Essentials

Yes	**Oui**	wee
No	**Non**	noñ
Please	**S'il vous plaît**	seel voo **play**
Thank you	**Merci**	mer-**see**
Excuse me	**Excusez-moi**	exkoo-**zay** mwah
Hello	**Bonjour**	boñzhoor
Goodbye	**Au revoir**	oh ruh-**vwar**
Goodnight	**Bonne nuit**	boñ-**swar**
morning	**le matin**	mat**añ**
afternoon	**l'après-midi**	l'apreh-**meedee**
evening	**le soir**	swah
yesterday	**hier**	eey**ehr**
today	**aujourd'hui**	oh-zhoor-**dwee**
tomorrow	**demain**	duhm**añ**
here	**ici**	ee-**see**
there	**là bas**	lah bah
What?	**Quel/quelle?**	kel, kel
When?	**Quand?**	koñ
Why?	**Pourquoi?**	poor-**kwah**
Where?	**Où?**	oo
How?	**Comment?**	kom-**moñ**

Useful Phrases

How are you?	**Comment allez vous?**	kom-moñ tal**ay voo**
Very well, thank you	**Très bien, merci**	treh byañ, mer-**see**
How do you do?	**Comment ça va?**	kom-moñ sah **vah**
See you soon	**A bientôt**	byañ-toh
That's fine	**Ça va bien**	Sah vah byañ
Where is/are…?	**Où est/sont…?**	ooh ay/soñ
How far is it to…?	**Combien de kilomètres d'ici à…?**	kom-**byañ** duh keelo-**metr** d'ee-see ah
Which way to…?	**Quelle est la direction pour…?**	kel ay lah deer-ek-**syoñ** poor
Do you speak English?	**Parlez-vous Anglais?**	par-**lay** voo oñg-**lay**
I don't understand	**Je ne comprends pas**	zhuh nuh kom-**proñ** pah
Could you speak slowly?	**Pouvez-vous parlez plus lentement?**	voo pwee-say par-lay ploos **loñ**tuh-moñ
I'm sorry	**Excusez-moi**	exkoo-**zay** mwah

Useful Words

big	**grand**	groñ
small	**petit**	puh-**tee**
hot	**chaud**	show
cold	**froid**	frwah
good	**bon**	boñ
bad	**mauvais**	moh-**veh**
enough	**assez**	as**say**
well	**bien**	byañ
open	**ouvert**	oo-**ver**
closed	**fermé**	fer-**meh**
left	**gauche**	gohsh
right	**droite**	drawht
straight on	**tout droit**	too drwaht
near	**près**	preh
far	**loin**	lwañ
up	**en haut**	oñ **oh**
down	**en bas**	oñ**bah**
early	**tôt**	toh
late	**tard**	tar
entrance	**l'entrée**	l'oñ-**tray**
exit	**la sortie**	sor-**tee**

toilet	**toilette**	twah-let
occupied	**occupé**	o-koo-**pay**
free (vacant)	**libre**	leebr
free (no charge)	**gratuit**	grah-**twee**

Making a Telephone Call

I would like to place a long-distance telephone call	**Je voudrais faire un interurbain**	zhuh voo-dreh faire uñ añter-oorbañ
I'd like to call collect	**Je voudrais faire un communication PCV**	zhuh voo-**dreh** faire oon kom-oonikah-**syoñ** peh-seh-veh
I will try again later	**Je vais essayer plus tard**	zhuh vay ess-ay-eh ploo tar
Can I leave a message?	**Est-ce que je peux laisser un message?**	es-**keh** zhuh puh les-**say** uñ meh-sazh
Could you speak up a little please?	**Pouvez-vous parler un peu plus fort?**	poo-**vay** voo par-**lay** uñ puh ploo for komoonikah-**syoñ** low-**kal**
Local call	**Communication local**	komoonikah-**syoñ** low-**kal**

Shopping

How much does this cost?	**C'est combien?**	say kom-**byañ**
I would like…	**Je voudrais…**	zhuh voo-**dray**
Do you have…	**Est-ce que vous avez…**	es-**kuh** voo zavay
I'm just looking	**Je regarde seulement**	zhuh ruh**gar** suhl-**moñ**
Do you take credit cards?	**Est-ce que vous acceptez les cartes de crédit?**	es-**kuh** voo zaksept-**ay** leh kart duh kreh-**dee**
Do you take travellers' cheques?	**Est-ce que vous acceptez les chèques de voyage?**	es-**kuh** voo zak-sept-ay lay shek duh vway**azh**
What time do you open?	**A quelle heure vous êtes ouvert?**	ah kel urr voo zet oo-**ver**
What time do you close?	**A quelle heure vous êtes fermé?**	ah kel urr voo zet fer-**may**
This one	**Celui-ci**	suhl-wee **see**
That one	**Celui-là**	suhl-wee **lah**
expensive	**cher**	shehr
cheap	**pas cher, bon marché**	pah shehr, boñ mar-shày
size, clothes	**la taille**	tye
white	**blanc**	bloñ
black	**noir**	nwahr
red	**rouge**	roozh
yellow	**jaune**	zhownh
green	**vert**	vehr
blue	**bleu**	bluh

Types of Shops

shop	**le magasin**	le maga-**zañ**
bakery	**la boulangerie**	booloñ-**zhuree**
bank	**la banque**	boñk
bookshop	**la librairie**	lee-**brehree**
butcher	**la boucherie**	boo-**shehree**
cake shop	**la pâtisserie**	patee-**sree**
chocolate shop	**le chocolatier**	shok-oh-lah-tyeh
chip stop/stand	**la friterie**	free-tuh-ree
chemist	**la pharmacie**	farmah-**see**
delicatessen	**la charcuterie**	shah-koo-tuh-**ree**
department store	**le grand magasin**	groñ maga-**zañ**
fishmonger	**la poissonerie**	pwasson-**ree**
greengrocer	**le marchand des légumes**	mar-**shoñ** duh lay-**goom**
hairdresser	**le coiffeur**	kwa**fuhr**
market	**le marché**	marsh ay
newsagent	**le magasin de journaux/tabac**	maga-**zañ** duh zhoor-**no**
post office	**le bureau de poste**	boo-**roh** duh pohst
supermarket	**le supermarché**	soo-pehr-**marshay**
travel agent	**l'agence de voyage**	azhons duh vwayazh

Sightseeing

art gallery	**la galérie d'art**	galer-**ree** dart
bus station	**la gare routière**	gahr roo-tee-yehr
cathedral	**la cathédrale**	katay-**dral**
church	**l'église**	aygl**eez**
closed on public holidays	**fermeture jour férié**	fehrmeh-tur zhoor fehree-ay
garden	**le jardin**	zhah-**dañ**
library	**la bibliothèque**	beeb**leeo**-tek
museum	**le musée**	moo-**zay**

railway station	la gare (SNCF)	gahr (es-en-say-ef)
tourist office	les informations	layz uñ-for-mah-syoñ
town hall	l'hôtel de ville	ohtel duh vil
train	le train	trañ

Staying in a Hotel

Do you have a vacant room?	est-ce que vous avez une chambre?	es-kuh voo zavay oon shambr
double room with double bed	la chambre à deux personnes, avec un grand lit	la shambr uh duh per-son uh-vek uñ groñ lee
twin room	la chambre à deux lits	la shambr ah duh lee
single room	la chambre à une personne	la shambr ah oon pehr-son
room with a bath	la chambre avec salle de bain	shambr ah-vek sal duh bañ
shower	une douche	doosh
I have a reservation	J'ai fait une reservation	zhay fay oon ray-zehrva-syoñ

Eating Out

Have you got a table?	Avez vous une table libre?	avay-voo oon tahbl leebr
I would like to reserve a table	Je voudrais réserver une table	zhuh voo-dray rayzehr-vay oon tahbl
The bill, please	L'addition, s'il vous plait.	l'adee-syoñ voo play
I am a vegetarian	Je suis végétarien	zhuh swee vezhay-tehryañ
waitress/waiter	Monsieur, Mademoiselle	gah-sohn/ mad-uh-mwah-zel
menu	le menu	men-oo
cover charge	le couvert	luh koo-vehr
wine list	la carte des vins	lah kart-deh vañ
glass	le verre	vehr
bottle	la bouteille	boo-tay
knife	le couteau	koo-toh
fork	la fourchette	for-shet
spoon	la cuillère	kwee-yehr
breakfast	le petit déjeuner	puh-tee day-zhuh-nay
lunch	le déjeuner	day-zhuh-nay
dinner	le dîner	dee-nay
main course	le grand plat	groñ plah
starter	l'hors d'oeuvres	or duhvr
dessert	le dessert	duh-zehrt
dish of the day	le plat du jour	plah doo joor
bar	le bar	bah
cafe	le café	ka-fay
rare	saignant	say-nyoñ
medium	à point	ah pwañ
well done	bien cuit	byañ kwee

Numbers

0	zero	zeh-roh
1	un	uñ, oon
2	deux	duh
3	trois	trwah
4	quatre	katr
5	cinq	sañk
6	six	sees
7	sept	set
8	huit	weet
9	neuf	nerf
10	dix	dees
11	onze	oñz
12	douze	dooz
13	treize	trehz
14	quatorze	katorz
15	quinze	kañz
16	seize	sehz
17	dix-sept	dees-set
18	dix-huit	dees-zweet
19	dix-neuf	dees-znerf
20	vingt	vañ
21	vingt-et-un	vañ ay uhn
30	trente	tront
40	quarante	karoñt
50	cinquante	sañkoñt
60	soixante	swahsoñt
70	septante	septoñt
80	quatre-vingt	katr-vañ
90	quatre-vingt-dix/ nonante	katr vañ dees nonañ
100	cent	soñ
1000	mille	meel
1,000,000	million	miyoñ

Time

What is the time?	Quelle heure?	kel uhr
one minute	une minute	oon mee-noot
one hour	une heure	oon uhr
half an hour	une demi-heure	oon duh-mee uhr
half past one	une heure et demi	uhr ay duh-mee
a day	un jour	zhuhr
a week	une semaine	suh-mehn
a month	un mois	mwah
a year	une année	annay
Monday	lundi	luñ-dee
Tuesday	mardi	mah-dee
Wednesday	mercredi	mehrkruh-dee
Thursday	jeudi	zhuh-dee
Friday	vendredi	voñdruh-dee
Saturday	samedi	sam-dee
Sunday	dimanche	dee-moñsh

Belgian Food and Drink

Fish

fish	poisson	pwah-ssoñ
bass	bar/loup de mer	bah/loo duh mare
herring	hareng	ah-roñ
lobster	homard	oh-ma
monkfish	lotte	lot
mussel	moule	mool
oyster	huitre	weetr
pike	brochet	brosh-ay
salmon	saumon	soh-moñ
scallop	coquille Saint-Jacques	kok-eel sañ jak
sea bream	dorade/daurade	doh-rad
prawn	crevette	kreh-vet
skate	raie	ray
trout	truite	trweet
tuna	thon	toñ

Meat

meat	viande	vee-yand
beef	boeuf	buhf
chicken	poulet	poo-lay
duck	canard	kanar
lamb	agneau	ahyoh
pheasant	faisant	feh-zoñ
pork	porc	por
veal	veau	voh
venison	cerf/chevreuil	surf/shev-roy

Vegetables

vegetables	légumes	lay-goom
asparagus	asperges	ahs-pehrj
Belgian endive /chicory	chicon	shee-koñ
Brussels sprouts	choux de bruxelles	shoo duh broocksell
garlic	ail	eye
green beans	haricots verts	arrykoh vehr
haricot beans	haricots	arrykoh
potatoes	pommes de terre	pom-duh tehr
spinach	epinard	aypeenar
truffle	truffe	troof

Desserts

pancake	crêpe	crayp
waffle	gauffre	gohfr
fruit	fruits	frwee

Drinks

coffee	café	kah-fay
white coffee	café au lait	kah-fay oh lay
milky coffee	caffe latte	kah-fay lat-uh
hot chocolate	chocolat chaud	shok-oh-lah shoh
tea	thé	tay
water	l'eau	oh
mineral water	l'eau minérale	l'oh meenay-ral
lemonade	limonade	lee-moh-nad
orange juice	jus d'orange	zhoo doh-ronj
wine	le vin	vañ
house wine	vin maison	vañ may-sañ
beer	une bière	byahr

Tips for Pronouncing Dutch

The Dutch language is pronounced in largely the same way as English, although many vowels, particularly double vowels, are pronounced as long sounds. *J* is the equivalent of the English *y*, *v* is pronounced *f*, and *w* is *v*.

In Emergency

Help!	**Help!**	help
Stop!	**Stop!**	stop
Call a doctor!	**Haal een dokter!**	Haal uhn **dok**-tur
Call the police!	**Roep de politie!**	Roop duh poe-**leet**-see
Call the fire brigade!	**Roep de brandweer!**	Roop duh **brahnt**-vheer
Where is the nearest telephone?	**Waar ist de dichtsbijzijnde telefoon?**	Vhaar iss duh **dikst**-baiy-zaiyn-duh-tay-luh-**foan**
Where is the nearest hospital?	**Waar ist het dichtsbijzijnde ziekenhuis?**	Vhaar iss het **dikst**-baiy-zaiyn-duh **zee**-kuh-hows

Communication Essentials

Yes	**Ja**	yaa
No	**Nee**	nay
Please	**Alstublieft**	ahls-tew-**bleeft**
Thank you	**Dank u**	dhank-ew
Excuse me	**Pardon**	pahr-**don**
Hello	**Goed dag**	ghoot dahgh
Goodbye	**Tot ziens**	tot zins
Goodnight	**Slaap lekker**	slap **lek**-kah
morning	**morgen**	**mor**-ghugh
afternoon	**middag**	**mid**-dahgh
evening	**avond**	**av**-vohnd
yesterday	**gisteren**	**ghis**-tern
today	**vandaag**	**van**-daagh
tomorrow	**morgen**	**mor**-ghugh
here	**hier**	heer
there	**daar**	daar
What?	**Wat?**	vhat
When?	**Wanneer?**	vhan-**eer**
Why?	**Waarom?**	vhaar-**om**
Where?	**Waar?**	vhaar
How?	**Hoe?**	hoo

Useful Phrases

How are you?	**Hoe gaat het ermee?**	Hoo ghaat het er-**may**
Very well, thank you	**Heel goed, dank u**	Hayl ghoot, **dhank ew**
How do you do?	**Hoe maakt u het?**	Hoo maakt ew het
See you soon	**Tot ziens**	Tot zeens
That's fine	**Prima**	**Pree**-mah
Where is/are...?	**Waar is/zijn...?**	vhaar iss/zayn
How far is it to...?	**Hoe ver is het naar...?**	Hoo vehr iss het nar
How do I get to...?	**Hoe kom ik naar...?**	Hoo kom ik nar
Do you speak English?	**Spreekt u engels?**	Spraykt uw **eng**-uhls
I don't understand	**Ik snap het niet**	Ik snahp het neet
Could you speak slowly?	**Kunt u langzamer praten?**	Kuhnt ew **lahng**-zarmer-praat-tuh
I'm sorry	**Sorry**	sorry

Useful Words

big	**groot**	ghroat
small	**klein**	klaiyn
hot	**warm**	vharm
cold	**koud**	khowt
good	**goed**	ghoot
bad	**slecht**	slekht
enough	**genoeg**	ghuh-**noohkh**
well	**goed**	ghoot
open	**open**	open
closed	**gesloten**	ghuh-**slow**-tuh
left	**links**	links
right	**rechts**	rekhts
straight on	**rechtdoor**	rehkht dohr
near	**dichtbij**	dikht baiy
far	**ver weg**	vehr vhekh
up	**omhoog**	om-**hoakh**
down	**naar beneden**	naar buh **nay**-duh
early	**vroeg**	vrookh
late	**laat**	laat
entrance	**ingang**	**in**-ghang
exit	**uitgang**	**ouht**-ghang
toilet	**wc**	vhay-say
ocupied	**bezet**	buh-**zett**

free (vacant)	**vrij**	vraiy
free (no charge)	**gratis**	**ghraah**-tiss

Making a Telephone Call

I'd like to place a long-distance telephone call	**Ik wil graag interlokal telefoneren**	ik vhil ghraakh **inter**-loh-kaal tay-luh-foh-**neh**-ruh
I'd like to call collect	**Ik wil "collect call" bellen**	ik vhil " collect call" **bel**-luh
I will try again later	**Ik probeer het later nog wel eens**	ik pro-**beer** het later laater nokh vhel ayns
Can I leave a message?	**Kunt u een boodschap doorgeven?**	kuhnt ew uhn **boat**-skhahp **dohr**-ghay-vuh
Could you speak up a little please?	**Wilt u wat harder praten?**	vhilt ew vhat **hahr**-der **praat**-ew
Local call	**Lokaal gesprek**	low-**kaahl** ghuh-**sprek**

Shopping

How much does this cost?	**Hoeveel kost dit?**	hoo-**vayl** kost dit
I would like...	**Ik wil graag...**	ik vhil ghraakh
Do you have...?	**Heeft u...?**	hayft ew
I'm just looking	**Ik kijk alleen even**	ik kaiyk alleyn **ay**-vuh
Do you take credit cards?	**Neemt u credit cards aan?**	naymt ew credit cards aan?
Do you take travellers' cheques?	**Neemt u reischeques aan?**	naymt ew **raiys**-sheks aan
What time do you open?	**Hoe laat gaat u open?**	hoo laat ghaat ew opuh
What time do you close?	**Hoe laat gaat u dicht?**	hoo laat ghaat ew dikht
This one	**Deze**	**day**-zuh
That one	**Die**	dee
expensive	**duur**	dewr
cheap	**goedkoop**	ghoot-**koap**
size	**maat**	maat
white	**wit**	vhit
black	**zwart**	zvhahrt
red	**rood**	roat
yellow	**geel**	ghayl
green	**groen**	ghroon
blue	**blauw**	blah-ew

Types of Shops

antique shop	**antiekwinkel**	ahn-**teek**-vhin-kul
bakery	**bakker**	**bah**-ker-aiy
bank	**bank**	bahnk
bookshop	**boekwinkel**	**book**-vhin-kul
butcher	**slager**	slaakh-er-aiy
cake shop	**banketbakkerij**	bahnk-**et**-bahk-er-aiy
chip stop/stand	**patatzaak**	pah-**taht**-zak
chemist/drugstore	**apotheek**	ah-poe-**taiyk**
delicatessen	**delicatessen**	daylee-kah-**tes**-suh
department store	**warenhuis**	**vhaah**-uh-houws
fishmonger	**viswinkel**	**viss**-vhin-kul
greengrocer	**groenteboer**	**ghroon**-tuh-boor
hairdresser	**kapper**	**kah**-per
market	**markt**	mahrkt
newsagent	**krantenwinkel**	**krahn**-tuh-vhin-kul
post office	**postkantoor**	**pohst**-kahn-tor
supermarket	**supermarkt**	**sew**-per-mahrkt
tobacconist	**sigarenwinkel**	see-**ghaa**-ruh-vhin-kul
travel agent	**reisburo**	**raiys**-bew-roa

Sightseeing

art gallery	**gallerie**	ghaller-ee
bus station	**busstation**	**buhs**-stah-shown
bus ticket	**strippenkaart**	**strip**-puh-kaart
cathedral	**kathedraal**	kah-tuh-**draal**
church	**kerk**	kehrk
closed on public holidays	**op feestdagen gesloten**	op **fayst**-daa-ghuh ghuh-slow-**tuh**
day return	**dagretour**	**dahgh**-ruh-tour
garden	**tuin**	touwn
library	**bibliotheek**	bee-bee-yo-**tayk**
museum	**museum**	mew-**zay**-um
railway station	**station**	stah-**shown**
return ticket	**retourtje**	ruh-**tour**-tyuh
single journey	**enkeltje**	**eng**-kuhl-tyuh
tourist information	**dienst voor tourisme**	deenst vor **tor**-ism
town hall	**stadhuis**	**staht**-houws
train	**trein**	traiyn

Staying in a Hotel

Do you have a vacant room?	**Zijn er nog kamers vrij?**	zaiyn er nokh **kaa**-mers vray
double room with double bed	**een twees persoons-kamer met een twee persoonsbed**	uhn **tvhay** per-**soans**-ka-mer met uhn **tvhay** per-**soans** beht
twin room	**een kamer met een lits-jumeaux**	uhn **kaa**-mer met uhn lee-zjoo-**moh**
single room	**eenpersoons-kamer**	ayn-per-**soans** kaa-mer
room with a bath/shower	**kaamer met bad/ douche**	**kaa-mer** met baht/doosh
I have a reservation	**Ik heb gereserveerd**	ik hehp ghuh-ray-sehr-**veert**

Eating Out

Have you got table?	**Is er een tafel vrij?**	iss ehr uhn **tah**-fuhl vraiy
I would like to reserve a table	**Ik wil een tafel reserveren**	ik vhil uhn **tah-fel** ray sehr-**veer**-uh
The bill, please	**Mag ik afrekenen**	muhk ik **ahf**-ray-kuh-nuh
I am a vegetarian	**Ik ben vegetariër**	ik ben fay-ghuh-**taahr**-ee-er
waitress/waiter	**serveerster/ober**	sehr-**veer**-ster/**oh**-ber
menu	**de kaart**	duh kaahrt
cover charge	**het couvert**	het koo-**vehr**
wine list	**de wijnkaart**	duh **vhaiyn**-kart
glass	**het glass**	het ghlahss
bottle	**de fles**	duh fless
knife	**het mes**	het mess
fork	**de vork**	duh fork
spoon	**de lepel**	duh **lay**-pul
breakfast	**het ontbijt**	het ont-**baiyt**
lunch	**de lunch**	duh lernsh
dinner	**het diner**	het dee-**nay**
main course	**het hoofdgerecht**	het **hoaft**-ghuh-rekht
starter, first course	**het voorgerecht**	het **vhor**-ghuh-rekht
dessert	**het nagerecht**	het **naa**-ghuh-rekht
dish of the day	**het dagmenu**	het **dahg**-munh-ew
bar	**het cafe**	het kaa-**fay**
café	**het eetcafe**	het **ayt**-kaa-**fay**
rare	**rare**	'rare'
medium	**medium**	'medium'
well done	**doorbakken**	door-**bah**-kuh

Numbers

1	**een**	ayn
2	**twee**	tvhay
3	**drie**	dree
4	**vier**	feer
5	**vijf**	faiyf
6	**zes**	zess
7	**zeven**	**zay**-vuh
8	**acht**	ahkht
9	**negen**	**nay**-guh
10	**tien**	teen
11	**elf**	elf
12	**twaalf**	tvhaalf
13	**dertien**	**dehr**-teen
14	**veertien**	**feer**-teen
15	**vijftien**	**faiyf**-teen
16	**zestien**	**zess**-teen
17	**zeventien**	**zayvuh**-teen
18	**achtien**	**ahkh**-teen
19	**negentien**	**nay-ghuh**-tien
20	**twintig**	**tvhin**-tukh
21	**eenentwintig**	**aynuh**-tvhin-tukh
30	**dertig**	**dehr**-tukh
40	**veertig**	**feer**-tukh
50	**vijftig**	**faiyf**-tukh
60	**zestig**	**zess**-tukh
70	**zeventig**	**zay**-vuh-tukh
80	**tachtig**	**tahkh**-tukh
90	**negentig**	**nayguh**-tukh
100	**honderd**	**hohn**-durt

1000	**duizend**	**douw**-zuhnt
1,000,000	**miljoen**	mill-**yoon**

Time

one minute	**een minuut**	uhn meen-**ewt**
one hour	**een uur**	uhn ewr
half an hour	**een half uur**	een hahlf uhr
half past one	**half twee**	hahlf twee
a day	**een dag**	uhn dahgh
a week	**een week**	uhn vhayk
a month	**een maand**	uhn maant
a year	**een jaar**	uhn jaar
Monday	**maandag**	**maan**-dahgh
Tuesday	**dinsdag**	**dins**-dahgh
Wednesday	**woensdag**	**vhoons**-dahgh
Thursday	**donderdag**	**donder**-dahgh
Friday	**vrijdag**	**vraiy**-dahgh
Saturday	**zaterdag**	**zaater**-dahgh
Sunday	**zondag**	**zon**-dahgh

Belgian Food and Drink

Fish

fish	**vis**	fiss
bass	**zeebars**	see-buhr
herring	**haring**	**haa**-ring
lobster	**kreeft**	krayft
monkfish	**lotte/zeeduivel**	lot/seafuhdul
mussel	**mossel**	moss-uhl
oyster	**oester**	**ouhs**-tuh
pike	**snoek**	snook
prawn	**garnaal**	gar-nall
salmon	**zalm**	sahlm
scallop	**Sint-Jacoboester/ Jacobsschelp**	**sind**-yakob-ouhs-tuh/yakob-scuhlp
sea bream	**dorade/zeebrasem**	doh-rard
skate	**rog**	rog
trout	**forel**	foh-ruhl
tuna	**tonijn**	tuhn-een

Meat

meat	**vlees**	flayss
beef	**rundvlees**	**ruhnt**-flayss
chicken	**kip**	kip
duck	**eend**	aynt
lamb	**lamsvlees**	**lahms**-flayss
pheasant	**fazant**	**fay**-zanh
pork	**varkensvlees**	**vahr**-kuhns-flayss
veal	**kalfsvlees**	**karfs**-flayss
venison	**ree (bok)**	ray

Vegetables

vegetables	**groenten**	**ghroon**-tuh
asparagus	**asperges**	as-puhj
Belgian endive/ chicory	**witloof**	vit-lurf
Brussels sprouts	**spruitjes**	spruhr-tyuhs
garlic	**knoflook**	**knoff**-loak
green beans	**princesbonen**	prins-ess-buh-nun
haricot beans	**snijbonen**	snee-buh-nun
potatoes	**aardappels**	**aard**-uppuhls
spinach	**spinazie**	spin-a-jee
truffle	**truffel**	truh-fuhl

Desserts

fruit	**fruit/vruchten**	vroot/vrooh-tuh
pancake	**pannekoek**	**pah**-nuh-kook
waffle	**wafel**	vaff-uhl

Drinks

beer	**bier**	beeh
coffee	**koffie**	coffee
fresh orange juice	**verse jus**	**vehr**-suh zjhew
hot chocolate	**chocola**	sho-koh-**laa**
mineral water	**mineraalwater**	meener-**aahl**-vhaater
tea	**thee**	tay
water	**water**	vhaa-ter
wine	**wijn**	vhaiyn

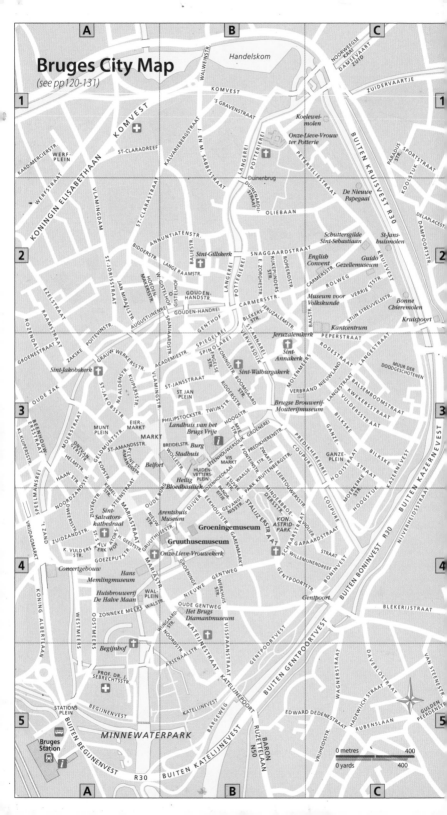

Bruges City Map

(see pp120-131)

Handelskom

A **B** **C**

1

KOMVEST
WALWEINSTR.
'S GRAVENSTRAAT
KOMVEST
NOORWEEGSE KAAI
DAMSEVAART ZUID
ZUIDERVAARTJE

KARD.MERCIERSTR.
WERF-PLEIN
ST-CLARADREEF
Koeleweimolen
Onze-Lieve-Vrouw ter Potterie
PETERSELIESTRAAT
BUITEN KRUISVEST R30
PARADIJS STR.
SPORTSTRAAT

WERFSTRAAT
KONINGIN ELISABETHAAN
VLAMINGDAM
ST-CLARASTRAAT
Duinenbrug
DUINENVAARDI-STRAAT
OLIEBAAN
De Nieuwe Papegaai
KOOLSTUK
DELAPLACESTR.
DAMPOORTSTR.

2

BIDDERSTR.
ANNUNTIATENSTR.
LANGE RAAMSTR.
BALIESTR.
Sint-Gillskerk
SNAGGAARDSTRAAT
RUIKPLINDERS STR.
E. ZORGHESTR.
ROPEERDSTR.
Schuttersgilde Sint-Sebastiaan
English Convent
CARMERSSTR.
Guido Gezellemuseum
St-Janshuismolen
KRUISVEST
DAMPOORTSTR.

ST-JORISSTRAAT
JAN MIRAELSTR.
HOOGEN MAEKERSSTR.
W. GESTELMAN O. GISTELHOF
SPANJAARDSTR.
AUGUSTIJNENREI
GOUDEN-HANDSTR.
GOUDEN-HANDREI
GENTHOF
LANGEREI
POTTERIEREI
CARMERSSTR.
BLEKERS STR.
JERUZALEMSTR.
ST-ANNAREI
Museum voor Volkskunde
BALSTR.
STIJN STREUVELSSTR.
VERRIESTR.
ROLWEG
Bonne Chieremolen
Kruispoort

EZELSTRAAT
RAAMSTRAAT
ROZENDAL
GROENESTRAAT
Sint-Jakobskerk
OUDE ZAK
GRAUW WERKERSSTR.
POTTENSTR.
ZAKSE
ACADEMIESTR.
VLAMINGSTR.
SPIEGELREI
ENGELSE STRAAT
KONINGSTR.
VEERVERSDIJK
ST-ANNAREI
Jeruzalemkerk
Sint-Annakerk
Kantcentrum
PEPERSTRAAT
RODESTRAAT
LANGESTRAAT
MUUR DER DOODGESCHOTEN

3

BEENHOUW.EESTSTRAAT
K.K.KUIPERSSTR.
MOERSTRAAT
MUNT PLEIN
GELDMUNTSTR.
ST-JAKOBSSTR.
NALDENSTR.
KUIPERSSTR.
ST-JANSSTRAAT
ST JAN PLEIN
RIDDERSTR.
TWIJNSTR.
BOOGAARD
Sint-Walburgakerk
MOLENMEERS
VERBRAND NIEUWLAND
Brugse Brouwerij-Mouterijmuseum
LANGESTRAAT
BALSEMBOOMSTRAAT
KWEKERSSTRAAT
VULDERSSTRAAT
BILKSKE
BUITEN KAZERNEVEST R30

EIER-MARKT
MARKT
ST-AMANDSSTR.
EIERMARKT
PHILIPSTOCKSTR.
HOOGSTR.
MEEL STR.
GROENEREI
PREDIKHERENREI
GANZE-PLEIN
HOOISTRAAT
MOERKERKE STR.
HOOGSTUK
BILKSKE
GANZESTRAAT

Landhuis van het Brugs Vrije
Burg
BREIDELSTR.
Stadhuis
Belfort
WOLLESTR.
HUIDEN-VETTERSPL.
VIS MARKT
BEENHOUWERSDIJK
PREDIKHERENSTR.
Heilig Bloedbasiliek
ZWARTE LEERTOUWERSSTR.
COUPURE
COUPURE
KAZERNEVEST

Sint-Salvatorskathedraal
Arentshuis Museum
Groeningemuseum
Gruuthusemuseum
Onze-Lieve-Vrouwekerk
ZILVERSTR.
ST-SALV. KERKHOF
H. GEESTSTR.
GRUUTHUSESTR.
DIJVER
ROZENHOEDK.
GEVANG.
PANDR.
NISSTR.
EEKHOUTSTR.
GENTPOORTSTR.
MINDERBROED. DERSTR.
KON. ASTRID PARK
GAPAARDSTRAAT
STALIJZERSTRAAT
GARENMARKT
SCHAARSTRAAT
AZIJ. VOLIER.

4

Concertgebouw
Hans Memlingmuseum
Huisbrouwerij De Halve Maan
MARIASTRAAT
ZUIDZANDSTR.
K. VULDERS STR.
GOEZEPUTSTR.
NIEUWE STR.
GROENINGE
NIEUWE STR.
WERKHUIS STR.
WILLEMIJNENDREEF
GENTWEG
Gentpoort
BUITEN GENTPOORTVEST
BLEKERIJSTRAAT

KONING ALBERTLAAN
WESTMEERS
OOSTMEERS
ZONNEKE MEERS
WALPLEIN
WALSTR.
WIJNGAARD STR.
NOORDSTR.
KATELIJNESTRAAT
Oude Gentweg
Het Brugs Diamantmuseum
VISSPAANSTRAAT
KATELIJNEVEST
DAVERLOSTRAAT
WAGNERSTRAAT
HADEWICH STRAAT
VAN STEENESTR.
GULDEN PEERDENSTR.

5

Begijnhof
PROF. DR. J. SEBRECHTSSTR.
ARSENAALSTR.
KATELIJNEVEST
KATELIJNEVEST
BUITEN KATELIJNEVEST
BARGEWEG
BARON RUZETTELAAN N50
EDWARD DEDENESTRAAT
VRIJHEIDSSTR.
RUBENSLAAN

STATIONS PLEIN
BEGIJNEVEST
BEGIJNEVEST
Bruges Station
MINNEWATERPARK
BUITEN BEGIJNEVEST
R30
BUITEN KATELIJNEVEST

0 metres — 400
0 yards — 400

A **B** **C**